We Are Not Alone

We Are Not ALONE

A Complete Guide to Interdimensional Cooperation

Atala Dorothy Toy

WEISER BOOKS
San Francisco, CA / Newburyport, MA

First published in 2009 by
Red Wheel/Weiser, LLC
With offices at:
500 Third Street, Suite 230
San Francisco, CA 94107
www.redwheelweiser.com

ISBN: 978-1-57863-448-4
Library of Congress Cataloging-in-Publication Data is available upon request.

Cover and text design by Donna Linden
Typeset in Perpetua and Neutra
Cover photograph © Stockbyte/Getty Images
Bhuvaneshvari Yantra and Sri Yantra illustrations on pages 90, 109 and 110 are reproduced
with permission from *Tantric Yoga and the Wisdom Goddesses* by Dr. David Frawley, Lotus
Press, a division of Lotus Brands, Inc., PO Box 325, Twin Lakes, Wisconsin 53181, USA,
www.lotuspress.com. ©2003 All Rights Reserved.
Merkabah and toroid illustrations on pages 88, 91 and 247 are reproduced courtesy of
Andy Furgal.
Author photo on page 279 at the Olcott Labyrinth at the Theosophical Society in America
Headquarters, Wheaton, Illinois © James Daley.

Printed in Canada
TCP
10 9 8 7 6 5 4 3 2 1

Out beyond ideas
Of wrong-doing
And right-doing
There is a field.
I'll meet you there.
—Rumi

Field is the only reality.
There is no physical matter,
only denser and denser fields.
–Albert Einstein

CONTENTS

ACKNOWLEDGMENTS

This work is a cosmic thank you to the life forms of the universe who work in partnership for the greater benefit of us all. Special thanks to Archangel Metatron, the cosmic scientist; Archangel Melchizedek, the cosmic teacher; Archangel Michael, the cosmic warrior of this age; Thoth, the scribe; and Jesus, the Christ. And thanks to to the feminine energies of Holy Mother Mary, Sekhmet, Hathor, Kuan Yin and Kali.

Special thanks to those members of the Melchizedek lineage who have each been working in their own way to bring forth different aspects of the vast change in consciousness we will all be experiencing in the near future. These people, some of them controversial, have inspired me with their dedication and their personal adherence to the highest levels of truth, as personally understood by them. They include J. J. Hurtak and the Academy of Future Science, Drunvalo Melchizedek and the Spirit of Ma'at, Grace Marami and James Germain of the Church of the Creator, Alton Kamadon of the Melchizedek Academy and Ashayana Deane and the Azurite Temple. These people also include the seminal consciousness explorers Gregg Braden, Zecharia Sitchin and Doreen Virtue.

Much gratitude to the American Society of Dowsers (ASD), the Labyrinth Society, the Theosophical Society and the Association for Research and Enlightenment (A.R.E.), where I have found receptive homes; to the United Nations and the United Nations Development Programme, where I worked for several years and grew to deeply admire the selfless service of all these committed international civil servants; to Swarthmore College, which schooled me in detached observation and analysis; to Abington Friends Meeting in Pennsylvania, which gave me my

Quaker upbringing; to those who helped me in my many years of yogic training; and to the Unitarian Universalist Association of Geneva, Illnois.

Many thanks to the colleagues and teachers whom, over the years and in many different areas, I have learned from and investigated consciousness with, including Starr Fuentes, Peter and Debbie Roth, Laura Nina Zealey, Marianne Somers, Diana Stevens, Tarak Kauff and Jeff Toy. To Virginia Litza, with whom I co-founded The Institute for the Study of Interdimensional Co-operation (ISIC). To the staff of Crystal Life Technology, Inc., past and present; each staff member is a special person who is an expert in their own area and who taught me a great deal about their aspect of energy. They include Tami Tredinnick, Karen Kimbell, Gary Lupton, Andy Furgal, Jeff Furgal, Tara Wilgues, Marcia Foster, Anna Robinson, Yana Tolstunova, Gunilla Bradshaw and Kim McDuffee. To the amazing technical experts who have fashioned subtle energy tools that have been of great assistance to me in my work, including Bob and Charmion McKusick and Geoff and Kathleen Condit of Biomagnetic Research; Slim and Katharina Kaffl Spurling of the Slim Spurling Light Life Tools; Marie Allizon and Christianne, who create the Flower of Life tools; and Victor Barr of Energetic Jewelry, who creates the merkabahs.

To my friends in the dowsing community, including Barbara Anne Hughes, Sandy Isgro and Irene Paquin, with whom I've spent many happy hours dowsing and talking energy. To my dowsing teachers, especially Walt Woods, Don Taylor, Janet Dunlap and Marty Cain, who taught me a great deal about the subtleties of energy. To my fellow ASD board members: Bess Cutter, George Weller, Keith Schaffer, Bill Bonnell, Tipi Halsey and Will Clark and to ASD Operations Manager Arvid Johnson.

This work would not have come into its final organized linear shape without the unique combination of expert dowsing knowledge, energy knowledge and editorial knowledge that belongs to Sybil Carey, ASD's managing editor and a longtime colleague and friend. Many thanks to my Red Wheel Weiser editor Caroline Pincus, and copyeditor Amy Rost, who turned this work into its final printed form.

And especially a profound thank you to my family, from whom I learn so much, who share my world-view of a positive cooperative universe, and with whom I have spent many happy years exploring this wonderful earth: my sons Steven Toy and Brian Toy, my brother Chet Perry and my sister-in-law Eve Perry.

INTRODUCTION

Several years ago a friend and I were joking about the magnetic attraction of earth. We talked of the many different galactic civilizations that have visited us and the complex stories that have taken place in this rare world that has embraced solid form.

"Yeah," he said, "It's the great universal carnie call: 'Come on down—you won't believe your eyes. All you have to do is forget who you are.' And then the fun begins."

Ours is a world based on forgetfulness of who and what we really are.

And now it is time to remember.

Remembering

There is no doubt that many of us are remembering. We are becoming aware of who we truly are at our source and of the place we should rightfully hold in a vast interdimensional society that has long existed.

Our current time period marks the end of earth's infancy and the start of our conscious re-entry into interdimensional society. It is the end of a long dark age in which we were solidly locked into the third dimension and thus forced to focus our attention on this dimension's strata of consciousness. With no way out for most of us, we could go only into this frequency and master its potentials on both the dark and the light sides of the spectrum of consciousness. We fashioned many objects to adjust to the parameters of this third dimension. These include tools ranging from hammers and nails to institutions such as the military, the government and religion.

Today, as our consciousness expands, we can easily see that our issues go beyond the solution capacities of our current solid tools and forms. Do we throw these tools away or adjust them to more effectively serve the larger vision we are now acquiring? The answers are up to each of us to decide for ourselves. Various options are discussed in this book.

Our world is experiencing the end of one level of perception and the start of a new expanded vision. This is why all the previous generations of soothsayers of all traditions have said they cannot predict the outcome of this period. We are crafting for ourselves a new level of consciousness, and we do not know yet what it will bring. It is a grand experiment, and we are the fortunate few (million) who will be determining its outcome for our world.

Many in our world today feel isolated and alone, yet this perception is one of the furthest from reality that we humans can ever hold. We are connected to everything in the universe; we have all spun forth from the same unified source, and thus we are all related. We can learn to communicate with any part of the whole that we choose, if we learn the proper protocols and work to absorb these into our personal consciousness, or energy field. Whether this work is communication with the cells of our own body, with the animals, plants and nature spirits in our backyard, or with the vast cosmic consciousnesses that have themselves spun forth universes and worlds, it does not change.

This book will show you what substantive issues are involved in communicating with other parts of the unified source and what your own personal options are going forward. We are remembering. The breadth of this growing remembrance is easily seen on a visit to any broad-based bookstore. A look at its shelves shows books about contacting angels, fairies, extraterrestrials, metaterrestrials, our own higher selves, our animal, plant and mineral totems and God, the source him/her/itself. There are books explaining the commonality of all fields from the viewpoint of science, politics, religion and self-help.

How do all these perceptions tie together? What is the common thread running through this tapestry? How do we learn to communicate and cooperate with all these life forms that are occupying the very same space in which we—solid, third-dimension humans—also live?

These questions inform the subject of this book: multidimensional perception, awareness, communication and cooperation. These pages offer information on many aspects of interdimensional cooperation, from personal to land to intergalactic politics. The book ranges from the subtle science of interdimensional cooperation to the personal thoughts and emotions that are involved.

The Core Concepts Explored in This Book

We are going to explore the fields that exist behind form. These fields are known in various traditions as the net, the web, the grid, the merkabah, consciousness, universal love, universal mind, the source and the void; choose your own semantic variation for these fields.

We also will be working with the following terms:

The source. That ultimate point, or field, from which all has emerged. We consider this point to be simultaneously the fullness and the void.

Merkabah. A force field composed, at its base level, of two or more simultaneously projected polarities that hold the construct in place to self-examine, explore, define and develop itself. Merkabahs exist in all sizes and levels of complexity.

Consciousness. The aware substance of the universe from which all is created. Consciousness is composed of many merkabahs united for a common purpose. Consciousness has many segments that are all, at an ultimate level, equal to each other, as all are aspects of the source and each is taking responsibility for growing and perfecting a specific aspect of the whole.

The field. A segment of consciousness that has organized it-self to perform a specific task. The merkabahs have formed a collective consciousness, and consciousness has assigned an aspect of itself to a specific field, or task.

Consciousness, energy, frequency, vibration, resonance. Consciousness is the substance of which the entirety of creation is formed. Energy is its active component. Frequency is the pitch at which an object exists. Vibration is the action that occurs as the polarities of the pitch interact with each other. Resonance is the movement of a fully developed field or merkabah formed by— in descending order of form—consciousness, energy, frequency and vibration.

Energy workers. People who understand some aspect of the substance that permeates all existence. They can work with this substance, called consciousness or energy, to improve the health and abilities of their clients, who can be any life form: land, animal, human and so on. They often understand and have mastered an aspect of energy and can assist with this aspect of a client's situation. They do not claim to have mastered all existence, as a guru might claim. All energy workers have the ability to communicate with other life forms, although they may not yet think of themselves as being able to do so.

Interdimensional communicators. A subdivision, or type of, energy worker. Interdimensional communicators have mastered the ability to communicate with life forms other than humans and are aware that they are doing so. They are always extending their knowledge because this universe is large and because different clients or situations interface with different realms of consciousness. They do not claim to know it all; however, they do say that by using their capacities and their inner contacts (colleagues), they can most likely locate the situation, the cause and the path for resolution.

Shape-shifters. A type of interdimensional communicator; a type of empath. Shape-shifters can shift their consciousness, either internally identifying with a field they wish to work with or physically shifting their shape into that of another life form. When done internally, shape-shifting enables the practitioner to understand the motivations and energy of widely diverse situations. On the physical level, Merlin taught Arthur how to shape-shift. The Crow medicine women are alleged to have this capacity, and many of the so-called gods and goddesses use this ability to visit earth as humans or as animals.

Interdimensional communication. The art of communicating with life forms other than the humans who exist in the third-dimensional reality. It requires coordination of one's mind, heart and emotions. That is, one uses the purified heart to travel to any location in the universe; the purified mind to observe, catalog and analyze what is observed in this location; and the purified emotions to permit the life forms in the world one is approaching to understand that the communicator will not harm anything in their area of responsibility. Interdimensional communication takes place through the process of internal dowsing, in which the communicator locates the frequency of the field being sought, then enters into it.

Interdimensional cooperation. A methodology for working with the life forms in many worlds who are interfacing with each other, often unaware of each other, in the same field of action. Using arbitration, boundary setting and the authority that comes from union with the all-loving source, interdimensional communicators work like intergalactic United Nations members to foster interdimensional cooperation.

Guides, guardians, inner colleagues. The individuals with whom we all work and who exist in various other dimensions. The interdimensional communicator works consciously with these life forms, who in turn assist the communicator in locating the source of a situation and the life forms involved. These colleagues are essential to the communicator's work, for they know how to locate the life forms and dimensions with whom the individuals involved must communicate in order to achieve a resolution.

Dowsing. This ancient art, also called divining, is a method by which one can find the answer to any properly phrased question, wherever that answer is located in the universe. Dowsing, at the most basic level, involves locating water or minerals. At the advanced levels, it involves locating energies and then adjusting them via various dowsing protocols. All interdimensional communicators are dowsers. "Locating" or "entering" a merkabah means connecting with it via internal body or consciousness dowsing.

••••

We will be weaving back and forth between these core concepts to show how interdimensional communication and cooperation are a natural function of all life.

The descriptors "interdimensional communicator" and "energy worker" are often used interchangeably, depending on what aspect of the topic the term most relates to (e.g., the general field of energy work or the specific capacities of interdimensional communication).

This is a proactive, pragmatic book that examines how we can understand the functioning of the unified field and use this knowledge to improve our lives, correct our mistakes, protect our future and make a more beautiful "now" for ourselves, our loved ones and our world.

About the Organization of This Book

Reality is, at its core, based on very simple truths. In these pages, we are seeking to achieve that true level of awareness that is simple and easily understood by even a child. We are moving behind technical distinctions to core concepts.

• •

The "we" used throughout this book refers to the author in cooperation with the various parts of her own individual self (vital, mind, heart, spirit, higher self), her guides and inner colleagues and the great collective consciousness of which the reader is also a participant. The use of "we" may also refer to the collective, or group, that has assembled from many planes of consciousness to deal with a specific situation (other humans and their guides, elementals, devas, extraterrestrials and metaterrestrials or life forms and guardians of a specific occupation, such as finance or an energy such as peace).

• •

Interdimensional consciousness is not a linear concept. However, we are describing it through a linear medium, the written word. To do so, we have chosen to go into one aspect at a time, describe that aspect and then tie it back to the totality of its full field. None of the aspects grows in isolation to the others. Thus, this book is both a primer and an advanced text. If at times you feel lost, keep reading; the totality will emerge.

We will be giving overall snapshots of a section of consciousness, then looking more closely at some aspects of interest to the topic of this book. We are building a picture of the forest and the location of various plants and trees within it. There are always more trees than we can look at in a general walk-through. You may well find yourself stopping time and again, in your reading, to examine some concept just discussed, which just showed you a beautiful new flower you never saw before or a path through another section of the forest that you want to go explore. Do so! Have fun! We will be waiting for your return, to continue our exploration together.

Much of this book is a result of interdimensional discussions I have had with various life forms as we worked together to resolve a variety of interdimensional situations. Most of these situations occurred during the course of my work—consulting, teaching and preparing energy tools. Having spent many decades immersed in the metaphysical study of consciousness, I eventually was taught by my guides that, for me, at this time, the best way to master universal consciousness was to examine how it applies to a specific, concrete situation on earth. There is a world of energy involved in every single action on earth. My guides and I have a contract we energetically signed with each other: I am to take on assignments presented to me, if they say our group can handle it; when I have no idea how we will handle it, they show me the how. We jokingly refer to it as our interdimensional work-study program.

One method visionaries have traditionally used when receiving information from spirit is to express that information in a short verbal statement. Sutras and haiku are highly polished examples of this approach; they offer a world of information in a few words. Throughout the book we offer brief flashes of insight on various topics. However, my guides asked me to arrange the hundreds of informational merkabahs in a linearly understandable whole. They next asked me to expand the insights in a comprehensive linear manner. There will be, of necessity, some redundant concepts, but each aspect that is discussed slots into the overall field somewhat differently.

When you are new to energy work of this type, it helps to work on these concepts with an expert, and we encourage you to explore your local area for any workshops related to the development of subtle energy skills.

To help you integrate some of the concepts, we have included a chapter of exercises on the development of interdimensional skills and offered other practical exercises throughout the book. It is useful for you to have a basic understanding of the merkabah and consciousness before practicing the exercises in chapter 9, so we suggest that you be sure to read the chapters 1 through 8 before moving into these exercises.

Some of you who are reading this book may be unsure about your own ability to do interdimensional communication. Eventually, in some lifetime, every human being will be able to operate interdimensionally. But if for now you simply want to read about it and not attempt it, that is fine.

To further assist you, I have created a CD to guide you through some prime interdimensional exercises, which you can download from our website. Go to *www.crystal-life.com* and click on the front-page icon for this book. Inside this room you will find the CD, which you can receive for free by entering this code: YANA2012.

There will eventually be a second book available on this topic, containing stories about my work.

All of the information in this book reflects what we humans once knew how to do. We once knew how to travel through time and space, to surf the waves of consciousness as they move through the universe. We once knew how to identify with, learn from and even transform into other shapes when necessary for our work. These legends live on in the tales of our grandfathers and grandmothers, of Merlin the magician and the famous Crow medicine women who were shape-shifters.

I have taught the information in this book in many workshops. I have learned from this teaching that different people experience the same field of information in different ways. Some sense, others see, feel, smell, touch, hear, know. One way is not better or worse than another. Each of us has a particular energetic strength and that is where we first enter this work. Eventually, we learn to understand consciousness in all these ways. If the material in this book seems strange to you, but you feel compelled to read it anyway, consider translating the concepts into familiar energies for your own understanding and grow from there.

And now, as my guides like to say, let's go surfing! We'll pick up an energy wave and go for an inner ride.

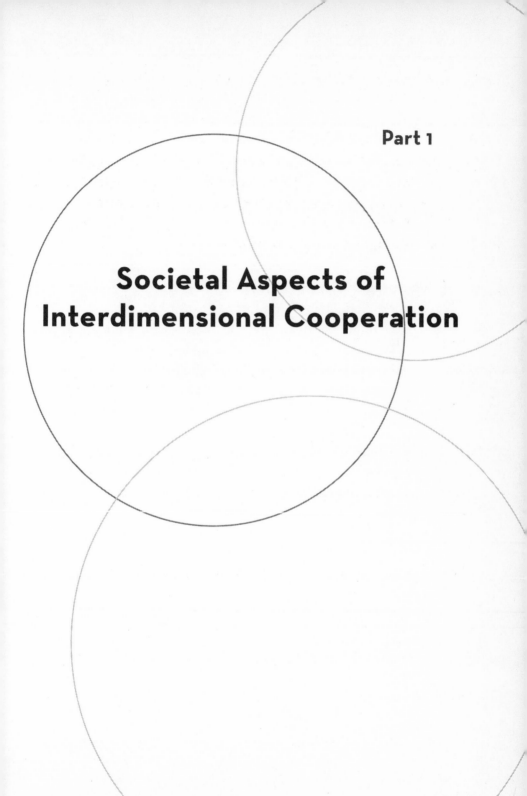

Part 1

Societal Aspects of
Interdimensional Cooperation

Chapter 1
My Own Journey to Interdimensional Consciousness

We have each gone through uncountable experiences. Each experience has required that we choose a course of action. Each choice has defined the direction from which our next choice will come. Each choice, made consciously or unconsciously, takes the undulating snake line of our soul's evolution on an increasingly unique course through time and space.

Several of my more mainstream human colleagues have observed that some people may find my knowledge of interdimensional society very strange. They suggested I tell the readers a bit about myself, so they can see that, like them, I had a very normal upbringing, shaped by the same societal forces as many others.

This chapter is meant to help you grasp the normalness of my capacities and the fact that we *all* have the same type of capacity latently waiting inside ourselves, ready to come forward as we develop. My intent is to show that the capacities I have developed are very real, very human and easily learned (by some). This autobiographical chapter provides a synopsis of my life and the perceptual changes that have enabled me to do the work documented here.

In chapter 15, Intergalactic Contact, I'll share with you my encounter with the larger community of which earth is a part.

As relatively straight and ordinary as this chapter is, chapter 15 describes my entry into the world of intergalactic and interdimensional knowledge from another perspective. The perspectives of these two chapters are each true, they simply emphasize different aspects of the same situation.

· · · ·

I grew up in a normal family, with a mother, father and younger brother, and as a Philadelphia Quaker. As a Quaker, I practiced meditation regularly on a private basis and in weekly community silent meetings. Through this religion, the closest of the Western Christian traditions to Eastern yoga, I learned about the spark of God inside all living beings and the inherent equality of all beings in the sight of God.

I attended Swarthmore College, an ultraliberal, Quaker-founded institution outside Philadelphia. It emphasized equality in an era when women and minorities were not accorded that right elsewhere. It emphasized intellectual, objective analysis and community service and freed me from a belief in the utter sanctity of mainstream cultural mores. After graduation I worked at the Massachusetts Institute of Technology (M.I.T.), publicizing its humanities programs for a year. Then I married another Swarthmore graduate, had two sons and joined a cutting-edge yoga community at the time when Eastern philosophy was just making inroads in the West. This was an era of dreams—the time of the Beatles—when the youth felt love and light would solve all.

As I was trying to decide whether or not to join the yoga group, I was given the inner message that the teacher was like an uncle to me—not my direct lineage, but "a part of the family"—and that a day would come when it would be time for me to leave and go in another direction. My husband and I decided to join the group and moved to its headquarters, which was set up as an in-city ashram in New York City. I was an active part of the group for over twenty-five years, teaching free meditation and philosophy classes, starting an evening school in Manhattan to bring free meditative activities to the community, writing many of the yoga group's brochures and press releases and serving as one of its media spokespeople. During this time, my sons grew into men and left to pursue their own dreams. My husband and I divorced, and I went to work at the United Nations Development Programme (UNDP).

The United Nations (U.N.) is a remarkable place. There, on the physical plane, the world is attempting to bring together people with radically different perceptions of the same situation. It is not easy to do. The most successful approaches come from finding common ground and being very flexible in perceptions regarding any situation. The need to negotiate a way forward when presented with differing views strikes home very clearly in the staff's everyday work. In our division, the staff came from twenty different countries, and we even had to negotiate how we were going to brew the morning pot of coffee! Working interdimensionally is much the same; it is negotiating for an equitable common ground.

I had entered the UNDP as a strong, athletic, twenty-four-hour runner. After five years, I was so sick I could barely walk to work. I was determined to discover why. After going to regular doctors without success, I found a chiropractor who used an alternative diagnostic device called a vegatest. This test showed that I was electromagnetically sensitive and filled 90 percent with electromagnetic radiation poisoning—a result of my particular energy type living and working in New York City. That is, I was someone who relates to creation via the electromagnetic bands of energy, has dry skin that conducts electricity and is living in an environment where most of the electromagnetic body frequencies were being usurped or polluted by machine, land energies and the powerful emotional/mental energies found in an international diplomatic community. All options for feeding my personal electromagnetic needs had one by one become affected.

The electromagnetic radiation poisoning had, by this time, filled my body to the point where I had continuous nausea, diarrhea and emotional stress. I had carpal tunnel syndrome so severe that my hands were claw shaped, and the mainstream doctors had recommended surgery.

Electromagnetic sensitivity was not well known at that time, and no one knew what to do about mine. The chiropractor, a kind man, told me gently that I basically had two choices: quit my job or die (because the work environment was so toxic to my particular energy type). My yoga teacher told me to stay, which added another layer of distress to the situation. This life-or-death situation was the transformative goad that helped me break with the "rules" of ordinary third-dimension perception and also with the "rule" of obedience to external authority figures.

The actual break with third-dimension perception occurred one day as I sat looking at my computer—the device to which, I was told, I was allergic. I was praying for assistance in understanding what was occurring in me when the thought popped into my mind: "If something is killing me, I should be able to see it." I experienced a conscious shift of perception, like a quarter turn of a kaleidoscope. Suddenly, a very new picture formed. I could see and feel the energy coming towards me from the computer. As I watched, I thought, "If I can see it, I can do something about it."

Like many others who were at that time developing new modalities in the field of subtle energy and resonant technology, I broke with the standard perceptions of our society because of the simple necessity to survive.

During this difficult period, I also came into contact with an intergalactic group called the Arcturians. Immediately following this contact, I retained only the vaguest recall of the incident, but it changed me forever. (See chapter 15 for this story.) My comprehension of subtle energy expanded, and I reconnected to the larger consciousness family to which I had always belonged, but had not been consciously aware of. Through their help, I began to understand the nature of consciousness more clearly. They helped me take control of my own life, a right that until then I kept handing over to others, and value more highly the feminine, cooperative aspect of consciousness.

Prior to contact and the escalation of my illness, I had been interested solely in subtle energy as it affected the practice of yogic meditation and the ascension into the more rarefied planes of consciousness above the earth experience. I had applied this knowledge to my running, learning to keep going by rising above the body and watching it perform its athletic duties on the physical plane. Now I began researching everything I could find on subtle energy as it affects the human body. Because my health issue was coming from new technologies—computers and cellphones—I was drawn into observing how the earth itself was being affected.

The first thing I had to do was to find the courage to challenge the authority figures of society at that time. The fact that I could see and affect subtle energy was not acceptable among the people I then knew. No ordinary people I then knew, not even the members of the yoga group I belonged to, could affect human energy in such a way. If I broached the subject with someone, the other person would invariably indicate I was out of line to be talking like this. So first I had to take the very huge step of acknowledging to myself that I *was* seeing subtle energy, that I was not crazy and that I would not be punished by God or society if I quietly admitted these things to myself.

I began finding, tucked away here and there, individuals and groups who could see and work with subtle energy. I took classes and initiations via many different lineages.

The next step was to learn from these groups and individuals how I could avoid, remove or change the noxious energy fields around myself or how I could protect myself from them. Then I needed to clear out the electromagnetic radiation poisoning that had already invaded my body system. And finally, I needed to establish a method of functioning successfully in a difficult environmental situation that was not going to go away.

I realized there was not going to be a worldwide change, at least for now, in the energetic premises upon which our modern technology, with its unconscious manipulation of pervasive electromagnetic and microwave fields, is based. Since, like many earth lovers, my personal method of contacting the universe was through these same electromagnetic wavelengths that technology was usurping, I would have to adjust to remain alive.

For the next several years I searched out every bit of alternative knowledge that I could find on how the earth really functioned—not how we had been taught that it functioned. I checked out everything with my own inner guides; some of these guides came and went, instructing me in specific energy forms, while others remained as my long-term teachers.

Learning how to successfully work with inner guides and teachers was also part of my internal training during these years. I learned, gradually, to distinguish between the real messages and the ones my mind or emotions created from my desires to have a rapid answer. I learned to distinguish between the forces and guides of darkness who serve our world and the forces of light who serve in a more loving and beneficial manner.

I learned to continually turn the kaleidoscope of perception. Only after I had relaxed the cultural coulds and shoulds of our third-dimension world and allowed myself to accept other perceptions as equally valid could I proceed to make sense of the information I was receiving.

Then the time came when, for further progress, I needed to understand my own soul's growth. The universe responded. I experienced a sudden energetic readjustment of my consciousness—a rush that traveled up my spine, unlocking blockages and permitting the snake energy of awareness to course through my energy field—a process known in yoga as awakening the kundalini. Energy instantly realigned inside my existence, and doors opened that for millennia had been firmly shut. I saw, moving up from the base of my human existence, my own past. Significant incarnations, each built on the experiences of preceding lives, came before my eyes and snapped into place, so that gradually there emerged a very full-bodied and uniquely defined individual, who is my current self.

That experience taught me that I am unique, as are we all, for no one else can possibly be exactly like any one of us. We have each gone through uncountable experiences. Each experience has required that we choose a course of action. Each choice has defined the direction from which our next choice will come. Each choice, made consciously or unconsciously, takes the undulating snake line of our soul's evolution on an increasingly unique course through time and space.

We may have started from the same brood as many others, from the same part of the one source, and each member of our brood may have the same ultimate goal. But the direction by which each of us arrives at this goal is different. It is, in large part, determined by what we individually face in the broad, complex playing fields of life and by what means and direction we have chosen to move forward with our lives.

I did heal myself, with the help of many energies in many fields of consciousness. I then took a stand, a very brave one for the me of that time. I decided to devote myself to subtle-energy work full-time. I began making subtle energy jewelry such as I had used to heal myself. In 1996, I founded my company, Crystal Life Technology, Inc., and started one of the earliest websites for esoteric products (*www.crystal-life.com*). Then, taking a big gulp, I quit my job at the UNDP. I dedicated myself to finding solutions to common energy and consciousness issues that fell within the domains of my particular soul family and circle of guides.

I was inwardly guided to exhibit Crystal Life Technologies products, which I called Resonance®: Products with Purpose®, at a wide variety of shows across the length and breadth of our beautiful country. These shows gave me the opportunity to become friends with, meet or observe the pioneers in consciousness who were bravely coming forward with books and products dealing with subtle energy. The members of this core group were aware of alternate means of perception, which had become part of their knowledge via one or all of three main avenues. For some, that avenue was the need to heal themselves of illnesses mainstream medicine could not handle. For others, it was contact with positive or negative life forms from other dimensions who are seeking to interact with earth. And some, such as those we now call the Indigoes and Crystals, were born with alternate perception and were struggling to integrate this perspective with the far differing one of mainstream society.

All of us were aware that what we were doing was the wave of the future, of where humanity was going, and that we were all being consciously guided to contribute our own new human knowledge as part of the solution. Two years later I began writing a book, which was eventually published as *Explorations in Consciousness.*

A few years later, I joined the American Society of Dowsers, a venerable organization that provides information on how to access information located anywhere in the universe using the simple science called divining, or dowsing. All dowsers work interdimensionally, connecting to whatever energy of the light is required to complete the job they have undertaken, whether that is locating water, oil or lost children and pets, or clearing spirits and ley lines on a piece of property.

Eventually, as my consciousness expanded, I was able to have fully aware discussions with my own personal inner team. There are many different life forms on every individual's interdimensional team. These team members include our higher self, our incarnational and energetic lineal families and the inner forces we contract, before birth, to work with while on earth. They also include the guardians of whatever fields we choose to work with at any time. While I began by referring to these life-forces as my guides, they eventually asked me to acknowledge the reality that we are a collective—an interdimensional team, of which I am an equal partner. They asked me to shift my perspective to work with them as a fully equal colleague. I now refer to them either as colleagues—when being technically correct—or in the more colloquial term of "guides," meaning as among equals, each with a specialty they are contributing to the whole.

I also have an energetic lineage that is always available for me to work with. In my case, this lineage includes the three archangels Metatron, Melchizedek and Michael. It also includes Thoth, a human who has transcended the bonds of death and is known in others of his incarnations as Valmiki, Hermes, Mercury, Paracelsus and St. Germain. This group is one of those focused on helping our earth successfully transition into the new world now upon us. I work with other colleagues as the situation requires. There is no one on earth without similar groups of colleagues.

Metatron, Melchizedek and Michael are each a vast consciousness composed of many aspects. Each of their existences is similar, on very high planes, to our body. Our body is a group effort composed of life forms that have agreed to work together to form bones, flesh, liver, mind, etc. If you ask the liver who it is, the answer will be slightly different than if you ask the bones, although the overall unit is the same. This is also true of the vast cosmic beings. This is why when different people convey information from, say, Archangel Michael, their messages sound slightly different although the core concept is consistent. Each is connecting to a different aspect of the same life form.

We are a part of all the larger life forms from whom we have descended, existing as a part of their consciousness "body." This "body" functions somewhat like our own body. A cell in our body exists complete unto itself and also as a part of a unit called the liver which is part of the digestive system which is part of the human being. In the same way we humans each exist as complete unto ourselves but are also a part of larger and yet larger units of consciousness that reaches full size only upon re-entering the original source itself.

Likewise, our inner colleagues have their own roles to play, and it is very useful for us to understand what they are. For example, in my group it was explained that Archangel Michael is the warrior, Melchizedek is the teacher and Metatron is the scientist. Thoth, on the other hand, has explained to me that he is a human being who evolved up into cosmic consciousness. He works specifically and consciously with individuals—work that takes up a portion of his very vast individual attention. Thoth comes and goes in my life, but is always with me quiescently and available consciously when I need him, such as when I need a specific human explanation because I am not comprehending the energies of a situation.

Metatron and his merkabah energy are especially present in my existence when I am working with core-level consciousness issues. He comes forward very solidly to explain these issues to me. When I need to learn about an aspect of the merkabah, either for this book or for a project in which I am involved, Metatron brings a full merkabah of information about the topic into my being. Some topics I grasp instantly, and others present themselves a part at a time. Once I understand them and am ready to teach the concept, Melchizedek approaches me with the energy of the detached instructor. Melchizedek helps me to teach others.

When I am ready to act, such as when I am clearing a piece of land, then the team member present is Michael, the great warrior of the angels. The three archangels are often affectionately called the 3Ms by those who work with them. I and many others are part of the 3Ms' efforts on behalf of the earth grids—that is, stabilizing, clearing and energizing the earth field during this critical period of evolution.

The 3Ms have a great sense of humor and will often joke with us humans. Their humor is distinctive. When I meet another earth grid worker with the same lineage, we sometimes exchange stories about jokes the 3Ms have told us and instantly recognize the similarity in energy. This group uses humor as a way to lighten up the human, especially at the start, when the enormity of what we are learning and how it is significant to humans can cause us to become too serious.

These guides are especially fond of poking holes in puffed balloons of human pomposity. When we started working together, they often showed me what people I was in awe of were really thinking. They wanted to show me that I had no need to feel inferior to people who were pretending to be spiritually elevated and were using this pretense as a power device to control others. And, on the other hand, they would show me the true spirituality of very humble life forms that classic religions often look down on, such as flowers; a quiet, humble mother; ants going about their work; or a fairy tending its flower or tree.

I had, by this time, started attending meetings of other spiritual groups. One of my favorite experiences occurred at a meeting where a so-called inner group of supposedly spiritual people were fawning over their leader. My guides asked me if I would like to see what was really happening; when I said yes, they opened up my third eye. They showed me how these people had given away their own capacity for universal centeredness to the will of the not-quite-perfect leader. Thus, their own crown chakras were now limp and hanging down the side of their heads, or the very strong ones had the chakra squashed down and crumpled on top of their heads. I was horrified at this sight, but my guides joked with me.

"Not to worry," they said. "Why, look—some of the women have even made this into a fashion statement." They directed my attention to several who had put a bit of a saucy flip to their collapsed chakra, which now hung on the side of their head like a cluster of old-fashioned rolled curls.

At every point along my path of growing self-awareness, I was offered the free-will choice of several options. I could have chosen to do nothing about my new comprehensions, or I could have made vastly different choices. If I had been interested in some other aspect of human endeavor and not the understanding of spirit, what I chose would have been different. As we are all infinite, in the larger sense, it does no one on our teams any good should they make the choice for us.

There are millions of humans who have had contact with some type of more spiritually evolved interdimensional life form. The choices different people make after their individual experiences are very personal. I had already committed myself, in this lifetime, to understanding more thoroughly the nature of God. Now the universe is a balance of give and take. When you help life forms in other dimensions, there is usually reciprocity: subtle life forms are generous, grateful and gracious. Once the situation has been solved, and the energy is back on track, the life forms generally return to thank you and ask what it is they can offer you as a gift. My inner colleagues recommended I ask the life forms to teach me more about themselves and their world.

The life forms have always been surprised and delighted by this response, and proceed to teach me more about how the source works through their world.

While I do not have a background or interest in science and mathematics, what I have been shown jibes very well with the principles of quantum and chaos physics. Although I do not understand the technical details that interest scientists in these fields, I do understand how the energy works. We have wonderful conversations about our similar experiences, learning from each other and thus helping extend the current bridging between spirit and science.

As I grew in awareness, there came a time when my guides explained that I needed to formally make a contract. When I asked what that was, they explained that I needed to commit myself to some course of action. What I chose would determine how I would grow from then on out.

They opened up a path of light to a place deep inside myself, where I could see what I really wanted from existence. I saw that I could not continue along the traditional spiritual path that saw life as inferior to spirit. I saw that I believed, to the very core of my being, that life on earth is the greatest of blessings. It holds within it the opportunity for the one ultimate source to manifest itself consciously in a very specific manner, through each beloved part of itself, of which I am one. I am, like everything else in existence, a very specific aspect of the source as it is seeking to fully manifest itself inside its own existence.

I saw that we all make contracts, consciously or unconsciously, and these contracts determine what part of infinite knowledge we explore. With the help of my guides, I formulated my own personal contract, which was then jointly accepted by myself, my soul family, and my guides. This personal contract is to positively assist any life form that wishes to participate in the positive evolution of the earth experience. This assistance is undertaken by the entire team, of whom I am the human, earth-steward part.

Whatever action is needed to resolve an issue is worked with by the entire group, who can call in assistance from whatever life forms we deem appropriate.

Before accepting a client, I always check with my team to see if this is something we should handle. My team told me not to be concerned about working with any client or situation we had agreed together to assist, no matter how strange or bizarre the situation may initially appear. I have trusted them on this and in every case have been shown a resolution that would work, usually one that teaches me totally new (to me) energetic "rules of the universe."

My acting and understanding is my growth. It can be as vast or as limited as I choose it to be. This does not make the situations I encounter any easier to deal with or my own life any easier to handle than any other human being's life. It does give me clarity, hope and a destination. And that is useful for a human being to have.

Shortly after formulating my own contract, I knew it was time for me to strike out on my own, to work specifically with my own guides. This was a very difficult time for me. I kept trying to see what would lie ahead if I took different courses, but I could not discern an answer. I asked my guides why I could, by now, clearly see into various of my own past lives, but sometimes I could not see the immediate future before me. My current situation was particularly difficult, they explained, because I was faced with many options going forward that right now looked very similar but in the future would lead me in far different directions. It was my free-will choice to choose the way forward.

Sometimes the future facing us at a juncture is so strong that we can clearly see which way we wish to proceed. At other times there are too many options for any to dominate. At a juncture such as I was now facing, my guides explained, it was like a traveler reaching a fork in the road from which many other paths branch out but the destinations were obscured by heavy fog. To further clarify the energies of this type of situation, my guides went on to show me the palm of my hand—one unit from which five fingers spread out. Each finger is different from the other, although emerging from the same source, just like the choices one makes in life. For a short time going forward, the energies may appear similar and one can even cross over to another path, but with distance the energy of the different choices begins to dominate and it is too late to then change.

The situation is actually more complex than this, my inner colleagues explained, because included in such a major decision are the energies of past and future options, parallel universes and multiple dimensions. At every moment in our lives we are making choices—some smaller, some larger. Every decision we make affects the direction from which the next choice will appear.

After much inner turmoil—each of my options were so different and so major—I finally decided to leave the yoga group and focus on working exclusively with my own family of guides. I sold my house and moved from New York City to the Midwest— to the heartland of America.

Here, where there is a great connection to the earth and a great gentleness of spirit, I began to intensely explore, in partnership with my inner colleagues, the nature of Mother Earth.

In 2001 I became a consultant on personal and subtle land-clearing issues. Four years later, I cofounded the Institute for the Study of Interdimensional Cooperation (ISIC) and, expanding on the business I had previously begun in New York, opened the Crystal Life Technology subtle-energy and stone store in Geneva, Illinois. In 2007, I was elected to the Board of Trustees of the American Society of Dowsers, and my fellow board members then elected me to serve on its executive committee as executive secretary.

My work now includes land and building energy clearing. People call me in for several reasons, such as finding out why a home will not sell, the feeling that there are geopathic issues affecting the family's health or the sense that there are spirits in the home.

Above time and space all life exists simultaneously in the same field. The particular time, space and place that is perceived comes from the focus or identification of a particular life form with a specific frequency. Shift your frequency and a totally new image emerges. This can be as simple as a shift from seeing the jealousy with which someone approaches you to focusing on their hunger to know, and responding to that. It could be more complex, such as seeing the origins of the battles between the members of a home as not actually emerging from their current feelings but from the energy imprinted there from an ancient, violent battle between two Native American tribes. The ability to locate the source of the issue, through time/space, is the work of an interdimensional communicator.

When I am contacted to work on a home, on arrival I first ask its owners exactly what they feel the problem to be, or what they need to have resolved. I then focus only on the energies related to the specific topic at hand. I do not concern myself with the multiple other issues that exist there and might bother people other than my client.

Once I have clarified the issue the owners want investigated, I go by myself for a walk through the home and check out the property as well. I listen to the complaints and problems and aspirations of the many kinds of life forms connected to the issue at hand. These life forms may include the house spirit, the resident deva and nature spirits, the energies present in the ley lines, and all the other life forms from other dimensions who feel they have a right to be heard on the matter at hand.

Each home has one overall deva as well as subsidiary spirits for each room. They are charged by their world to see to the well-being of everything and everyone concerned with the house. Once these energies know I can communicate with them, they are very firm yet helpful in explaining the situation and the problem from their point of view. Usually what has happened is that humans have unwittingly unbalanced the energies of the area. These nature forms ask for my assistance to help them get their area of responsibility back in balance. This includes discussing the situation with the owners then connecting the two parties together so they can communicate with each other (like an old-fashioned phone operator plugging cords into lines). Once connected, the two parties can come to a common understanding. Now that they know each other's "frequency number," they can talk back and forth as they wish.

Technically, I have created this space by providing a very large, clear, contained space—a merkabah in my tradition—that, in energy work, is called holding space. When necessary, I also work remotely on these issues, although I prefer to be physically present. Remote work is a common option for dowsers, as we can connect to the energies of a situation above time and space and look into the situation from wherever we are.

Chapter 2
Connecting to Other Life Forms

The Golden Age of Awareness that earth is now moving into is affecting all life on earth. Whether we are mineral, plant, animal, human or elemental, we are recognizing that each other exists, that we can communicate with each other and that we need each other to perfect the multidimensional world in which we all live.

We say we live in a solid, normal, third-dimensional reality. But if we stop for a moment and consider the various ways in which different people interact with the forces of this universe, what is "normal"?

We are part of a very large, very old and very diverse universe. Many intergalactic and interdimensional issues abound in this vast society. As we on earth mature and move into this larger space, we will need to learn how to deal with issues that are arising in a vast variety of ways.

Many Different Worlds

There are many dimensions and many worlds, extending in perceptual range from those close to our frequency to those that are extremely different. The life forms in all these worlds are just as real as we are, and, like us, they are each directly connected to the one ultimate source of all.

The ability of humans to perceive these other worlds is cyclical in nature. Many visionary traditions around the world have documented these varying cycles of awareness, including the Navajo, Mayan, European esoteric (including Nostradamus) and the Hindu and Buddhist cultures. Each tradition, because of the way it has culturally evolved, terms this cycle, or rotation of ages, slightly differently. Yet most are in agreement that right now we are on the cusp of a new age, one of spirituality, which may occur relatively peacefully or cataclysmically, it is up to humans to make that choice.

In the yogic tradition where I received many decades of training, we refer to this process as a cycle of four ages, proceeding from the highest Golden Age (Satya Yuga), when humanity has its greatest access to spiritual consciousness, to the darkest Age of Iron or Age of Darkness (Kali Yuga), when humanity is the farthest from awareness of its spiritual origins. It is believed via my yogic lineage that we are near the end, or at the end, of the thousands of years-long Kali Yuga and are transitioning to the start of a new and higher cycle—the next Golden Age.

Whenever this Satya Yuga occurs, humans are able to perceive life forms that exist in the higher frequencies. We can see levels of energy that we have not been able to see in many thousands of years. These energies, life forms and structures have always been there, but because they exist in faster, higher, more subtle frequencies than the energy that forms the Kali Yuga, most humans could not perceive the forms.

During the Kali Yuga, some visionaries have stated that evidence proving the existence of previous, very high earth civilizations was right in front of our eyes, but we had not been able to see it or, if we saw it, to understand what it meant. For example, the sleeping prophet Edgar Cayce, working in the early years of the twentieth century, often made comments about various physical structures that would prove the existence of ancient civilizations, saying that these structures would suddenly be discovered at specific years in the future. He said that the steadily expanding human consciousness would suddenly be able to vibrationally access the level of awareness during which these structures were built. Until then, although this evidence was already there, it would not be understood and hence would remain "unseen." Cayce specifically predicted the discovery of sites off the coast of Bimini and Cuba that would prove the existence of Atlantis and the discovery of a secret chamber under the Sphinx in Cairo, Egypt, that would prove the antiquity of that structure. Both these situations have come to pass; scientists are discovering, exploring and sometimes photographing these structures.

This same expansion of consciousness has brought about a significant change in the way I teach interdimensional communication. At the turn of the millennium I needed to explain to audiences that other dimensions really do exist. A few years later the public believed in these worlds and wanted to know how to enter these for themselves. Today attendance at workshops has steadily increased, and members of the public are eager to discuss exactly what they are observing or communicating with and want to learn how they can work with the situation.

Our efforts do affect others. Over three years, I took students on annual trips to an Illinois prairie to work with the nature spirits on some energetic alterations that needed to take place because of ignorant human land stripping and house and road building nearby. Each year returning students saw a positive change in a once-discordant situation. Each year several students have been able to take actual photographs of the energies with whom we are cooperating.

Every age has its reason for existing. In the recent Kali Yuga, because we humans could only see the gross physical, we were forced to find gross physical solutions for issues that began in spirit. If someone stole something from a store, they were put in jail or fined and given a warning. That physical solution now underlies all the other spiritual, moral solutions of previous ages. That is, if people don't behave correctly for moral reasons, there is now a specific, unpleasant physical result that will deter them.

Life forms existing in other more subtle dimensions have greater energetic mobility. However, often they are not able to get down below the situation and hold the solution in the physical for it to take effect. This is one reason nature spirits often need human assistance to correct a situation: they cannot affect the physical aspect of the problem.

I learned this first-hand one summer while attending a conference in the Maine woods. While I was walking in the woods, a woodland fairy approached me and pleaded for my assistance. When I followed him, I discovered that several small saplings had fallen over his community's core "sweet spot" or energy-emitting vortex. The saplings were blocking the energies of that area, and it looked very weak, rundown and energetically messy. I took some time to move the saplings aside and continued on my walk. That night there was a full moon, and the next day, on my walk through that area, I could not believe my eyes!!! The faery community was totally transformed, filled with light and energy. The faery representative greeted me and invited me in to sit at the center of the circle. Then he and his compatriots graced me with the vision of the entire community having danced late into the night before, in celebration.

The faeries graced me with greater awareness, and when I asked if they had any message for the students I was about to teach, they replied: "Yes. Tell them we need them. We cannot do the work without them. Humans are the arms and legs of this earth."

During the Kali Yuga, we humans have so thoroughly explored the gross physical reality of our world that we have formed very specific methods to deal with a wide variety of physical abuse and opportunities. This knowledge will serve us well when we enter intergalactic society, where there will be many types and levels of life forms interacting with us and requiring a wise response from our side.

However, the human effort to stabilize the energies of the third dimension has also fenced us into its perceptions. This is a dynamic inherent in a visit to any specific location. First we are a visitor, then we start to settle in. Soon we identify so solidly with the place that we may not want to leave, until the restrictions present in any single field of energy may cause us to want to leave it to explore other options. There are ways subtle energy workers throughout history have recognized and worked with this situation. This book presents one method to do so.

The Golden Age of Awareness that earth is now moving into is affecting all life on earth. Whether we are mineral, plant, animal, human or elemental, we are recognizing that each other exists, that we can communicate with each other and that we need each other to perfect the multidimensional world in which we all live.

Right here on earth there are many, many worlds interfacing with our human one. When you sit in your backyard on a summer day, enjoying the peaceful sun, notice how many other worlds, just on the gross physical level, are interacting with ours. Look around at the trees and plants, grasshoppers and raccoons; the air forms, such as birds and flying insects; and the subterranean life forms, such as worms and moles. We have, until recently, existed as separate energy systems. How much more effective we could all be if we consciously worked together.

In a similar fashion we coexist with other frequency domains. Above time and space, we all exist in the same space. By shifting frequency and angle, we can see into these worlds. This is interdimensional communication. Throughout the book, we provide you with specific exercises to show you how to communicate interdimensionally and guide you through the process.

If something can be imagined, it is a reality in some world. If we can enter into a world, we have the possibility of manifesting its purpose on earth. We unconsciously create worlds with our thoughts at every moment: "I am no good," "I am the greatest," "Only Christians/Muslims/Hindus have the *real* God," etc. Our thoughts become so solid and real that we are fenced into that world, and it takes great effort on our part to get out. Interdimensional communicators, shamans and occultists know how to consciously create or enter into forms with their thoughts and energy and also how to exit. They are very careful to always know the exit site before they enter a new world. Some energies seem likeable in their subtle form, but have disguised components that can create problems.

Like all interdimensional communicators, I have been in conscious contact with life forms from many other dimensions. These life forms are real and able to interact with humans on projects of joint benefit, or detriment, to both worlds—ours and theirs. Each domain has many types of forms within it. Most humans are in contact with other worlds every day. We don't think of these realms as being other dimensions, but they are. Once we can accept this, it becomes easier to extend our perception a bit farther and accept the reality of worlds farther away from ours. Just some of the many dimensions and universes that interact with earth are discussed below.

Life Forms Who Have Helped to Physically Manifest Earth

Nature Spirits
These beings include the devas and the tree, plant, water, fire, air and stone peoples. They also include the faery folk: the gnomes, trolls, fairies and elves (known by different names in different cultures). These life forms care for our earth on a subtle, higher

frequency level than ours and sometimes need our help to handle a task that exists in the solid third dimension, such as moving logs and eliminating pollution of a stream.

Very often we are aware of these contacts in several ways that we have largely learned to disregard. Should we see or experience any of the following, there is most likely a life form from another realm somewhere around: A sudden chill comes over you for no outer reason. You hear a sound, word or voice, and no one is outwardly nearby. You see movements out of the corner of your eyes, but when you turn your head, no one is there. You see strange lights or forms. You sense a presence. Objects have been moved, and no one has outwardly been at that location. You take photographs and find mists or "orbs" of light with faces or grids weaving through them.

Life Forms from Other Dimensions Who Have Caused Alterations in the Human Genetic Code

There are many life forms who have interacted with earth and whom our folklore has lumped together and called gods and goddesses. This was because, during the Kali Yuga, most humans did not have the ability to distinguish what was occurring. The statement that the visitor was a god made it easier to acquire acceptance and obedience from the humans. This group actually includes a wide variety of life forms with a wide variety of motivations. Many of these life forms intermarried with humans, resulting in children and lineages with exceptional abilities.

In many cultures there are myths and fables about beings who materialized or descended from the skies and either contributed to the rapid advancement of that culture by establishing better forms of government and moral codes such as is found in the Assyrian, Native American and Mayan legends or who intermarried with men or women from that culture and whose offspring were exceptional in their leadership such as in the Egyptian dynasties. Today many speak of extraterrestrials who specifically wanted to alter the human gene pool for some reason, either with a high or nefarious motivation. Sometimes they want to make their group a part of the versatile human genetic pool, and other times they want to utilize the broad human genetic pool to assist their own troubled race to survive.

There are stories of elemental forces (such as the thunder god Zeus) who descended and sired heroes such as Hercules and beings who descended and sired "monsters" such as the Minotaur. There are stories about humans who transcended death and reappeared time after time in different guises to assist earth in times of need; the ancient Lemurians and Atlanteans are said to have known how to do this and one of these was said to be Valmiki, later known in Egypt as the scribe god Thoth; the Essenes were also said to know how to do this, and the appearance throughout the ages to Native American nations of a man known as the Peacekeeper is said by some to be of that lineage.

There are also time travelers and advanced human beings who appear in certain times to affect the gene pool of humanity and also the political, cultural and religious orientation of a particular society.

"Mythic" Creatures (Centaurs, Unicorns, Dragons and the Like)

Fables usually state that certain fantastical creatures, such as the Minotaur and Chiron the centaur, were born to human women who mated with "gods." Some fantastical creatures actually once existed on earth but disappeared because they were life forms who were not able to survive in the rough arena of our volatile earth. If we re-examine the folklore descriptions of the origins and disappearances of these creatures, we can sometimes decipher what may have occurred.

Life Forms of Other Worlds Who Interact with Earth to Assist Us

Inner Colleagues

Our guides and guardians are life forms in other dimensions who are working with us to solve various issues. Although these life forms exist in subtle realms, that does not make them "higher" or more worthy than we are. Once you have begun learning about energy, a true guide will discuss the equality of all members of your group, explaining you are all colleagues with different tasks to perform for the whole. To get the group's work done, you need each other, each working from free will for the collective whole.

A very fast way to tell if you are working with a real guide is whether they honor your free will and spiritual equality. If *any life forms* attempt to command your obedience, threaten to destroy you, attempt to make you grovel before their magnificence or state that they will elevate you to power above all others, politely decline to work with them. They are not of the light. In this free-will universe, we have the source-given right to refuse to work with any life form, and they *must* accept that decision and leave. They will sometimes seek to stay by attempting to convince you that you are powerless to do anything about them, but that is not true.

Higher selves, soul families and parallel realities are aspects of ourselves that exist in other dimensions. You simultaneously exist in parallel realities, alternate earths, and other worlds in which you have sometimes quite different life situations. This is an area I have not delved into, yet, in any great depth; you can search the Internet for writings on this topic. However, the basic principle is that our life form is very complex, and it is possible (for I have done this) to separate yourself into different parallel aspects, each of which exists as a whole being able to communicate with the others. Being aware of your own parallel existences can result in illuminating interpersonal discussions on various matters of great importance in your life. You can learn from these other parts of your own existence how they are handling, or would handle, the matter in their world.

You exist as separate but equal "faces" of a higher-dimensional being who has separated itself into twelve or so clocklike positional energies—like a Native American medicine wheel—to experience and work on life-perfecting issues simultaneously; each face focuses on a specific aspect of the issue. Thus, for example, some people may totally believe they were once Cleopatra and even have access to private information on her life that no one else knows about; it is possible that they are part of the same family that evolved Cleopatra and, on the energetic combined level above her life, are partaking of that evolved knowledge in their own current life. It could also be that they have entered the morphogenetic field of the Cleopatra energy and mistake that for their own personal field.

You exist as a separate individual, but you are also connected to many other aspects of yourself. How you handle your life situations affects all the other parts of your family. When you are facing a crisis and want to give up, believing your response will not affect anyone else but yourself, remember that your response actually does affect many others, so choose it bravely and wisely.

Extraterrestials

In chapter 15, Intergalactic Contact, I discuss my own interactions with other galactic life forms. Many of these beings have made great sacrifices to either be birthed into earth form or to communicate with us in order to assist us during this crucial period of our rejoining galactic society. These beings may come from related or unrelated, friendly or hostile domains. Many in the universe value earth and what it is offering and seeking to offer to the universe. Earth has taken on the challenge of solid physical form; this is relatively rare in the universe, most other life forms existing in subtler realms. Our physical form, and the opportunities it provides to experience all other energies while in the physical, attracts life forms from other realms who are eager to experience this for themselves.

Angels

Angels are closely akin to us. There are many different types of angels with many different levels of capacities. Angels often look after and protect humans. They include Archangel Michael, a vast being of many parts who is in charge of ushering in the new world that is now appearing. Angels are a huge kingdom, and I recommend the books of Doreen Virtue, should you wish to know more about them.

Cosmic Beings

Some cosmic beings are the source forms from which earth has evolved, such as Metatron. Some, such as groups called the Ascended Masters, the Great White Brotherhood and Melchizedek, were once human but now serve through spirit. Some cosmic beings, such as Archangel Michael, serve the white light, and some, such as Lucifer, serve the dark light. Both the white light and the dark light ultimately serve the one and only source and assist us with our transformation. The function of the dark light beings is largely misunderstood in our current Western culture.

Life Forms of Other Times/Space/ Dimensions Who Interact with Us

Disembodied Spirits

Disembodied spirits were once human, plant or animal and are stuck between worlds—that of humans and that of the light. For some reason there is blockage that must be cleared or resolved so that they can move on and transition to the light. The blockage may be emotional, such as an animal being cruelly slaughtered. Sometimes humans don't look for a way to the light because they don't believe they are dead; their belief system says life ends with death and they know they still exist, ergo they are not dead. Sometimes the humans were focused on a task when they died and keep feeling they must finish the task before they can leave, but since they are not in the physical anymore, they cannot accomplish this.

Whatever the reason, it is important for these spirits to transition to the light, for their own progress to perfection and for that of their soul family as well. Progress for all these parties is stalled as long as the life forms remain in these in between worlds.

These spirits are often confused or ignorant as to where they are. Many interdimensional practitioners have the job of helping the spirits get back on course by transitioning them on to the light, so that they can resume their individual journeys and their soul families can continue to evolve. True energy workers and interdimensional communicators do not "ghost bust" or curse the life forms or punish them, but help them get back on their evolutionary track.

Sometimes people contact me, asking me to check out their house to see if they really have a ghost. When I explain that if I find one, I am obligated to assist the ghost to transition to the light, they don't proceed. They say they like having the ghost there. I once had an assistant who had a ghost cat who had frozen to death and would come into her bed to snuggle at her feet, and warm up. Several people, including myself, helped her send the ghost cat on, but it kept coming back. I asked her if she was calling it back, and she sheepishly said yes, because she liked the sweet nature and the companionship of the cat. I learned then that if a person asks for help removing the ghost but secretly harbors a desire to have the ghost remain, it has a hard time leaving. Once the ghost is sent on, it is important not to focus on the ghost for about three days or so, so that it can break all ties and move permanently into the light.

On another occasion, some colleagues and I helped a client assist their house ghost to go to the light. The woman was dressed in the prairie style of the late 1800s and pretty much stayed in a den section of the client's home—a location that once housed the original homestead kitchen. The ghost would often be seen standing in the same place, washing dishes, where she had been when the Indian attack occurred and she had been killed. Here the spirit had become bound to a place because it had not completed a task it believed was essential. The task represented a specific energy it felt it failed to master: protecting and caring for her family. The ghost could move about, although not far from its prime location and the task. She could not transition until the task was completed, and she could never figure out how to do so. In this situation, it is the job of the communicator to help the spirit resolve the issue and complete the task. We did so, helping her wash, dry and stack her dishes—that is, straighten the energies. Then she was at last free to go to the light, and did so.

Disembodied spirits also include a category known as "vital breakoffs." These are actually pieces of the person's energy field that were trapped at a specific traumatic point in time/space. The soul transitioned to the light, but part of the energy field was so traumatized it could not break free and transition. This can occur in an intense emotional situation, such as a war or death, when part of the energy separates and is locked into a location. The energy is holographic, in a way—that is, it looks like the original field, but it is not a full energy form, such as a ghost. A breakoff is capable only of repeating the crisis situation over and over, like an instant replay. It is not capable of changing the action or communicating on an original level. This breakoff can function to a certain level of complexity, but no further. It does not interact with humans as ghosts sometimes do.

One of the most well-known examples of breakoffs is the famous phantom brigade at Gettysburg, Pennsylvania. Here, many, many people have seen a squadron of Civil War-era–soldiers—in various states of civilian dress, such as that of farmers and hunters—assemble under the leadership of a captain, who guides them through a military drill in preparation for that sad battle that saw the death of thousands of brave men. Everyone who sees the brigade sees the same scenario. It never changes, and the solders are never aware of nor do they interact in any way with the living humans who are observing them.

Time Travelers

While there is a universal non-interference protocol that prohibits interference on other worlds and other time/space locales, such as was recounted often on *Star Trek,* there are always extenuating circumstances and life forms who won't comply. Time travelers will sometimes go back in time to attempt to change circumstances that had disastrous results. We discuss this in detail in chapter 3, A Multidimensional Social History. One of the most serious situations involving time travel deals with scientists whose worlds have been destroyed. They are seeking ways to remedy the situation by going back in time.

There are all the usual energetic reasons for time travel, as we discuss several times throughout this book. These include scientific study, adventure and attempts to correct or to understand and energetically rewrite the significance of various disastrous situations.

Humans are also capable of creating time tunnels that connect different points in time/space. I know this first-hand for it has happened to me on several occasions.

One time occurred when I was in college, and having a very difficult time emotionally I went to a favorite cliff, called Alligator Rock, and spent a long, long time considering my life, what if anything it was worth, what lay ahead for me and what might occur should I try suicide. Suddenly a shaft of clear energy went through me, head to toe, and I felt a very warm, comforting, mature and self-confident feminine energy move into and strengthen my own energy field. "Don't worry," she said. "You will do fine. You will do well." She sustained me with this powerful column of energy which, when I was again calm, gently dissipated. Never again did I have that sense of aloneness, helplessness and disconnect I had just passed through.

Over the years, I would occasionally return to the college campus and be inexorably drawn to that site, where I would once again go into the same column of energy. Try as I might, I could never get the energy to respond and tell me who it was. Then on a visit about ten years ago, now a seasoned interdimensional communicator, I returned and suddenly found myself at the other end of that tunnel/column of energy. I felt myself at the same time that young, confused woman and heard myself telling her, "Don't worry, you will do fine." I was the one, the me of the future, who had been reassuring that sad young woman. We had formed a strong column of energy that had gone through time and which energetically kept calling me back, until that day. The action through time had been completed. The other "me"s over the years could move into the column, but it had not focused on their presence. Since then, I have returned to the college campus but on visiting the rock cliff find it very ordinary, with no magnetic pull left at all.

Dimensional Crossovers

These are life forms from other dimensions who have somehow crossed over into ours, on purpose or by accident. For example, detonating explosives during war, mining operations or highway construction can open up portals into other realms, suck the beings of those realms into our world and then rapidly shut the door, leaving the life forms stranded. I have encountered some of these bewildered spirits and have taken photographs of them. One type I've encountered on many occasions in the Great Lakes area is a very large, bulbous, dark form, whose appearance is frightening but who is actually extremely gentle. These are water spirits and are found near water.

When forms such as these sense I am aware of them, they keep following me, nagging to get my attention. They are hoping I can help them.

One of these beings pleaded with me to "tell the humans to stop the destructive work." He explained that when detonating dynamite to clear land for roads, there is a specific frequency nodule—he demonstrated it for me—in the sound of the detonation that opens a portal into their world. If someone is near that doorway, such as he, alas, was—they are pulled into our world, the door is slammed shut and they are stranded, unable to return. He was so sad-eyed I felt very unhappy for him. After we discussed matters for a while, I asked my guides for assistance. We opened a portal. He was so happy! He waved good-bye and walked through to his home.

••••

In addition to being accidentally brought into our dimension by human mistakes that open doors between our worlds, dimensional crossovers may purposely come here to do research, to explore or to exploit our dimension.

Dimensional crossovers often appear to humans as a globe of light. This is a merkabah. It is commonly called an orb. Seeing a life form as an orb usually indicates we have not identified fully enough with the being to see its actual shape. It is like seeing the human aura or grid, but not being able to descend far enough into the specific frequency of the human body to see its physical form.

There are many more conscious life forms in this vast universe of ours. All are capable of communicating with us.

Energies and Life Forms Who Affect the Human World

The Human Energy Field

Interdimensional life forms of the human aspect of earth include our own existence: the many aspects of our own body, mind and spirit. Just in the physical body itself, some of us have learned to talk to our body to soothe, optimize and heal it.

For example, many top athletes now consider it perfectly acceptable to work with sports consultants who teach them how to use affirmations and self-talk to relax and optimize their sports performance. Many books discuss the effectiveness of talking positively to heal injured body parts. There was a Hollywood movie on Patch Adams, a doctor who uses humor to help sick people heal themselves. When I myself was ill with radiation poisoning in the mid-1990s, I was greatly helped by Norman Cousins' book *Anatomy of an Illness.* Cousins helped start the mind-body revolution of the 1980s, using humor and laughter to heal himself physically, when doctors had given up hope.

There are forces emanating from humans whenever we interact with others. These thoughtforms and emotional forms exist both as energy and as beings we can communicate with. Some are very aware life forms, which is why they can affect us so strongly, even when the person housing them is totally unaware of the situation.

I am occasionally called in to assist people whose health has been affected by Native American guardian thoughtforms. Areas where residential homes are being built on old Native American sites are especially affected by such situations. A thoughtform had been created to guard a site, such as a spring. When the spring was destroyed, the life forms still existed but now wandered about lost, without purpose. They could become destructive. Poor things! I send them "home," to be with others of their kind, in the light.

Be careful what you think! Thoughts are realities in some world and focusing our will on them can call them into existence. Occultists and medicine people know this. They can consciously use this innate human ability to manifest a thought into a form and give it life. This can be used to create a guardian for a treasure or a location. The life form has a simple level of awareness and when existing under the control of their creator can stay on task. The problem is, their existence also is a part of the source and over time they start to evolve. The thoughtform has no lifespan such as a human does, unless their creator specifies this. So they remain, century after century, and can cause problems. Ancient Egyptians would create spiritual guardians to protect the graves of Pharaohs. This is what occurred when King Tut's grave was opened. It activated protective energies. Within a short span of time, all but one of the discoverers had died. The one who survived had been wearing an antique ring decorated with an Atlantean symbol for protection $\triangleleft = \!=\!=\!=\!= \triangleright$. This ring design has become a famous psychic protection talisman.

Powers of Transformation

These include such life forms as resistance, servitude, oppression and anger. These powers must be mastered for us to become detached and open to energy. The powers of transformation also include silence, love, peace and many other qualities that permit us to see into energy without any effort. As discussed in the previous section, focusing on any of these energies helps bring them alive, for you. They start to control the direction in which your life energy flows.

Morphogenetic Fields of Consciousness

These are group thoughtforms. They gather strength from many individuals adhering to the same thought or energy. They layer a frequency, or consciousness, into the universal grid, ready to be accessed by whoever seeks it. Morphogenetic fields can be sometimes dormant and sometimes active.

Remember, above time and space, all always exists. Thus, we should be careful what we consciously create, for it becomes a part of our world and our future. This is true whether our creation is a horror movie or novel or an inspirational tale. Curses become energy fields we must work through. Praying and participating in world prayer groups, saying affirmations, establishing sacred ground and sacred space—all of these acts become fields of consciousness. Once formed, they stay in our earth consciousness in some form forever. These fields can affect millions of others for all time.

Earth Energies

These include so-called ley lines, which exist at multiple levels and are actually the light fields which, overlaying each other, make our world appear solid. To grasp this concept, consider the multicolored balls of rubber bands that some people like to make. On the surface, the balls look like a simple array of crossing lines. But these lines run many, many layers deep, and are filled with separate rubber bands. Just as the balls are made of overlapping rubber bands, our world is made of overlapping fields of energy. Each field carries information along its own set of lines at a specific frequency band unlike any of the others. Where ley lines cross each other, vortexes are formed. A vortex can occur any time two forces cross each other, thereby spinning the energies in the middle in different directions that eventually evolve into a spiral moving out from the starting point in an enlarging cone. When ley line junctures are aligned through several levels, the vortexes are even stronger. If a ley line becomes polluted or takes sick for some reason, problems can occur on one or multiple levels of the overall field, depending upon the depth, breadth and extent of the situation and its intersection with other fields.

In today's world, humans have unconsciously contributed to the deterioration and pollution of many levels of grids by ignorantly adding an ever-expanding range of "artificial" frequencies, such as those emanating from electrical and microwave devices. The frequencies being usurped are those that are used by our machines, computers, power lines, transformers, cellphone towers, submarine communication devices, wireless routers—the list expands continuously.

What has not been acknowledged by our scientists is that these manufactured devices are usurping energy frequencies already occupied by some other life form. What happens to the ability of that energy to fully function, when they have been kicked out of their home? Today, more and more plants and animals are no longer able to thrive in areas affected by these frequencies—witness the efforts being mounted by many on behalf of the whales and porpoises whose sonar communication systems are being interfered with by submarine communication devices. Many people, such as myself, are experiencing frequency-related health issues, such as high levels of stress and depression, immune-system deficiency, leukemia and other cancers.

Microscopic Life Forms

These include particles of energy that float through the air, viruses and airborne diseases, protons, neutrons and so on down through the many levels of smallness our hard sciences keep discovering. All these energies are conscious and, as physics has proven, can be affected by human thoughts directed to them.

Because we do not value this level of awareness, my guides have told me that this is a potentially very serious situation, and where the "next invasion" will come from. These life forms, my guides say, seem small and inconsequential but they are vast, complex universes at their level of magnification, with their own social system and own methods of surviving which are often far different from the human ones. They work with group thought and are able to morph their form as required.

We are beginning to see the effects of interfacing with this universe now, particularly as our scientists attempt to manipulate cellular matter, resulting in issues such as Lyme disease and AIDS. When we stop attempting to conquer and manipulate this kingdom without really understanding their conscious nature, and start working cooperatively with them as an aware life form, we will have greater success.

Ancient Traditions

Lemuria, Atlantis and the ancient Assyrian and Egyptian cultures were each profoundly evolved in their ability to move through space and manipulate matter in ways far different from the protocols our contemporary world has evolved. Much of this work was accomplished with assistance from other dimensions. The downfall of all these traditions occurred as they abused the knowledge, first for curiosity and personal gain and then for increasing levels of power over others. These cultures were not afraid to work with all the forces, dark and light, but ultimately they failed to keep the two in balance. Each ended as corruption overwhelmed the forces of balance.

In the generations since, earth has worked hard to master many different ways in which the dark forces have overwhelmed those of peace and love. Our current world cultures, especially America and other technologically based countries, are currently in a critical stage similar to that which brought the downfall of other great civilizations in the past. However, we also have on earth right now lightworkers who have conscious memory of the downfalls of past civilizations of which they were once a part. They are working very hard, often unseen and unnoticed, to strengthen and sustain positive energy in the face of the over-whelming onslaught of negative forces.

I myself am from the Atlantean lineages, with conscious recall of having lived during the final days of that great civilization. I have often discussed Atlantis with others who remember having lived on that continent. Atlantis began with great dreams, but over time its society degenerated. In many ways, it is similar to our current world culture, with its ability to manipulate matter and the abuses that come with that capacity. There are many Atlanteans who have returned seeking to help our current world escape from the fate of that wondrous culture, and also a return of spirits with allegiance to the most ancient human culture we remember, that of Lemuria, which was located in the Pacific region near modern Hawaii. Virtually all of us with conscious recall have been assured of the determination of our collective guides and guardians, and of galactic forces, to avoid a recap of history. Our guides of the light have assured each of us: "This time we will not fail."

Far Eastern Traditions: Yoga, Hinduism and Buddhism

These cultures excelled in the development of mandalas and mantras for graphing energy fields in light and sound. They developed the knowledge of body structuring—of vortexes, chakras and meridians. They graphed the structure of their particular universe with the many levels of consciousness existing there.

Mediterranean Traditions

This area specialized in the moral development of the human being. Judaism contributed Kabalistic knowledge, Christianity emphasized the self-offering and self-sacrifice of human love and the Greek and Roman traditions developed philosophy and ethics. Islam came later, working also with the moral understandings of universal energy.

Indigenous Traditions Around the World

Indigenous traditions focus on the interrelation of humans with nature in their specific area. They have lived in their region through many ages and understand how to affect, balance and enhance life in relation to nature or to the larger natural patterns of the universe. Many have, in their fables, tales of contact with teachers from the skies who helped them shape holistic lifestyles based on simple but profound wisdoms. Some are renown for particular knowledge that they have evolved. This includes the Mayan people of South America with their profound knowledge of astronomical time and the Huna people of Hawaii with their profound knowledge of healing. It includes the many indigenous traditions of Africa, European paganism and Native American nations.

Contemporary World Culture

For the past several hundred years, the Western-based cultures have focused on the fine details of manipulating gross physical matter. We are dissecting, dividing, observing and categorizing all aspects of form to understand how it has come into existence and what is required to successfully change it for the better.

••••

In all these traditions, the wisdom keepers and spiritual adepts tell the same tales. They speak of a living earth—one in which the life forms can communicate with each other and where the greatest life form of all is Mother Earth herself. She can and will communicate with and assist those of her children who wish to communicate with her and to use action to follow through on her objective, which is a peaceful perfection for all in her domain.

All who can access and exist in rarefied forms of consciousness tell of advanced beings—humans, animals, stones, metaterrestrials and/or extraterrestrials—who can bring the teachings of truth and gifts from other worlds for humans to use and work with.

All tell of battles between forces from outside the domain of third-dimension earth. All tell of some interdimensional beings who oppress earth life forms and other interdimensional beings who support earth forms.

All impart teachings and training about how to survive and thrive. These teachings include devices and methods for honoring and cooperating with the energies of the land and of other beings.

Understanding the Same Energy from the Viewpoint of Different Disciplines

Within our various earth cultures during this recent dark age, we have developed many disciplines that have sought to dissect gross physical matter into its component parts, to see its patterns and to learn to manipulate or work with these patterns for the benefit of our world. The following are some of the ways we humans have used the inherent qualities of grid technology to chart, stabilize and adjust energy. It is just one more step to adapt any of these sciences to the more subtle levels with which the interdimensional communicator works.

Science has sought to understand structures, groupings, patterns, waves and premises. Mathematics has understood that the universe is made of patterns that can be broken down into equations. Physics has explored quantum mechanics, chaos theory and string theory, to mention a few. Astronomy has discovered repeating patterns in the movements of the planets and of distant galaxies. Earth sciences have explored the mapping of the weather and the biology of living life forms.

The esoteric sciences have developed dowsing, radiesthesia, radionics, astrology and divining systems such as the I Ching, Tarot, palmistry and facial and postural reading.

Medical knowledge has expanded, forming such divisions as Western mainstream medicine, alternative medicine, Oriental medicine and Ayurvedic medicine.

Business has evolved its own principles, including stock-market analysts who track the patterns of stocks.

Some historians focus on analyzing patterns of human events so that we can avoid repeating those that were destructive or devastating.

Athletics delights in mapping statistics to follow trends and spot winners. Sports and fitness groups create graphs to chart ways to enhance individual performance.

The arts are fully capable of dipping into a varied range of frequencies and consciousness. However, right now the tendency is to explore the lower frequencies: either the vital realms of sex and power or the dark forces of the universe. In periods of high consciousness, the arts are more inclined to work from a point of comprehension instead of exploration. We can expect the art of our future to fully explore and accurately map the fields of consciousness that are going to become accessible to us all.

Dowsing land energies uses knowledge of the earth's electromagnetic fields and energy lines (called ley lines) to clean and adapt the energies to improve the health and disposition of all in the environs. It has learned how to overcome interference from geopathic fields, nature, technology, other people and what has been imported into the home. Dowsing land energy includes the clearing and energizing of the grids and energy fields to positively affect health, productivity and creativity.

Help Is Coming in Many Ways

Today, we are seeing a new civilization emerge as we step forward into a significant new level of earth evolution. We are moving into a new world perception, one in which we have the knowledge of power and its abuse as it evolved through all these previous civilizations. We see how to develop positive methodologies, what types of abuse can occur, and how to counter abuse from many different merkabahs, or civilizations. This is good: it is our base. Now, as we begin to recover conscious awareness of all time and space, we are bringing together all this knowledge, sequentially evolved, into one full, more complete understanding of consciousness.

Some of our earth groups spearheading this work are receiving help from other dimensions. Also coming in to serve are masses of children, currently known variously as the Indigoes and the Crystals. Whatever succeeding waves of these children will be labeled, we know they will have extended or alternate forms of awareness, shaped in part by the altering frequencies of our earth environment. These altered frequencies result from cosmic changes as well as from the alterations that our advanced technologies, including chemical and frequency pollution, are exacting on all who are living on earth.

Other cosmic lineages are quietly coming to earth and "upgrading" their offsprings' DNA/genetic coding to adapt to the demands of this new world. Among these is my lineage, known as the Melchizedeks, whose main sages are Metatron, Melchizedek and Archangel Michael.

Other life forms from intergalactic, other-dimension civilizations, intent on helping us evolve correctly, are incarnating on earth. And many, many earth beings—humans, elementals, nature spirits, et al.—are waking up to a greater awareness than we have exhibited before in recent history.

There is a commonality to this new knowledge—this new age of awareness that is coming in. It is the knowledge of the shape and form of energy. Technically speaking, some see this energy as plasma and others as grids. Plasma and grids are interconnected: the grids form the Oreo cookies that hold the white plasma cream filling in place.

Much of this new knowledge is being transmitted in full packets of information called merkabahs. When looked at, merkabahs resemble balls of light packed with geometrical forms—the language of light. When comprehended at the level transmitted, they impart a full experience of the totality of the concept being expressed. When downgraded to accommodate the capacity of the recipient, much of the fullness is lost, and only parts are received. At the most solid third-dimensional level, they become a single strand of information, a phrase or an inspiration.

Humans have worked throughout the ages with the knowledge of how merkabahs are shaped and used, although under different names. Mandalas, yantras and mantras are representatives of this knowledge, as is sacred geometry and the circle diagrams of all indigenous traditions. Today we are experiencing another manifestation: authentic crop circles, which are complex geometric merkabah imprints placed in earth's energy field by advanced intergalactic civilizations. Most of these imprints are seeking to stabilize beneficial frequencies on earth for our benefit and growth.

We humans have been working with the merkabahs' grid structure all along. We just need to upgrade this awareness to see how the grids perform on subtle levels.

How to Travel Between All These Energies

The interdimensional communicator works from the premise that the source of all is all-accepting. It trusts its own self—its own creation—to eventually master whatever challenges the source sets up, creates or permits to occur and evolve. The source is seeking ultimate full comprehension and manifestation of itself through its own existence. No way is superior to another in this viewpoint—

each way is just different. Different ways will lead to different re-sults. Eventually, all ways will lead back to the source.

We interdimensional communicators enter into many different ways and may "take on" another's grid reality as a form of energetic clothing. We do this to understand and work with a situation. When the work is completed, we step back out and into our own realm. We can choose not to accept a particular assignment if we and our inner colleagues believe the solution lies beyond the human's or the group's current capacities.

As interdimensional perception is developed, the practitioner eventually learns to move above time and space and map the pattern of energy fields. On a personal level, this includes the necessity to revisit and examine our own significant past and future lives. Another necessity is to chart our own descent from the source via our particular lineage, which may take us into many other dimensions, worlds and even universes. This interdimensional work helps us "rewrite" our understanding of who we are, why we act and have acted as we do, and to correct energy flows and move on in a positive manner.

At a very advanced level of interdimensional communication, you will find the yogis and other adepts in many cultures who develop various *siddhis,* or energetic capacities, through their intense practices. Some, to assist their followers, will appear in subtle or even physical form at various places around the world while still also remaining at their distant ashram. Some masters will manifest themselves from the spirit realm. These humans have the ability to work with energy as a pliable substance and can, should the need arise, shape-shift from one reality to another.

Communicating Among Different Dimensions

The interdimensional communicator knows that *all* existence is capable of communicating with us, should we only ask, locate their world and intend to work in partnership with their life form (not autocratically demanding or seeking to control them). *All* existence can communicate with each other through the common universal language, accessible through the higher fields of consciousness and specifically through the oneness-heart (or oneness-mind, depending upon semantics) that pervades all existence.

It does not matter whether this existence is our liver, our pet dog or cat, the flowers and rocks in our yards, the electromagnetic fields in our place of work, the waters of Mother Earth, the elemental kingdom, the stars in the skies or the other worlds of beings that exist in this vast universe we all occupy together. If we find the right frequency, approach with a loving heart, as a friend and not one seeking to dominate, we will find life forms eager to work with us for the common good and betterment of all.

We are also going to encounter life forms who have chosen to work for the dark forces or who are destructive. Knowledge, education and guides—and our own attitude of humility and a constant prayer for protection—are therefore important parts of this emerging cosmic science.

It is simple to say that the universe will offer to us all that we wish to know. It is, frankly, another situation altogether to know how to receive this information in a personally digestible form. As a species, we humans will eventually solve this issue. But it will take time.

As more and more people on earth understand the process of interdimensional cooperation and work through it themselves, the process will become increasingly accessible to all. We are, right now, developing this consciousness. Those who first start a work are visionaries, able to see high into spiritual consciousness. They grasp the concept, and like a balloon, it is held in place by a thin string of energy. Next the technical experts come to explore and develop the field. Finally the masses come. They are able, in varying degrees, to reach up into the field and adapt it for their own use. This accessing the field by so many people weaves the energy into a broad morphogenetic web, or grid, that becomes a new part of the earth consciousness itself.

Without the dream that such a reality can exist, we cannot find it. What we go seeking for, we find. If we have been conditioned to see only certain truths, then we will see only those "truths." If we then use what we see to justify our perceptions, we limit what we can discover. We put on energetic blinders.

For example, if surgeons have been trained that the answer to a health issue lies only in flesh and bones, they may not be willing to see that a better solution might lie above the flesh, in thoughts and feelings. Fixing the flesh and bone may solve the result of the issue, but if its cause is an energetic disturbance, that disturbance may eventually descend into some other physical ailment, because energy, good and bad, will move around obstacles so that it can ground itself in physical matter.

If an individual is a fundamentalist Christian, Jew, Muslim or Hindu, he or she has been trained to perceive the source as manifesting in one set way and may not be able to see the source's manifestation in other ways. Yet individuals of all religions and philosophies, when seeking the source through personal mystical understanding, come to know the same truth: the source is present everywhere, including in *all* religions.

The knowledge of the principles of multidimensional communication can help us, as a global society, to bridge our current cultural and religious barriers.

Information Transfer

There are a vast number of ways in which consciousness can travel to transfer information and to accommodate the needs of a particular situation. Instead of being prejudiced against some ways, we should re-examine them for the true knowledge they have evolved. This re-examination includes looking at many of the so-called primitive and pagan cultures. It also includes applying the so-called esoteric sciences to practical, everyday reality.

Some of the old, secret sacred societies now coming out into the open are offering extensive knowledge about the workings of what we call *sacred geometry*. Sacred geometry is known in energy circles to be grid-defining forms referring to specific movements of energy. Sacred geometry is also the basis of intergalactic, interdimensional language and communication.

The basic sacred-geometry form for the interdimensional communicator, as practiced here, is the merkabah. This is a round globe of energy, a self-contained packet filled with geometric light forms of information. As an information packet, the merkabah can be from one's inner world guides, from some intergalactic civilization that is making contact or from the higher levels of consciousness of any field. We can comprehend this information in many ways. At the start, it pretty much depends upon the most developed aspect of the recipient's consciousness: visual, auditory or sensory. The interdimensional communicator will enter into the merkabah and find the forms swirling around like light beings. We become one with the information, and it flows through our existence, top to bottom, filling us with the experience of its message.

The higher the consciousness at which we perceive the information, the more fully we comprehend the topic. If we cannot comprehend the information in its fullness, the living, conscious merkabah attempts to reach us in a variety of ways. It may take the form of light beings who will verbally or visually impart the information to us. It may take the form of a being culturally acceptable to us, such as an animal totem, god/goddess, preceptor or teacher. If it must descend further yet, we will grasp parts and phrases of information or flashes of insights, often while we are in a relaxed or meditative, tranquil state. The more the information must descend into the linear third dimension, the more it must string out into a linear form, and the less of the whole we will receive.

Pushing Your Own Limits

Currently, an interdimensional communicator learns on the job. If a situation they are dealing with requires it, they will learn from and with their team the appropriate way to handle the job. Sometimes these ways can be so different from what the human is used to that they push the limits of the communicator's own personal belief system.

At the start of their work, interdimensional communicators are always checking: Can this be real? Am I making it up? Since every time in the past successful action has resulted from a truthful interchange between myself and my guides, and they are telling me about this situation, can I trust the information? Or have I gone off course and am now working with tricksters and not my real guides? What does my "gut" say is right?

This situation reoccurs from time to time if the communicators are true explorers and are continually pushing the limits as to what they can do. The universe is infinite. The more practitioners learn, the further the parameters of their work are extended. If these parameters are suddenly radically expanded or there is a sudden scrambling of energies (such as from astrological alignments or conscious attempts to interfere by various forces), the practitioners must go back to the basics. They must re-examine their work from the source out and step by careful step ascertain the presence of their energy council in the new situation. They need to decipher the new situation and be certain their team is securely, honestly and forthrightly working together.

Many Patterns

Consciousness is multidirectional. There are self-contained energy fields (merkabahs) on all levels of consciousness. All energy fields are held within larger fields, up into their final enclosure inside the source itself. All energy fields have, or have the potential to contain, additional fields inside themselves. Therefore, energy fields have the potential to exist in a vast range of sizes and forms, from the most microscopic to the most macroscopic levels.

Any issue being studied has numerous energy fields affecting it. The merkabahs may be arranged in clusters within the same parent field; they may consist of overlapping fields. All these fields coexist, although they are working at many different frequencies. Each way, as it evolves, affects all the other ways that interconnect, descend and ascend from it.

The practitioners are dealing with time lines, parallel futures and cyclical, linear and transcendent time and consciousness beyond time/space considerations. When energy workers get together, the issue is not whether other worlds exist, for the workers know this experientially. Rather, it is what aspect of consciousness has each energy worker mastered and what can be shared to expand our common goal of broad awareness. Mastery of consciousness is a science as well as an art form. One progresses in levels of expertise and has areas of specialization and areas one has chosen not to explore for various reasons, such as the need to focus on specific issues. There will always be more levels and areas of expertise to explore. On earth, we are at the infant stage of this science.

To succeed at any interdimensional task takes enormous willpower, focus and concentration in the physical form. Whom and what are we listening to and working with? This takes time to discover clearly.

When practitioners go into a new dimension, we are first aware of a shift in energy. This shift can appear as light or darkness, depending upon the point of focus, point of entry, what we are doing there, why we are going there and what we want to accomplish. At first we see light, or nothing, or a shimmer. Then our eyes start to adjust to that particular frequency, and we begin to see objects. What we see depends on where we land, just as on earth: is it a desert, ocean, city or forest?

It is so much more effective and quick if we have guides we can trust to show us around the place. We can rely on their taking us to the spot where we need to go.

Thus communicators are usually working with a team, made up of ourselves, our higher self/selves, our long-term guides, the guides who assist us generically (such as the medical Medical Assistance Plan [M.A.P.], an inner world committee of spiritual healers and nature spirits who help heal people; the ascended masters; and the Melchizedek lineage) and the guides that are specific to this field. We will discuss these issues later, in chapter 11, Support from Guides, Guardians and Inner Colleagues.

Chapter 3
A Multidimensional Social History

Earth is an aspect of creation that has actually succeeded in grounding its consciousness into the physical.

My inner colleagues have asked me to provide a simplified understanding of the nature of intergalactic society.

The perspective related here was told to me by Metatron and my soul family and is the viewpoint of this lineage. Just as with human history, perceptions can change according to what group, nation, or race is telling the story. If this topic interests you, I recommend the books of the following authors. Each has specialized in a particular aspect of this topic, and I find all to be very accurate. Each has provided hard physical facts such as ancient sculptures, paintings, mathematical formulae and historical references supporting their position that our contact with other worlds has been going on through the ages. These authors include Drunvalo Melchizedek, Zecharia Sitchin, J. J. Hurtak, and Gregg Braden.

There are many different paths of descent from the unmanifest source into form. The source is infinite, and it cannot be locked in by its own creation and forced to proceed by one method alone, even though we sometimes pretend this is so. Through the ages, some groups have even made laws specifying how we may and may not state how the process occurs. Examples from today's world are fundamentalists of all religions and the hard-science disciplines that maintain a gross physical approach to the exploration of existence. These two groups are actually working at the same level of consciousness.

There are many different ways to perceive the growth of the universe. All can successfully coexist with each other and expand the knowledge of the others, *if* we comprehend the process multidimensionally. The same scene from the perspective of another discipline or life form can initially look very different from our own, until we link all the puzzle pieces into one overall image.

Here is my Metatron lineage's description.

A spark goes forth from the source. It knows, inherent to its own structure, its purpose for being. It has a mission to fulfill. That mission is the full conscious awareness and expression in form of a specific aspect of the source's own infinite perfect potential. It is an expression of source's question to itself: who am I and what can/will I be?

The spark's core purpose serves as a homing signal. When this spark, this merkabah, this life form stays on track, it is happy and content at its core, no matter what is occurring externally. When it meets obstacles or veers off course, it may temporarily enjoy the diversion, but its own inherent structure eventually becomes sufficiently unhappy so as to make it veer back on course. Looked at this way, "mistakes" are simply directional diversions, such as might occur when steering a craft to its specific location on a distant shore. The craft can be detoured to take a side trip to a scenic island, but it must eventually make a course correction and continue on its original journey. It has a mandate to reach a specific location and cannot forever ignore this.

All that occurs to that original spark of the source—all the billions and trillions of years of its development—is that particular spark's unique contribution to the richness of the perfect source's own transcending perfection.

When the source descends into manifestation, it does so by degrees of consciousness. It creates a world of frequency—a merkabah (our "spark" as described above). This original spark, or merkabah, plays with its many options until it realizes that for any more progress or fulfillment, it must expand, divide, or create, to include yet another vibratory field of consciousness. The game gets increasingly complex as each newly explored frequency of consciousness begins to develop its own choices internal to its field and thus further multiplies the options that influence all the levels of all the forms involved.

For example: Metatron was originally a spark from the source who, over an uncountable period of time, evolved from his life form countless universes and worlds, all of which evolved their own life forms, which further subdivided until one of these lines of descending energy manifested me, and probably you the reader. We each have our own lineage leading back to this original spark yet we are each probably connected as one life form at some point along the way. We also each have descending from us our own creations that are uniquely our own.

The process reminds me of the tiny clown cars in a circus. When the doors of our consciousness open up, out of this one tiny vehicle pour many, many "clowns," all in different garbs. The trick is getting them all back in!

As consciousness descends, it becomes denser, a form that has been self-created to accomplish increasingly specific tasks of manifestation. This density works as a frequency fence, keeping the life form intact inside its field, but also obscuring what exists outside its form. It is as if the life form is in a forest in a fog. The fog (planes of consciousness) obscures the more distant objects.

Technically speaking, the life form inside the merkabah has several choices by which it can proceed: It can develop its capacity to see farther into other frequencies. It can develop the ability to detach from its frequency so that it can escape that world's sustaining fence. Or it can learn to enter into the heart of that merkabah—the source—and travel via that wormhole into whatever other place in the universe it chooses to go. The combinations of these three choices make interdimensional communication and cooperation possible.

Councils

There were, and continue to be, many efforts made by consciousness to manifest physical form in the universe. This process is extremely difficult, for a solidification of consciousness has inherent dangers, not the least of which is the polarization of light and dark and the release of uncontrollable destructive energies into the universe at the lower levels of consciousness. Destruction and perfection on any plane can ripple up, down, within and across dimensions.

Destructive forces have destroyed many worlds, with far-reaching ramifications. When a world is destroyed, the higher levels of every life form that was tied to the destroyed worlds is now lacking their particular line of descent, or physical aspect or vehicle. The evolutionary progress of all the families tied to the destroyed world is now delayed until they solve this issue. Therefore, when highly evolved life forms see such a disaster impending in some area of the universe under their care or area of responsibility, they have learned that it is necessary to gather and discuss what course of action to take. On earth, our esoteric knowledge banks refer to these gatherings by such terms as the Councils, the Brotherhoods, and the Masters.

These councils are real. Mature consciousness does not seek to isolate itself, but rather to expand and unify. These councils can be considered the referees and coaches of the various games being played out around the universe. They set the rules and often punish or reward the players—they might send a player to sit out a round, or bump them up a notch from local to regional to intergalactic conferences.

The councils are very necessary organizations because their business is to find the solutions for the work being done in the realms of consciousness under their care. These realms can be higher and lower in scope. Our own third-dimension judicial systems reflect this same principle, at our earth level. In all dimensions, there will be renegades and outlaws who will not abide by the decisions of the councils, frequently causing considerable grief to any well-laid plans.

Our earth is part of the Galactic Federation. Life on our earth is a combined form, assembled from the genetic strands of twelve different races (hence the twelve-strand DNA). Earth was envisioned as a unifying laboratory where the best of the best would be genetically bonded to create a new life form—humans—who would genetically understand the different races and could thus serve as intergalactic diplomats.

Many races wanted to be included in this mix, as whoever was selected would have an automatic "in" with the future diplomats of the universe on a very basic core genetic level. Therefore, the selection of these genetic strands was placed in the care of a Council of Nine, selected for the wisdom of their races. Selection was a very difficult process and included a great deal of diplomatic maneuvering, as well as threats if some group's genetic make-up was not included.

The Council of Nine selected twelve races to be included in the new life form, and a representative from each of these races sat on a Council of Twelve to oversee the development of this new species. The planet was put in quarantine, which meant no one except specifically selected officials were supposed to visit the planet to check on progress.

And now the plot began to thicken. Those races who were not selected included some renegade races, who thereafter sought to introduce their genetic lineage illegally, via abductions, impregnation and many other means. Galactic enforcement units were created to patrol the area to prevent this. When the renegades would succeed in altering some aspect of earth, the federation would step in and seek to correct it.

Life Forms That Interact with Us

Earth is an aspect of creation that has actually succeeded in grounding its consciousness into the physical. This is a tremendous achievement, and every life form on earth is to be congratulated for their family's part in this great experiment. During this process, we have evolved many, many different approaches to working with the life-force energy.

Earth's physical form, and the powerful emotions we have learned to harness to achieve and master physical form, makes us very attractive to other life forms. Just to be in physical form as a human being is an enormous achievement for consciousness to make. We on earth have the opportunity to consciously ground and work with all the energies of the universe in a single body. We on earth have not yet mastered this, but the potentials are so significant that many other worlds seek to interact with us to harvest this potential in some way for themselves or for the advancement of the universe.

If we look carefully at the people around us, we can find traces of these interdimensional worlds; we all have seen people who look like angels, gods, beasts or even e.t. grays.

Those attracted to earth include life forms who have chosen not to wrestle with the vital energies that precede the creation of physical form and who must therefore remain for the time being in subtle physical form. They enter into humans or are birthed into humans to experience density of form, which offers sensations not available in the higher realms.

Others attracted to earth include beings from worlds which have unsuccessfully wrestled with vital issues and ended destroying their own physical planet.

Many life forms from worlds without solid form have visited earth either for personal pleasure or for scientific harvesting of our genetic matter.

There are also other reasons. Some life forms come to learn. They include angels who incarnate so that they can better understand the humans they are assigned to assist. Some worlds may send a member to earth as a gift for good behavior; other worlds might send life forms here as a punishment for arrogance or bad behavior.

All, like the normal resident humans, are here for a purpose. They all have something to do or learn, and when a form completes their task, they move on.

Visitors to earth include:

The servers. These are highly evolved, compassionate beings who take birth specifically to assist us or who serve us from the subtle planes.

Interdimensional life forms who are related to us. They contributed to the common gene pool that makes up the present human prototype. These include the original races who formed the Council of Twelve as well as the renegade worlds who rebelled or adventurously sought to interact with and affect us. These races come as family to check in with the kids and see if they need anything else to help them along, to grow, for comfort or to keep discord stirred up. Just like various members of a family, some believe in tough love, some want to do it all for us, some want to teach us to stand on our own two feet and some are abusive. But they all are facing the fact that the child is growing up and must be taught how to survive in an adult realm of consciousness with its many options. These groups include the Sirians, the Pleiadians, and the Arcturians.

There are also advanced beings from other worlds who have been sent or have chosen to come to assist earth in comprehending consciousness as it evolves to the next higher level. To do so they have either incarnated via birth or directly into a physical body. But the human body is enormously complex, and the process of shifting from one embodied form to another is often not successful. Many healers have had as clients extraterrestrials whose human bodies do not quite fit them. Some specialists help these individuals realign their bodies to more appropriately adapt to the earth's atmosphere.

Other earth life forms. Here on earth there are many other life forms and planes of consciousness coexisting with us. Should we humans succeed in destroying our world, they and their worlds would suffer as well. Many of these other worlds once coexisted with us, and we could communicate with them.

During the Kali Yuga, humans lost the capacity to communicate with other life forms—the animals, rocks, plants, nature devas, et al. As we are only now beginning the new cycle, the Satya Yuga, its pattern cannot yet be discerned. However, we are already seeing that our capacity to communicate with other life forms is reappearing.

Other categories of interdimensional beings. Some interdimensional beings serve as guides, mentors and inner colleagues. The ones who do so are often related in some way to the human whom they are helping, or to the topic the human wishes to master. See chapter 11, Support from Guides, Guardians and Inner Colleagues for in-depth information about this group.

There are also interdimensional scientists and military personnel who act from a similar array of motivations as their earth counterparts.

The adventurers. This group is looking for adventure, and earth has plenty of it at this time. We are like the rough and rowdy West during its heyday of exploration; lots of exciting emotions and thoughts and stories are being played out. Life forms from other worlds drop in or incarnate and play awhile then return to their native home. Some of these beings are from the vital realms; they include those whom various cultures interpret to be gods and goddesses and also the lower-level dark forces. This group often enjoys the vital pleasures that they are able to experience here in the third dimension of solid form. Once satiated—they bore easily, fortunately—they disappear, leaving turmoil of some sort in their wake, including the devastation of wars, as well as progeny who bear the genetic marks of each parent.

Multidimensional predators. They are just as real and prevalent as the third-dimension variety. Just like country hicks going to New York City, we don't want to buy the Brooklyn Bridge on the interdimensional level, or get caught up in a shill game, or become a pawn for someone's ego-oriented power trip. Many UFO specialists consider the Reptilian and Dracos civilizations to be working in this manner, contesting the rights of the Galactic Federation to supervise earth's development. However, my inner colleagues have shown me that the situation is much like the cold war between Russia and the United States: a competition between rival cultures that will one day end.

Beings in need of earth's energies. The lessons we are learning from these unfortunate visitors are very valuable to us at this present time. These are beings from worlds that have been partially or fully destroyed by themselves or others. These beings may have destroyed their physical planet and also part of the heavenly system around it, or destroyed their atmosphere, or selectively bred themselves into a nonreproductive species.

This group has discovered that they still exist, in subtle form, even though their physical form or world does not. They are now faced with a very serious situation: having to reestablish form so that they and their entire lineage can continue their journey. They are here to get or wrest assistance from earth to help their life form resume its journey to self-perfection and thus to a conscious remerging with the source, which is the ultimate goal of all life. Of course, who is to say that this experience itself is not something chosen for or by them, as their life form's contribution to the vast panoply of experiences that result for different uses of the same universal free will that governs us all?

Some Aspects of Concern: What Happens When a World Is Destroyed?

Martians are one example of beings in our solar system who are in this situation. They destroyed their planet's atmosphere, and hence all life.

Beings in need of assistance at this level also include some of the "dark grays." They are laboratory technicians serving races whose worlds have died or are dying and are seeking to re-establish strong physical form. The dark grays have in the past abducted humans to experiment on, in order to understand our physiology, in the hopes of either replicating it for their masters or creating hybrid life forms. The hybrids would contain the other race's genetic sequences along with the human ones, in a physical body that could exist on earth. In this way the other race hopes to re-establish a physical base that can continue their lineage's story and development. Some hope to continue to evolve via earth's field.

Right now, earth has good breeding stock, because it has mastered physical consciousness and fully brought down spirit to incarnate as physical form. We also have a broad genetic base formed from many other galactic lineages—the twelve strands plus the renegade strands. So there is enough commonality to potentially bridge the different worlds.

Many worlds have manipulated physical form and eventually created forms with highly advanced capabilities. However, this type of extended ability has sometimes come at the expense of vital life-force energy, which is necessary for reproduction. These worlds have found that they need to reintroduce strong life-force energy to their world. We are one option. Unfortunately, right now our own earth scientists are irresponsibly altering the genetics of our own species. Sometime in the future, we may well end up like some of the civilizations now circumspectly interacting with us and seeking a remedy for their dying world.

These other worlds hope our stock can save them, for we contain within our own fields those aspects of the universal web of consciousness that they require to repair their own fields. However, this interbreeding will significantly alter their own race, and their own race's capacities. It will also alter our human condition. Their, and our, original intent for proceeding from the source to the goal is now going off in a totally new direction. Of course, who is to say, in an infinite universe of possibilities, that this is not an intended variation on the story anyway?

This situation presents many fascinating but sobering scientific principles, the complexity of which I have not yet mastered. The basic situation is this: above time and space, these crippled or destroyed planets still exist. Therefore, at a different juncture point in their own evolution, they are alive, and that world can be worked with from there. Some of that world's scientists are attempting to travel through time to a critical point at which they hope to avert the destruction of their world, or their species. Others seek to transport beings from the pre-destruction world to the post-destruction world, to recreate the species. Some seek to introduce compatible genetic material from other worlds to re-energize their world. The latter is what many of the intergalactic scientists visiting earth hope to accomplish; they seek to splice genetic DNA from human and other earth species (plant, animal, mineral) onto that of their planet and so re-establish their world's existence and evolution.

These crippled or destroyed worlds are very large merkabahs. In some cases, their scientists have recreated their world at a lower frequency, so that their own life forms can continue. However, while the merkabah, or world, exists on a lower level as well as a higher level of consciousness, an interim level has been cut off or destroyed. In this situation the lower life form can only evolve up to a certain point, and the higher and lower levels must work to replace or bridge the interim level if that line of evolutionary growth is to proceed in a healthy manner.

In this case, one is looking at the flow of consciousness that exists when a spark goes forth from the source, evolves and returns to the source, perfected. Now remember—above time and space this whole process exists virtually simultaneously. So what happens when an explosion rips out a major portion of its flow of consciousness? All action, within time/space, is affected and in some areas halted, unless a method for bridging this space is provided.

On a lesser level, there is a similar situation when a singular or combined life form or merkabah is cut off from their source because they have been taken over by or possessed by a destructive life form. The first life forms are the puppets of these other forces unless and until some master of consciousness or a collective of inner colleagues, guides and guardians is able to rescue them and thus restore their connection to the core source within. We read in all traditions of the great spiritual masters driving out dark forces from people and reconnecting them to their soul, often described as "the light." It is often recorded how the masters were thanked profusely by all the affected individuals—both those possessed and those doing the possessing—who are once more in balance, at peace, and reconnected to their own source.

Interdimensional workers occasionally see a situation inside a client's energy field where some drastic action in a past life has disconnected the individual from their own source. We work to determine how to reconnect or clear them so that the energy once again flows smoothly.

There is a growing group of human energy workers who comprehend this type of situation, and a perusal of the Internet or a good alternative bookstore will lead you to many works on this subject. The information offered by these authors have both true and not so true information, and you will need to develop personal discernment to comprehend the truth for yourself.

The New Earth Children

Now, as I write this, the earth is seeing hundreds of thousands of children being born with extended capacities. In time, these children will be the majority, and as they grow up and become the world's leaders, our civilization will reflect their far different perceptions. Those of us who have lived on both sides—e.g., we started as humans with "normal" perception and were somehow thrust into the world of extended perception—frequently serve as advocates for these new children. They are known variously as the Indigoes and the Crystals; the names will keep changing as the numbers and known abilities of these children grow.

These children see and know in ways that are far different than those of the old mainstream. Many are coming with group contracts; each brave soul made the promise, before descending into the human body, that they would attempt the impossible— to peacefully change the frequency of earth itself, to upgrade our world into the galactic community. Educators are having a hard time learning how to work with these children, because many of them have non-linear modes of perception. Some of them have been diagnosed as autistic or bipolar, or as having ADD, ADHD and dyslexia—and who knows what other designations will come next. These children need to be taught it is okay not to be linear in their thinking and encouraged to successfully develop new ways to work with their different styles of internal wiring.

There are a growing number of advocate groups developing to do just this, some formed by young adults who were once the misunderstood "new" child. If you know of, or are, one of these people with an alternate mode of perception, it is less important than you think it is. Very soon most people will be thinking like you. That is, being unable to deny the multidimensionality of creation, they will start searching for that morphogenetic entry point that you helped link to and ground. The world is very fortunate to have you, and the hundreds of thousands similar to you, who can see into other worlds and have had to fight to make this alternate perception "normal." You are the Gandhis of this new world. You have peacefully changed our culture. You have extended your perception to bridge into the old world, and thus opened the gate for their world to come into ours.

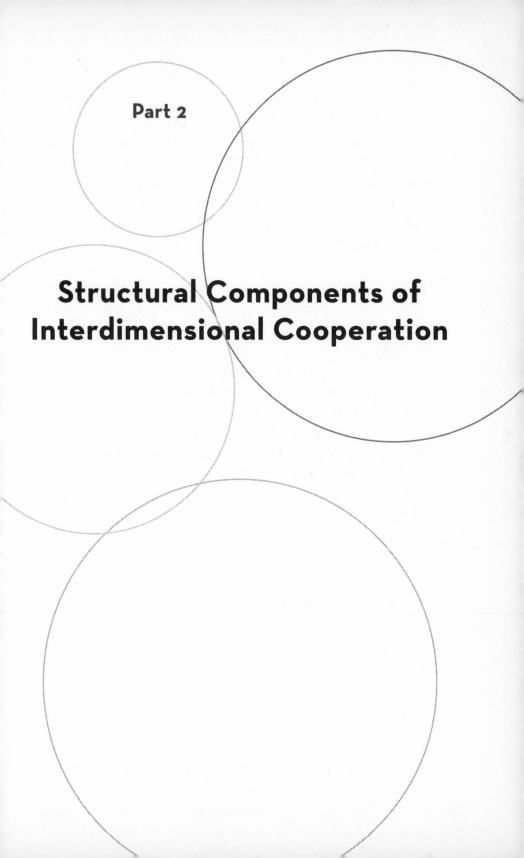

Part 2

Structural Components of Interdimensional Cooperation

Chapter 4
The Personal Nature of Interdimensional Consciousness

Right here and now, precisely where we are positioned, but above the realm of time and space, the entire universe exists in its totality. We are one. What we see, in the realm of time and space, depends upon which of the universal frequencies we tune ourselves to.

How can we learn to walk between dimensions? To meet and talk with the life forms of different worlds? To communicate with angels and land spirits; with ascended masters, and our own guides and guardians; with the life forms inherent inside water or earth; with animals, plants and stones; with the objects and implements of our life, such as tools and chairs; with our own family and friends?

Actually, all humans are already communicating interdimensionally as part of the process of understanding our personal environment. We just never considered that we could consciously develop this capacity.

When you decide on a bright, sunny morning to bring an umbrella to work, because your body is telling you that rain is on the way; when you ask the parking deva to have a parking space available for you on the busy street near a store, and the open space is there waiting for you; when as you're browsing the shelves at the library, a book drops off a shelf into your hands, and it's the very book you need to address some question or problem you've been thinking about; when you're rearranging the living-room furniture or creating a new garden and the couch or the new peony bush "tells" you where it wants to be; when the phone rings and you know who it is before you answer it—these are all common, everyday instances of interdimensional communication.

The only difference between people who say they cannot perceive interdimensionally and people who consciously communicate interdimensionally is intent and practice. Most people access interdimensional information unconsciously. When they experience conscious contact with a non-human energy, they tend to pass it off as a curiosity or as intuition, or they cancel out the experience as too weird to deal with. Interdimensional communicators, however, apply the principles of interdimensional existence to understand what is occurring; they explore the situation to learn from it.

When experiencing contact with life forms or information beyond that of external human conversation, the conscious communicator queries: What frequency did I just access? How did I get there? What are the inhabitants of this frequency like? How do I proceed? How do I return to this world when I wish to?

For an experience to be replicated, certain rules or principles must be identifiable in the process. The interdimensional communicator seeks to comprehend these principles, thus shifting the interdimensional contact from being an oddity to being a scientific observation.

Drugs can open up these windows between dimensions, but they also pollute the openings and can leave them open or close them tightly; drugs are not valid means for transportation and can create problems. (The sacred use of consciousness-altering plants by indigenous cultures is different, for these are used under strict controls by experts working within their cultural experience of consciousness.)

Violent, ecstatic and devotional emotions can open up windows between dimensions, but what is seen will usually be an inaccurate, incomplete vision. This is because individuals in these situations have been "snared" by intense energies that are seeking a specific object. These people are not interested in seeing the full field of energy itself, but only a specific object within that field. They will connect with energies directly related to their intent or to subconscious directives they have received from others. They are defining an entire world by one object in that world, which may or may not be a correct assumption. For instance, if they focus on one cactus plant, they might assume they are in a desert while they actually landed in a desert section of a botanical garden.

When devotees go exploring consciousness, they will connect with the energy of the tradition they are currently practicing, such as the Buddha consciousness or the Christ consciousness. They will proceed via the road mapped out for them by that tradition. However, as they proceed farther into spirit, their journey starts to become personal. They begin shifting from travels via roads built by others in their tradition to traveling via their own individual understanding.

Once any individual learns the parameters of that or any field, the journey turns personal. Even within established traditions, each person's way becomes unique to their own development and goals. No two journeys are ever exactly the same. It is at this point, however we arrive here, that the knowledge of the true workings of energy become predominate. Thus Lao Tzu said to his followers: "The way that is the way is not the way."

Interdimensional perception requires a broad acceptance of the nature of reality. The broader our acceptance, the more accurate the assessment of the situation can be. This assessment includes accepting the validity of a consciousness as it emerges in other cultures and life forms. It also includes valuing the contribution of both the so-called light and dark forces of the universe. If we "pull back" and reject some aspect of an energy field as inferior or "evil" or wanting in validity, we can create a blind spot in our accurate comprehension of the situation.

Right here and now, precisely where we are positioned, but above the realm of time and space, the entire universe exists in its totality. We are one. What we see, in the realm of time and space, depends upon which of the universal frequencies we tune ourselves to. Those life forms you are seeing around you right now are only perceivable because you and they have agreed to perceive existence through the frequency of the third dimension, magnified to the human energy field and to the time of the twenty-first century. We could, should we develop the capacity to do so, identify with life forms in other time/space frequencies, and these life forms would appear before our eyes.

Potentially, there is no end to the time/space travels or dimensional shifts we could make. It is important, however, to ask why should we want to do so and what do we want to accomplish.

Performing dimensional shifts for amusement or to gain power or for any other temporal, shallow reason is always eventually unfulfilling. It can lead to an extreme state of boredom, ennui, sated sophistication, sadism, voyeurism and so on. When done with the right intent or motivation, it can offer immense love, compassion, oneness and companionship.

We are antennas that attract specific ranges of frequencies into our field of perception or our pattern of resonance. Because of many issues coming together inside our own form, we are grounding a specific frequency or aspect of the source that no one else can accomplish in quite the same way. We are helping to ground on earth, in the solid third dimension, some subtle aspect of whatever frequency we turn our consciousness to explore. Our holding a consciousness on earth makes that consciousness more available to the next human being who seeks to master that particular issue and to go beyond their current level of perception to a more fulfilling or complete understanding. Thus, whenever we make progress, many others do, too; and when we fail, or go to the dark side, we enable those forces to become more active in our world. When we resolve any issue inside ourselves, we make viable solutions to that issue more readily available to all others.

Personal Qualities Needed to Perceive Interdimensionally

Often, when we begin perceiving interdimensionally, we experience a few key incarnations—ones that have had such a deep and profound effect on our composite energy field that they have bled over into others of our lives. Experiencing and working with our selves in our various aspects is one of the most intimate forms of interdimensional cooperation we can have. First we learn with our selves, and then we can assist others. This form of energy perception is part of our growing up and maturing as sentient energy forms assigned, in this time and form, to twenty-first-century earth.

Interdimensional perception is both an art and a science. Right now, it is a lifestyle choice and a philosophy; in the distant future, it will be a common method for achieving positive results in any given situation.

There are four qualities that humans need to develop for this practice:

- universal love
- *ahimsa*
- detachment
- cooperative spirit

Universal Love

The most successful interdimensional work is based on identification with the energy of universal love. In truth, this work can only be done through love. Universal, unconditional love is the interdimensional vehicle that has the broadest access to all the worlds. This means that while we can read about this subject and have some success at accessing it, there is a lock on what we can accomplish. The key to open all doors is love. This love is not a weak, overly tolerant or syrupy-sweet love. It is an eyes-wide-open, intelligent, wise, stable and mature love. It knows and sees all and still loves, no matter what the darkness or weakness.

Many interdimensional communicators perceive the universe as a love song being sung everywhere simultaneously. Anywhere we plumb the depths of the universe, we discover choirs singing tone poems of every possible configuration. It is the music of affirmation, offering the opportunity to experience self—the one self, our self—as existing everywhere at once. This cosmic self exists inside each of us. We are each a manifestation of the source seeking to fully experience its own potential.

The interdimensional practitioner finds a unity of design far beyond the imagination of anyone who believes the solid third dimension is the only place sentient life forms can exist and that we humans are the most sentient of all.

Successful interdimensional partnership cannot occur if we have a bloodthirsty, winner-take-all consciousness, because such an attitude creates barriers between energy fields. The most successful method is one of partnership among equals. At the core we are all equals because we are all the same substance: the source. Knowing that the one source is everywhere enables interdimensional practitioners to locate, communicate and cooperate with the source of any field we need to reach—that is, unless the free will of that life form forbids it. If it does, we need to negotiate the situation with its higher self, locate an alternative route through that field, or back off for now.

Most people on earth have used their free will to forbid other life forms and other dimensions of their own existence to contact them. These life forms and dimensions have complied, and many blocks and gates have been created inside our own energy field (in this work our team calls this energy field a merkabah). Energy blocks need to be disassembled for us to proceed. Because of the demands of our recent past, most human blocks occur on the physical and subtle physical level. Therefore, most humans currently have access to interdimensional knowledge only when rising above the physical condition, such as when they are under duress and calling intensely for assistance, in prayer and meditation or so relaxed that information from other planes of existence spontaneously flows into their perceptual range.

When assisting humans—or any life form—interdimensional communicators and their guides first set and hold a common space (another merkabah) so that all life forms involved can consciously communicate with each other. My team calls this *doing lunch*: "My people will contact your people. We'll discuss the issue in a friendly manner over lunch."

Relationships are important even interdimensionally, and many an issue of conflict can be resolved by "doing lunch." For instance, a person having problems with their career or their love life may be focused on physical parameters, but the source of the problem may exist in a past life above time and space. These lives and experiences are all alive and must be harmonized, made friends with, resolved and released before any further progress can occur in this current lifetime.

The universe respects our right and our need to focus on the immediate issues at hand inside the third-dimensional field we are seeking to master. As soon as we are ready to expand our field of perception and wish to invite communication with other realms also involved in the common issue, there is plenty of assistance to be had.

Ahimsa

Another quality necessary for successful interdimensional communication is what the yogis call *ahimsa*—non-harm to any living thing. Subtle life forms can read the real thoughts and feelings of other forms much more easily than humans, who choose to block thought and who communicate mainly via physical sounds. If we harbor any wishes to dominate or hurt a life form we are seeking to communicate with, the form instinctively knows it and will take defensive action. If we come in the consciousness of love and service to the one source, the form will sense that as well and will be more willing to work with us.

However, this does not mean that the field we are seeking to communicate with will necessarily initially respond to us with love. It may be trapped inside a negative energy itself, which is why it needs assistance. The field itself may be a part of the dark forces of the universe that lovingly serve the source by holding the dark energies in place until the entire situation is transcended and the unity of the all is perceived.

Detachment

A third quality required for interdimensional partnership is detachment. This is the learned ability to stay separate from any particular reality so that we can experience whatever alternate ones require our attention.

We communicators need to stay detached from the field of perception we are exploring, or we risk being locked temporarily into its frequency world. We can experience this situation as a general unease, a manifestation of the issues of the client or an attempt by the offending energy to take control of our energy field. Lest anyone think this is spooky, understand that when an individual is overwhelmed by stress or depression, they are letting a life form (energy) overtake their own inherent soul-connected, peaceful balance. That type of possession is so common that most humans don't even recognize it.

Interference, whether from emotions or thoughts or other life forms, can manifest in many ways. It can range from uncontrolled anger to the client seeing contorted forms approaching or interacting with them. Interference is part of the reason all of us, and particularly communicators, need to consciously establish good field integrity. And one way to do this is to work with the merkabah, which is the main tool our team works with.

Being locked into a particular frequency means we have adapted our field to its field and have settled in. The natural grids that define every field have begun growing around and through us. This process gradually locks us into place. We have all at some point locked into the field of earth's frequencies, otherwise we could not sustain our presence in this world.

It is important to stay detached from the energy with which you are working. You must be able to clearly observe its structure so that you can decide how to move into and out of the field without getting trapped. Moving into and out of a frequency has many aspects. The interdimensional communicator knows there are conscious life forms guarding the energy field: border patrols whose job is to protect and seal entrance into and out of their world. The field also simultaneously exists as a light field grid; there may be complex spatial and geometrical relationships within the field that one must weave through.

An experienced practitioner has already gone through the process of detaching from the frequency "reality" of third-dimension earth and remembers well how difficult that was. This capacity to be detached is part of virtually all intense spiritual disciplines. Detachment involves seeing yourself and an energy or situation as separate from each other. Once you are able to see this way, you can define yourself as who you are at your core. You can then objectively see and precisely define what other energies are as well. Following this stage, you next learn to identify fully with other energies, work peacefully with them, yet remain unaffected by them and able to detach and move on at will.

Cooperative Spirit

A fourth quality needed for interdimensional cooperation is the willingness to diplomatically proceed through partnership among all life forms. The interdimensional communicator must choose to approach the field of interest in a spirit of detached, loving, *ahimsic* cooperation. Considering ourselves superior to other life forms or seeking to take advantage of them (or get the better of them) is not an option. Energy is potentially infinite. We can never, ever, lord it over *all* of the potential fields of energy that exist. Moreover, every life form we encounter has its own bigger brother or sister who may eventually appear to assist the energy field under attack.

Field Integrity

Every life form in the universe is, at its core level, a merkabah— a self-contained unit of energy. In this book, we devote several chapters to an understanding of this energy form. Healthy merkabahs have certain commonalities. The primary one is field integrity, meaning that the life form is self-contained, intact, clear, energized and permeable. What do these characteristics mean?

Self-contained. The merkabah is not leaking energy via rips and tears in its perimeter. These rips can occur when an energy attacks an individual, breaks through the perimeter and the resulting hole is never repaired. Thereafter, anytime the individual encounters a situation with the same type of energy, it is often able to enter through that original hole and the individual experiences similar feelings once more. Or the original attack may have been so traumatic that the individual built defenses around the hole and blocked any interaction with that type of energy, good or bad. When blocked by defenses, energy that wants to enter will often circle the merkabah to find another, less-protected entry point. The person is blindsided and attacked again. This category of energy continues to affect the person until at last, in some lifetime, the person tires of it, turns and confronts the energy head on, and masters the intricacies of that specific aspect of consciousness, after which it can no longer affect them.

Intact. The energy field is not frayed from rips, tears, scars and energetic detours to get around unresolved issues.

Clear. All debilitating issues and counterenergies that have waged war inside the individual have been resolved and put to rest, so that energy can pass smoothly throughout the entire light field.

Energized. All aspects of the field are clear and connected to the source and receiving the correct light food the field needs to operate properly.

Permeable. The life-force field is comfortable in the mastery of its own substance and existence, knows how to protect itself, is intact, has resolved its issues, and so can permit other energies to flow through it without affecting it. It can also relate to other merkabahs without being unfavorably affected by them.

These characteristics make up the scientific definition of field integrity. But in terms of human existence, field integrity basically means that we have resolved our own hang-ups, learned how to be good without being a pushover and learned how to protect our own needs and wants without being a tyrant.

As a world operating in the solid third dimension, earth is also a collective merkabah seeking to resolve these same issues within a very complex form. Our world has created many different disciplines to resolve various aspects of this situation and is working through the complexities that occur when attacks come in many unexpected ways. For example, we desire to share our handicrafts with others via a store, yet we have to contend with those individuals who wish to steal the products instead of paying for them. How do we prevent theft from occurring? How do we demonstrate to those who steal that there is a better way to acquire something?

We could establish physical field integrity by installing cameras that are visible to customers, so that they understand they are being watched and, if caught, they will face our third-dimension judicial system. We could set a force field in place and hold it via various objects in that area. We could set a thoughtform in place, as the Native American medicine people used to do, and give the thoughtform the job of scaring anyone who tries to steal. We could clear the area and place such a strong force of love and acceptance throughout the space that it overwhelms any negative energy that might try to emerge while in that space.

Frequency

Interdimensional activity can also be understood as a technology. In this approach, the communicator is focusing on the composition of the field being observed. Even as a technology, progress is better when the field is approached with respect and a spirit of cooperation rather than an attempt to force it to comply with the communicator's personal will.

When starting to practice interdimensional communication as a technology, we need to understand certain scientific concepts:

1. All existence is the manifestation of frequency or sound in one form or another.

2. All frequency emerges from a struck point or sound.

3. Locate that struck point, and we can move through to its source.

4. All sources eventually work their way back to the primary source, which some call God.

5. If we locate the primary source, we can potentially move into any secondary, tertiary, etc., points that have evolved out of it. If we travel only part-way back to the source, we do not have free access to every aspect of energy—only to those aspects we have thus far been willing to investigate and comprehend. Those aspects can help us to resolve some, but not all, issues.

For instance, in the Middle Ages, people believed the world was flat. No one could see that it curved on the horizon and what that curve meant, until some adventurous individuals dared to defy convention and learned the world was round.

Today, we believe we can communicate only with humans, so when an angel or a nature spirit talks to us, we refuse to recognize the interaction. Our data bank of beliefs does not include one that allows for this communication, so we create another reason for it, such as: "I *imagined* I saw an angel." We can see only as far as we have permitted ourselves to examine in an honest, detached manner, untinged by cultural taboos.

When individuals commit to understanding the source of all and focus on that, suddenly all of the unexplainable occurrences fall into their proper place and are understood. We see the true connectedness of all and its significance. We acknowledge that it was *not* our imagination; we really did communicate with our pets, a rock, a fairy or an angel.

To proceed, we need a purpose, not just curiosity. The function of purpose, or intent, is to direct the forward movement of consciousness through the cosmic fields of infinite variation.

Our entire universe is constructed of merkabah fields. One way to accomplish interdimensional communication and travel is to master the merkabah form. When working with the merkabah, we learn to create energy changes in the form, including shifting and spinning it at different rates and locating travel lines and portals through which we can pass into another dimension. In actuality, the entire universe is only one merkabah that has spun off, within itself, multiple aspects. Since above time and space all existence is one, we can instantly enter that field by simply refocusing what we choose to perceive (if we have done our basic work with consciousness, of course).

A kaleidoscope, with its translucent colored stones, is an apt analogy for the universe. Hold a kaleidoscope up to the light, and you will see an intricate geometric pattern. Touch it ever so gently, and the stones shift, forming a different pattern. In reality, existence, too, consists of the same base components, re-arranged. We are working with the same materials in every field. The puzzle that we need to solve, in a specific situation, is how they are arranged and for what purpose they are acting.

Our earth is currently shifting in frequency. This is a natural astronomical and astrological phenomena coming from our shifting relationship to the universe around us. At this particular time, we are experiencing a severe shift. This shift is so profound that it is altering all frequency fields connected to it.

Manufactured frequencies that we ourselves have brought into being are also profoundly affecting us. We are pouring into the earth grid ever-increasing amounts of electromagnetic and chemical pollution. These pollutants are usurping or altering space already occupied by some other life form. When a space is changed, what exists inside the space must adapt or perish from lack of sustenance.

Whales and dolphins communicate on the same frequency band being usurped for submarine communication, and many believe this is contributing to the mysterious beachings and deaths of these great animals. The human energy field is electromagnetic in nature. The proliferating electromagnetic technology in our modern offices and homes is becoming so pervasive that it

is blocking our bodies' autonomic connection to the natural re-
storative frequencies of nature, resulting in many immune-system dysfunctions, stress issues and possibly genetic alterations,
including nervous-system disorders such as autism and attention
deficit disorder (ADD).

Natural earth changes, combined with pollution, are altering
the frequency paths by which a soul has traditionally descended
into the body. These frequency alterations are contributing to the
growing numbers of children born with alternate modes of perception and behavior. Everything is being forced to adapt; the
results are sometimes successful and sometimes not.

Today, some interdimensional communicators are successfully resolving many issues by making contact and talking with
the life forms involved. Their efforts include asking cellphone
towers and electrical power lines to share their frequencies with
humans, and asking the human body to make space for the manufactured frequencies to pass through.

Pregnancy is a prime example of interdimensional cooperation. What makes the correct embryonic brain connect with the
correct liver, with the correct legs and so on? There is an un-
spoken interdependency on a common stabilizing energy field,
which in the field of interdimensional communication is known
as a grid or a merkabah.

Merkabahs can be a linked partnership of individual types
of energy fields working together to manifest a larger complex
form. Like a chameleon that can regrow a lost tail, a merkabah
can direct its energy fields to assume whatever form is needed.
When supporting fields such as the brain, heart and liver are manifested within the parent form, the overall merkabah encourages
the frequency to oscillate at just the right spin and velocity for
the needs of the collective, combined field. The new part needs
to work in harmony with the rest of the parts. A harmonious life
form is being manifested. If some part becomes off-pattern or

off-frequency, at any level of any of the partnering fields, for any reason, a change in the manifested life form will occur. Changes from the ideal norm can occur because of past-life energies that define what this merkabah can now become, by the environment in which the fetus is growing and many other causes.

Altering the frequencies of a life form changes the subsequent form, subtly or grossly. Once the energy has reached the physical level and locked in, it is more difficult to alter the form, although the subtle energies can still be altered.

It is in the area of energetic formation that the interdimensional communicators are well qualified to assist. They can look into the fields and locate points of origin. They can see and discuss with the life forms themselves exactly what options are available.

The changes occurring now on our earth are so serious that representatives from many of the earth's non-human realms are coming forward to work with us to find solutions. Think of this time as a sequel to the *Lord of the Rings*. Now the nature spirits are returning to assist our human realm because if we fail, all life in all earth dimensions will be irrevocably altered as well.

Many people are being contacted by universal life forces. Earth is a concern to the universal community, for we stand on the cusp of a change so profound that it can destroy us or create a new world. There is great concern that the change go well.

Chapter 5
On the Nature of the Merkabah Unit

*As each merkabah contains, at its source,
a spark of the divine source of all, each
merkabah is actually the one source seeking
to manifest itself in some way.*

What Is a Merkabah?

A merkabah is defined here as a field of energy emanating from a single core point and expanding out in a circular manner. The term is ancient Egyptian and originally referred to what the Egyptians considered to be the three aspects of the human being: *mer* (light), *ka* (spirit), and *bah* (body). The ancient Hebrew culture further defines the merkabah as an energy vehicle, or the vehicle of vehicles—the supreme vehicle for moving through existence/creation.

A merkabah can be simple or complex. It always emanates from a larger field (which might be the ultimate source itself), because it is formed from the polarity of forces emanating from a single source. It will often contain inside itself subsidiary fields.

Every merkabah contains the opportunity to express the unmanifested, inherent energies of its source and the ultimate source in some unique manner. It is up to the life force that is contained inside that merkabah to develop itself to the point of true and perfect fulfillment. Doing so requires mastery of all the evolving aspects of that field's purpose or intent. Doing so also requires protection.

As each merkabah contains, at its source, a spark of the ultimate source, each merkabah is actually the one ultimate source seeking to manifest itself in some way.

It is impossible to say that one life form emanating from the perfect, infinite source is inherently more perfect or better than another. We can say that one merkabah may be less mature or less aware of its true reality than another. But we cannot say that it is inferior, which implies a difference of inherent quality.

The merkabah is a core geometric form—a primary building block for all existence. It is the base of most geometric light fields and is central to understanding how the source has chosen to manifest itself in this universe.

Subfields

At its simplest level, a merkabah is a frequency grid that keeps a particular aspect of consciousness intact and in place. As any specific merkabah develops, it becomes more complex because it naturally forms subfields and subfrequencies. Each subfield is a merkabah as well. There are numerous layers or subfields inside a mature merkabah. These sub-merkabahs may grow in size, and sub-merkabahs grow in them as well. Usually, the larger the merkabah, the more subfrequencies it has.

Any field we enter is inherently a subfrequency field of a larger merkabah, right up into the original emission of the original form from the ultimate source itself. Any field we enter has the potential to spin out subfrequencies of its own, ad infinitum. As noted earlier, there can be trillions of sub-merkabahs inside any field. Vortexes and fields can emerge from any point within a merkabah construct, and a merkabah can become extremely complex in construction as it matures.

Sometimes separate merkabahs will link up to exchange information or energy. Morphogenetic fields develop when many merkabahs link together to be proponents for a specific common topic or energy. Their original partnership grows from a group into a collective, and then into a broadly accessible field of knowledge or information. Eventually this common field becomes a self-sustaining merkabah that remains even if its original founding members subsequently leave.

A third-dimension example of this principle would be a club that was formed by three founding members and grew in size to over 1,000. Should a founding member leave at the start, the impact could prove disastrous. Should the member leave later, after the club is well developed, the club will survive and go on.

Working with morphogenetic fields is a basic part of interdimensional communication. Once a form is established, it resonates with all other forms of its same shape and frequency anywhere in the universe or morphogenetic field. Interdimensional communicators can use this resonance principle to locate and work with different patterns of energy.

It is good to be cautious when working with morphogenetic fields. All fields exist by binding universal energy, and all are connected to ever larger and more powerful fields of various sorts. Therefore, interdimensional communicators try not to stay too long in a field, to avoid being trapped inside its energy.

Field Rules

Merkabahs are round globes of energy. In this free-will universe in which we all exist, they can be complete worlds unto themselves that create reality in any form they choose to perceive it. Every merkabah has the potential to become fully aware of itself and its own inherent perfection. However, the route to the fulfillment of that potential can be extremely long in duration. For example, every cell in the human body is a merkabah, *and* these cells themselves will someday in the far, far distant future be fully realized as to their nature and potential—but not now.

This means that as we perfect ourselves, we must eventually perfect even the base individual cells or merkabahs of our body. As these cells perfect themselves, when they replace or replicate themselves as cells do, they will replicate that perfection—a continuation of that consciousness. Because the cells are also part of the morphogenetic field called cells, their individual perfection contributes to their field's knowledge of how all cells can perfect themselves as well. As in any field, there are the pioneers who set the new consciousness and the settlers who move into the consciousness.

Once inside a merkabah of any long-standing nature, certain field rules, formed by that merkabah itself, apply. To successfully complete its objectives, any life form entering a formed merkabah needs to quickly discern and work in harmony with that world's distinctively evolved rules.

Merkabahs occur at many differing frequencies and in many different sizes. Our universe is a merkabah; there are many other universes in existence that are also vast merkabahs. Our merkabah-universe has evolved its own set of rules. These rules do not necessarily apply to other merkabah-universes who may have evolved significantly different patterns of energy.

The Geometric Structure of a Merkabah

Many call merkabahs "sacred geometry." Sacred geometry simply depicts what various visionaries see when looking into the light forms that exist behind matter.

Every field of consciousness, or merkabah, can be perceived as a geometric form and communicated with as a living form. Here we are focusing on understanding the merkabah in its aspect as sacred geometry. However, its existence as a living form is always present in our awareness.

Sacred geometry forms are patterns of light that are created as energy organizes itself to perform a task. These shapes gradually define themselves more specifically, as they work to achieve a particular objective, and may eventually descend into a solid form, such as an ant, human or table.

The core level of a merkabah, looked at geometrically, is usually graphed in one of two ways. One way forms the flower of life

and the other way forms the star tetrahedron.

The flower of life shows the field of a merkabah. The star tetrahedron shows the polarities of a merkabah.

The core form of almost all sacred geometry is the merkabah. When the merkabah is seen as a star tetrahedron, balance via the harmonized polarities of the field is significant. Two pyramids form the star tetrahedron. They counter-rotate to each other, creating a spinning ball of frequency, which is why a merkabah is usually depicted as a ball of light. This ball-shaped merkabah is sometimes shown with a line, signifying a column of light, extending through it top to bottom. This column of energy has at its center point, within the column of light, a core point from which the merkabah has emerged from its source. The column is every form's connection to the ultimate polar energies of the father (spirit) and mother (creation) consciousness of the universe. It also indicates that the merkabah is expandable along those lines.

When inspected in stop action, an active merkabah can look something like a map globe; the latitude and longitude lines of the globe represent the merkabah's grid. Sometimes a merkabah is seen in motion, in which case it looks like a glowing orb of light. When a merkabah is in full spin, it looks like a saucer spaceship (UFO). As the merkabah matures and develops light field connections internal to itself, those with extended sight have observed a fairly predictable array of shapes, each of which has a specific energetic function. The most fundamental, universal ones are called the Platonic solids: the tetrahedron, cube, octahedron, dodecahedron, and icosahedron. Other fundamental geometric shapes that occur are the cross, the flower of life, the tree of life and the vesica pisces.

Mandalas

Far Eastern yantras and mandalas are graphs of various fields of consciousness. Adepts can enter into very specific fields by the information these diagrams relay.

When we look at an authentic mandala, yantra or sacred geometry form, we are actually looking at a subtle engineering schematic of what is occurring inside a particular aspect, or merkabah, of consciousness. We are each a living merkabah, always changing in time-space dimensions via varying modulations, spins, frequencies and complexities. We can, if we wish, graph ourselves and how our own energy fields overlap and interact.

For some practitioners, mandalas exist simultaneously as a schematic description of a field of energy, a witness for the field, and the actual energy itself. A classic mandala graphs a specific energy. Adepts can look at it and read the symbols to understand the energies involved. Let's look at one of the classic mandalas of creation, called the Bhuvaneshvari Yantra.

The central form is the star tetrahedron. The center of this tetrahedron is the core source. The absolute source has been perceived as both a void and as an unmanifest fullness inherently containing all. When it is perceived as a void, the Eastern diagram of creation has nothing in the middle of the Star of David. When it is perceived as an unmanifest fullness, the diagram has a single dot in the middle, as shown in the illustration, indicating that point from which all else has emerged.

The mandala next shows a double circle around the star tetrahedron, indicating energy is infinitely expanding in a balanced way. Eight lotus petals indicate its frequency or sound. (In the Western musical scale this sound is the note of F or FA—the heart frequency.) The square indicates the energy of the mandala is being held in place so that it can be examined by the observer. A square and a cube are the energies of grounding and holding; that is their light field function. In sacred geometry there is a process called squaring the circle; this enables the practitioner to hold a fluctuating energy field (a circle or globe) in place for examination.

It is important to avoid being trapped inside a field of energy. Expert practitioners of all the subtle arts are very aware of this principle and always make sure they know how to exit from a field before they go into it. Thus this mandala, as most of the classic Far Eastern ones, has four doors for entry and exit. These signify the energies of the four directions, or the major energies of existence, and indicate that the observer can move into and out of the mandala at will, from any direction.

One can also always leave via the core source of the form. This point may be disguised, obliterated from sight, clogged, shut down or cut off, but this is only on the lower levels of frequency. At the highest levels, a clear access to the source *always* exists. Locating this point can sometimes be difficult.

. . . .

Intersecting Polarity and Merkabah Fields

When two polarity fields intersect and the parent fields are cooperative, the common area becomes a rich field of activity in which both poles grow and stretch their capacities within one object. Conflict in the parent fields results in chaos where the fields intersect. It is very difficult to make clear, real progress in this situation. The star tetrahedron depicts the polarities inside a merkabah.

The flower of life is a core-level geometric found in all the ancient cultures of the world. It depicts the field of the merkabah. There are different ways to depict its growth from the one to the many. All the Platonic solids can be graphed inside this field. The appearance of multiple vesica pisces, or portals, is of particular interest to an interdimensional surfer and shape-shifter.

In this schematic, the area where two of any circles intersect is called the vesica pisces. Vesica pisces create gateways through otherwise solid energy and can be used to surf through the waves of consciousness to any location in the universe. They can also be used to shape-shift into other worlds of being. The Masons understood this aspect of the shape and in medieval churches would often depict Christ or the saints emerging from a vesica pisces, indicating the emergence of new life from spirit.

Those knowledgeable in sacred geometry can combine geometry and symbols to graph pictorially what is occurring inside a specific field of energy. Other practitioners can then look at the schematic and understand what is occurring inside that specific field. They can read the schematic as a pictorial language that eloquently describes what is occurring. They can also interpret it to be a three-dimensional (or more) form one can enter via identification and directly experience.

Dowsers, medicine people, occultists and witch doctors know that a schematic, or sample of the field such as a strand of hair, can serve as a witness for the actual object. This means it stands in for the object being searched for or investigated. Practitioners use the witness to locate something and/or to affect something.

Thus, pertinent to the topic of this book, a schematic of a merkabah is understood by experts to also actually be the object itself. This full identification is how they can powerfully affect the field. I call this full field perception.

When discussing merkabahs in this book, I am working from the awareness that the schematic of *a* or *the* merkabah can be understood as a description, worked with as a witness and experienced as the object itself.

I myself, as an interdimensional communicator, can when I wish visualize an object and instantly inwardly transfer to that spot or identify with its energy. Some advanced individuals can physically or subtly transport themselves across long distances, or even bi-locate themselves. Among disciplines capable of doing this are the Hindu saddhus and gurus; they call this capacity one of the siddhis, which are advanced energy field abilities that humans can develop through spiritual practices. Some extraterrestrial civilizations, when traveling between dimensions, use merkabah ships; some of these ships are externally constructed and some of the ships are biologically formed, responding to the navigator's energy field.

Nested Merkabahs

A merkabah can nest inside many similar but larger merkabahs, much like the Russian dolls that nest inside each other. This is what people see when they are tracking the perimeters of the subtle physical, astral, etheric and spiritual auric levels.

When we become expert at observing grids, we see many, many levels nesting inside each other, each responsible for a specific frequency that contributes to the consciousness of the whole. An overlapping of many grids creates the illusion of substance. The solid matter of earth is actually only the overlapping of many, many grids working together inside a master field. As Einstein said, "There is no phyical matter, only denser and denser fields."

Mastering the Merkabah

Three things are necessary to master the use of the merkabah in interdimensional travel:

1. Our belief in the omnipresence of one source throughout the universe.

2. Our ability to detach from the world as we perceive it now and to allow ourselves to perceive other manifestations of the one universal source.

3. A commitment to working with all other life forms via cooperation and partnership among equals. We will not be able to master this subtle science as long as we desire, consciously or subconsciously, to manipulate or dominate any other life form. As we are all the manifestations of the one source, we are all, at our core source, equal to each other. Our manifestation of this core source is different and serves its own purpose. This manifestation can and should have the right to change as it masters its ability to accurately work with consciousness to achieve its own core objectives.

When we master working with the merkabah, we can safely journey anywhere we wish. We can communicate with any life form that exists. We can communicate with our pets, with the birds and with the flowers and stones—all living beings who are cooperating with us to develop and perfect this field of consciousness we humans call earth. We can visit the realms of the inner earth peoples—the fairies and gnomes, elves and dwarves—each of whom exist inside a different field of frequency from humans. We can know the realms of the dark forces or the realms of the angels, the cosmic deities and the many metaterrestrials and extraterrestrials who cohabitate our earth on other frequencies.

We can also travel far beyond this dimension and journey into the far reaches of space and communicate with the many life forms existing there. "All" that is required to do so is to locate and merge with the precise frequency of the merkabah, or life form, that is being sought, no matter where it is in the universe. "All" that is required to do this—to travel, speak and work with any life form anywhere—is to enter into the heart center (the geometric center from which our own merkabahs have emerged) and to then enter into the heart or geometric center of whatever frequency we are focusing on, or seeking. The "trick" is learning to do this. At this point in your reading, however, don't be discouraged! Exercises are provided throughout this book to help you learn this skill. First it is important for you to gain an understanding of the basic principles involved in working with the merkabah.

Knowledge of the merkabah permits us to energetically get back home when we are taken inwardly visiting by some life form, for whatever reason, and dropped off in a strange spot. Understanding the nature of interdimensional consciousness helps us to comprehend what is happening and to ask the life forms in the place where we have been transported exactly who they are, what they want or need, how to assist them or be assisted by them, and how to then get back home.

Many interdimensional travelers to earth use the knowledge of the merkabah to travel here. Many of the "extraterrestrial" vehicles seen throughout history are in reality consciously crafted merkabah-shaped vehicles that are applying merkabah principles to facilitate a group's interdimensional and intergalactic travel.

Meditation and
Interdimensional Communication

When we first enter into a new merkabah field, it often takes a bit of time to adjust our inner sight to its particular frequency and spin. Our capacity to adapt depends upon several factors, including our awareness that we need to adjust, our level of expertise in such work, what types of locks or guardians are protecting that field for some specific purpose and the attitude with which we approach that field (that is, whether we come in friendship and peace, or seeking to conquer and/or destroy).

When we enter into a new merkabah, we may initially perceive it as void of existence. It is as if we are standing in the dark, opening a door, and being blasted with the light inside that room. It takes a little time for our eyes to adjust and to see that inside the lighted room there are actually forms. Classical meditation uses will-power to see nothing inside such a field. This is similar to asking our children and pets to be silent, in the third dimension, while we get some peace.

Classical meditation is useful for training our minds to stay still. But next we must be flexible enough to look into whatever field we have chosen to enter. If we train ourselves to block the image of the field we are within, putting up walls, we will succeed in seeing nothing, even if that field of consciousness is rich in life forms.

There is no space within all existence that is not fully occupied by forms native to their world. Investigating these forms and their inherent value to the whole, or the source, requires identifying with the particular world.

One of the primary differences between interdimensional cooperation and the learning of classic meditation techniques is this: in interdimensional cooperation, we are learning to facilitate action or to work with a world; in classical meditation, we are often looking for an escape from our world—that is, to find a place of refuge.

Entering a Merkabah

Once a field is set in place within a merkabah, it begins spinning out its own frequency. There are numerous such fields inside a merkabah, and the larger the field the more subfrequencies exist.

Whenever we interdimensional communicators enter into a merkabah, whether to speak with an individual, go to the meeting of a group or travel interdimensionally to another world, we are first aware of a shift in energy. What we experience depends upon our point of focus, point of entry, what we are doing there, why we are going there and what we want to accomplish.

First we may see light or darkness, or nothing, or a shimmer. Then our inner eyes start to adjust to that particular frequency, and we begin to see the objects of its world. What we see depends on where we have landed; we may land in different environments, just like on earth, where we may land in a desert, ocean, city or forest. Interdimensional travelers will focus on the frequency we are seeking, or if we have encountered a world or energy far different from any we have worked with before, we may choose to travel with an inner guide or inner friend—a colleague we can trust to show us around the place. We already have learned we can trust them to give us the correct "scoop" on the nature of this place. A trusted interdimensional team is essential when we undertake this work professionally.

Any field will have its own toxic substances or areas. It is always wise to proceed with caution, working with our guides to make certain we correctly comprehend and understand the nature of the situation and the best method to proceed.

There is always a danger in focusing on a toxic substance for any length of time. However, working with the merkabah and grid technology mitigates this danger somewhat. In this discipline, we are looking behind the toxic substance to the source within it and the lesson it has to teach. We are seeking either to help the substance itself transform into a beneficial substance or to help it achieve its goal, in a positive way even for a negative substance, so that it can leave a situation because its work is done. The toxic substance has a mission—to teach about the source through darkness—and once the client has learned that the source is all-prevalent, the substance has completed its job. In cases such as this, we practitioners are actually energizing ourselves, because, to solve the issue, we must locate the internal light that is in all existence. I myself usually come back from a clearing highly energized. Not only that, when I go to my chiropractor for my regular adjustment, he finds me very well aligned—more so than on other days. The light I am working in heals me as well as the situation.

In the work of an interdimensional communicator, fear is a frequency that needs to be overcome again and again. Darkness and discord do exist, and in the face of these forces we interdimensional communicators must be courageous and cautious, not oblivious.

When we approach a dark or discordant energy, it may well send forth fear as part of its arsenal of defense. The aura of fear may also occur when the parts of the grid around an object that is holding a great deal of light, such as a religious house or a natural vortex, are pushed back. We need to clearly observe what is occurring. The interdimensional communicators do this by standing still energetically, calling in our guides and all of us observing the frequency. When we do this, the opposing energy also pauses. We are, in essence, calling a time-out while all the players examine what is occurring and what needs to happen next.

We can now examine the energy to understand its function and purpose for being present in this situation. If we cannot understand how the dark energy is serving the source, for they are now at work because the methods of light did not succeed or need to be harmonized with the dark, we can request the life form to please step aside so that we can see the source behind them. Once we see what aspect of the source the dark life form is working for, and they step back into place, we can comprehend more clearly how to proceed to an appropriate solution.

In this work, it is important to respect darkness and its very real capacity to injure, hurt and destroy. It is important to realize that darkness is an aspect of the ultimate source and is meant to help strengthen us for full mastery. Have a healthy respect for what it does and its valid opposition to the light. Be careful and do not focus on it to the exclusion of light, or vice versa. Identification with such a resonance, or total lack of identification and awareness of its qualities, can lead to significant problems in the overall mastery of the situation.

Moving Among Merkabah Fields

When we move into a field of coherent energy, we send out a call to the life forms existing within it. We are like a fox entering a prairie homestead, seeking the hen house. When we enter, all the dogs of the farm come out barking. All they are doing is protecting their property; this is their job.

When we start our multidimensional explorations, we need to ask ourselves some basic questions. Why are we seeking to enter that life form, and what do we want/seek/wish to accomplish? Are we truly going as a seeker of wisdom, as a petitioner or as a helper, or are we seeking to become a world conqueror? Are we still in the mindset of the Kali Yuga, or have we truly transitioned to the new cooperative way we will be living as this next world of ours emerges?

The preceding age worked primarily through domination, and, depending upon the field and its rules, the strongest survived and ruled. When we work this way, there is never any end to this pattern of perception, and it results in separation of parts of our own selves from our own selves and in numerous diseases of body, mind and spirit.

Eventually, as a master of energy, an interdimensional practitioner is able to enter into the energy field of any world and comprehend why the energy exists, without being affected by it. Until that point, if a field contains a reality we have refused to accept within our consciousness, we may be thrown into the fray in order to comprehend it on an experiential level. Then, once we have known and lived the energy, we will have mastered its frequency modulations, and it will no longer bother us in the future.

I have learned, over the years, that if I meet someone I do not like, I need to look at myself and see what quality they are embodying that I have not transformed inside myself. This person becomes a living lesson to me. I need to transform my own self in the weakness they are exhibiting, so that when their energy field is projected towards me, it can keep flowing on through me and into the universe; there should be no hooks in my field where it can get caught. Sometimes I can solve the issue easily, and other times the same issue comes back again and again, often through multiple people. For example, if someone is jealous, that energy flows through me quite easily; I can immediately help them, because jealousy is not a personal issue for me. But if someone relishes creating discord, I have a more difficult time—not because I like to create discord, but because I dislike it so intensely that I sometimes block the energy from approaching me. Blocking only means the energy will circle me until it finds a weak spot, at which point it enters and attacks. The only choice is for me to face the issue squarely, understand its purpose, make peace with it and let it flow through.

As we advance in consciousness, we have the choice of experiencing the field by living it or simply by identifying and energetically entering it for a while before stepping out again.

Many of the so-called gods and goddesses of antiquity were, in reality, very advanced beings who stepped into human bodies to experience something to help transform themselves, then stepped back out again. This is a very, very advanced state of interdimensional energy work.

Creating a Merkabah Frequency

Whenever a thought is sent forth, it becomes a merkabah, or field of energy, self-contained and self-sustaining. When two or more hold the same thought, the merkabah increases in strength, and as more and more people feed into it, it gains in strength and size. Soon it becomes a morphogenetic field of consciousness, so strong that anyone approaching this field immediately senses this consciousness and solution. Unaware of what is actually occurring, they very naturally fold into the consciousness and hold it in place through their own bodily antenna. They dial to that frequency and leave the radio tuned to that station.

This is what happens to people who are brought up in a strict religion or as a member of a specific social class, for example. They have a very hard time perceiving energy from another viewpoint because they have from childhood been trained to stay inside a specific thought-form frequency. It becomes almost impossible for them to change, unless some type of catastrophe causes them to reject their previous confines. When the catastrophe occurs, it breaks their bonds, and they have the opportunity to make new choices.

This catastrophe principle is why, very often, energy workers emerge from some serious life-threatening illness for which mainstream medicine has no cure. Rather than die, these people choose to break the mold and investigate other methods to heal themselves. In the course of doing so, they often make remarkable new discoveries.

Ultimately, when enough people get tired of a confining frequency, as a unit they will make a change. This new frequency then becomes an option, or it overrides the previous one and dominates the field. For example, simplifying this principle, let's look at the pattern of such twentieth-century movements as Indian Independence and, in the United States, women's right to vote and civil rights. All of these, when they began, were considered unachievable goals. The early pioneers of each had a dream they would not let go of. They kept their faith and high ideals in the face of violence from the opposition. Each gradually made their dream so real that first other visionaries joined in, and as more people held the thoughtform, others also began to believe. The thoughtform/energy/merkabah adjusted as it descended to the physical plane, and the dream became accessible to the common person. When the number of people joining each movement became large enough, the dream became a reality: nothing could stand in the way of the dream's fulfillment,

There are many groups struggling right now to achieve and make real on earth a new consciousness, or merkabah. What emerges now, during a change of age, is going to have a profound effect on the evolution of earth as it proceeds. Many groups from many dimensions are present around the earth right now, seeking to help their favorites emerge victorious.

The interplay of the emotional forces in this process is currently "entertaining" members of intergalactic society, some of whom have incarnated to experience the blood rush of battle for themselves. The interplay of the spiritual forces is interesting other groups, who are coming in to work internally with their genetic and spiritual lineages to strengthen the opportunity for light to prevail.

Chapter 6
On the Nature of
the Polarities of a Merkabah

*It is a basic principle of grid technology that
all of existence is the expression of a universe
capable of an infinite amount of expansion or
compression while exploring its own potentials.*

Polarity Constructs

Polarities and their many methods of interplay are base forms
interdimensional communicators work with in grid technology.
Polarities have been in existence since the start of creation. Every set emerges at the same moment from a common source. As
any set develops, it creates multiple subfields in which its basic
energies have evolved, through direct experience, at many levels
of frequency and spin. At the highest, most subtle levels of existence, each side of a polarity is a pure expression of its polar
principle. At the grossest level, each is inert.

Let's examine the process of polarities via its simplest form;
a split into two opposites. When a life form/thought becomes
awake and wants to comprehend itself:

1. It examines what it is and is not. This creates a triangle:
   the original point and its self-examination of its two
   polar opposites.

2. Each side also needs to examine what it is and is not, which means it splits into two internal polarities, each replicating the energy of the parent. The energy of this self-examination process creates a two-dimensional star tetrahedron, or Star of David.

3. The two parent polarities face each other and as each side examines the energies of itself and its opposite, the energies intersect. When the two sides are equal in strength and are compatible, there is awareness.

There is an interesting strictly energetic principle at play here. The two polarities of a merkabah can also be perceived as spiral cones or pyramids. When looked at from their point to their widest opening, the energy of each side will be spinning the same way, say clockwise. But when looked at from how they intersect, the spiral is going the opposite direction. In a healthy merkabah, these counterspinning spirals are spinning out debris from the other side, and the two opposing motions are keeping the form in constant movement. Should one side break down or weaken, the energy of its spin starts to slow and this weakening gradually leads to the weakening of the other side which has had to either speed up to compensate or has clogged up and slowed down itself.

Looking at this process energetically, you can now under-stand that where there is conflict, the chaos in the field can dull the energies to such an extent as to cause inconscience. This level of awareness is known as the "gross" level of consciousness.

For each polarity construct, the "gross level" is a constantly extending point. It is determined by just how far into its opposite the polarity pair is currently exploring. Once any gross-level point has been mapped and explored, a new level is discovered beyond it, and the process begins anew.

"The other" in a polarity construct is potentially infinitely expandable and thus ultimately unknowable, as long as we stay with the construct itself. Therefore, it is a basic principle of grid technology that all of existence is the expression of a universe capable of an infinite amount of expansion (or compression) while exploring its own potentials. Furthermore, the entire universe can be collapsed back to one core source, technically termed the void or the unmanifest fullness.

As long as the two poles within any construct seek to work in partnership, whether they are currently walking together or are at the cyclical point of opposition, their process of growth is relatively peaceful. When one side seeks to overpower and dominate the other, problems expand. As soon as "power over" becomes an issue, the joint polarity field is weakened.

The discord must either be peacefully resolved or escalate until the imbalance becomes so extreme that neither side can exist in peace. At this point, harmony and equilibrium become the goal for each. Balancing efforts will start and continue until such harmony is established. Therefore, discord can be a source of growth, for both sides of the issue.

For example, in the recent patriarchal age we are just now emerging from, the male polarity has oppressed its female polarity. The female, convinced she is, indeed, inferior to the male, has behaved according to his dictates, and her acquiescence appears to have brought peace to the situation. However, because the abuse has been too extreme, the victim is finding the courage to fight back. She has started to reclaim her natural, inherent, universal right to be treated as equal to her opposite polarity and, indeed, to all other energies, all of which have the same infinite source as she herself. Thus, as soon as the female polarity begins to understand that she is equal and deserves to be treated as an equal, the probability of dissension, anger or violence begins to grow, and peace is gone.

Whenever there is inequality, it will eventually have to be addressed before either side can progress any further in its own separate course of evolution and in relation to the other. The recent male patriarchy penalized the men just as much as the women, for to maintain their belief in male superiority, men had to negate, abuse or close off the feminine energies inside their own consciousness, resulting in the various personal and societal violence and imbalance we are working through today.

Imbalance eventually requires each polarity to examine its own motivation as it seeks to restore peace to a situation. This process of rebalancing can occur within a time-frame that is relatively short (as in the case of a personal relationship) or long (as in the case of a society's cultural transformation).

Comprehending via the Merkabah

When we can comprehend any situation from its source and see its polarities, we can begin to make headway. To gain this comprehension, we often have to proceed by first moving up from the issue to its source and then reversing the process to see how the issue manifested down from this source, or vice versa. Once we have explored both directions, we can consciously work within the full multidirectional field of energies to balance the situation satisfactorily.

The view of an issue descending is different from the view ascending. In ascent, we are moving towards unity of consciousness. In descent, we are following a line of specialization of consciousness to achieve a specific result.

It is only by going above the polarities involved in a particular situation that one can clearly comprehend the totality of an issue and the value each pole provides. It is only by descent into form that the communicator can consciously guide energy to a proper solution.

As Albert Einstein said, a problem cannot be solved at the same level at which it has occurred.

While the simplest and clearest way to understand polarities is through the opposition of two forces, there are also other means to progress. A single point can simultaneously fragment into a set number of parts. Some of the more common geometric segmentations of one point into many are four, six, seven, eight, eleven or twelve. (To grasp how this segmentation is possible, think of objects you know with various numbers of primary segments, such as a nine-pointed star or the twelve-position clock.) Sometimes consciousness will simultaneously fragment, like a puffball, into an immense number of particles.

Whatever method the one uses to separate into simultaneously created parts, the parts are known as faces or poles. They express different potentials of the whole, or multiple opportunities for the original energy to succeed in finding a solution to an issue or procedure.

Each aspect can, as it matures, choose to explore its own nature, either in the same manner as its parent or perhaps in some other manner of its own choosing. This alternate method can include combining its energies with those of another form and thus creating a third, combined form that offers the potentials of each of its parents and its parents' lineages. An example of this combined form is the human child.

Consciousness can also combine its energies with multiple other life forms, selecting one factor from each, as it deems important, to create a combined form it feels will provide the best opportunity to achieve a specific set of goals. Many say our human race was created this way, our DNA code formed from a selection of intergalactic cultures.

....

EXERCISE WITH THE NATURE OF POLARITIES

In your own life, explore how this need to balance opposing polarities affects you.

Sit silently and quiet the mind and emotions. Enter into your spiritual heart.

Now take any situation, from losing weight to exploring your career. As long as you approach the matter from a polarity viewpoint, focusing on only one side of the issue, you will eventually snap back to the other side and react to the pull. You may, for instance, go off the diet and eat every goody in sight, or you may angrily tell off that control-obsessed supervisor and kill your chance for a promotion.

Now detach yourself from this situation and observe the energies in play. See how they came into form and how they will continue on if left unchanged. Observe the options at each major stopping point along the spectrum from one end to the other. Now go above the situation. Rise like a bird and observe the energies going on below you. Watch for another route of descent that will take you into the same frequency field but in a different location, which will yield a different result. Try this again and again and let the energy flow, to see which path would be more productive for you.

Let us say that the main scale is your chosen professional field. What point on the scale have you chosen as your point of focus? If you select "office secretary" on the scale, but have not looked at the full range of options and what it means to get to different levels, then you are going to create a different series of cascading merkabahs than if you are aspiring to also vertically move up the scale to, say, "office manager" or "company president."

Put your vision into inner action via imagination. Then come back to the present and begin acting on this in the physical world.

....

What Happens When We Attempt to Proceed Through Only One Polarity?

Energy is self-correcting, always seeking the balance from which the source can be properly manifested. This self-correcting process is depicted in one of the most famous mandalas within the Far Eastern traditions. It is called the Sri Yantra ("most honored yantra or form").

The Sri Yantra starts with one triangle facing down. This triangle maps the procedure for the manifestation of energy: the feminine energies. The diagram shows three descending triangles that form in succession until the pull of these energies brings into existence a counterbalancing, upward-facing triangle. There is a play of energy back and forth, manifesting in varying sizes of countering triangles, until the whole finally achieves a stasis of balance—the full and equally sized sides of a star tetrahedron.

Precisely how the Sri Yantra is to be charted to show this growth is a topic that can excite a great deal of debate among sacred-geometry experts. The form can evolve and devolve in many ways. This goes to show precisely our point: it is the underlying principles that should concern us, and we should remain open to whatever path to manifestation that energy so chooses to take.

Based on this awareness, many consciousness groups in today's society are focusing on human progress not by retreating to ashrams and monasteries, but by balancing the polarities of spirit and matter throughout a seeker's growth.

Male and Female Polarities

In the Sri Yantra, downward-thrusting energy (represented by three consecutive downward-facing triangles) must eventually manifest the opposite polarity, an upward-thrusting triangle. Polarity has suddenly reappeared, as must eventually occur in any directed act within creation. Any directed action, no matter how intense, must eventually balance out and stabilize itself via the presence of its own polarity.

We see this situation in today's world, which is self-correcting many polarities that have grown imbalanced over time. An example is the male versus female perception. Our world is currently recovering from a very long period of male domination, which was itself preceded by a very long period of female domination. Hopefully, we are now rising above this situation, and both fields can cooperate in partnership.

The two methods of perception are two polarities, and each has the responsibility for holding firm its particular energy.

The current male position, or the line of energy entering and forming the father aspect of the merkabah, perceives the world from a hierarchical position best described as classically religious in the current perception of religion. This position states that the unmanifest source is the highest, and each descending round needs to conform to the dictates of the ones above. Physical life is inherently inferior in this perception.

The feminine approach means hierarchical observation from the feminine side of the merkabah. Here the life force is seeking full expression in form, and all evolving systems emerge from this cauldron and seek to work in partnership for the goal of perfect manifestation.

The two forces working together, vision and manifestation, are the ideal balance.

For example, the patriarchal force of classic religion, with its control and oppression of nature, has extended as far as polarity will permit without the incorporation of the opposite polarity, the mother or matriarchal energy. The needs of this opposing pole are surfacing everywhere, as the thrust of the patriarchal approach comes up against the abuses inherent in any energy form that is not balanced, whether that form is in nature, politics, or religion.

Attempts to focus on only one side of a polarity, whether it is matriarchal, patriarchal or some other combination of energies, eventually lead to abuses of control. This combination might be the desires of the green environmental movements versus the needs of the military and sciences, communism versus capitalism and so forth. Control versus cooperation is also a polarity, and neither of these ways will work to the exclusion of the other.

Issues Involved in the Spinning of Polarity Fields

Where polarities are equally balanced and in full play opposing each other, at whatever extension the field has so far accomplished, there is a counterrotation of forces present. This counterrotation enables any two polarities to sustain their action when they are working as a unit.

One is always spinning the other, both assisting and counterbalancing the other to keep the construct as a whole at work. This construction enables an automatic clearing of the energies if partnership is occurring, or a continual frequency of destruction if the two fields are battling.

At different points for each individual and any given topic, a life form can feel "trapped" in a field's density with fewer and fewer options for mobility. This occurs when one side of the polarity seizes up or rejects the energies of the other side. When one gear stops functioning properly, it slowly stops the other from functioning as well. The polarities shift from enabling growth and sustaining healthy movement to actually stopping all movement and glutting the energy of the whole form. As this occurs, the clarity of the merkabah form diminishes and with this the ability of those inside the merkabah/field of action to see clearly as well. Our consciousness becomes confused, and we do not know which way to turn. We have to then re-examine the parameters of that now-confining field; we must start sorting out its qualities, all over again, to figure out how to proceed.

An example of how this dynamic works is the eternal dance of the sexes. The attraction/rejection of male and female is a healthy, balanced energy. As long as one side is firm in its position, it serves as a magnetic attractor to the opposite force. However, this magnetic polarity also prevents its identifying fully with the opposite pole, hence the lack of comprehension for how the other half works. When the person learns to rise above the polarities of the sexes, they have the significant opportunity to either embody both energies inside themselves or to descend to polarity and ascend again at will.

What Is the Interrelation Between the Sides of a Polarity Field?

It is impossible to fully separate one side of a polarity pair from the other side. Therefore, if something major happens to the energy of one side of the pair, it affects the energy of the other side as well.

Working with this concept helps the interdimensional communicator resolve difficult issues. To understand the principles at play in this situation, let's focus on the biggest polarity in existence: the one that pairs off the dark against the light forces of creation.

A core level mistake for much of humanity during the Kali Yuga has been misunderstanding the function of the dark and light forces of the universe. Many religious people seek to "destroy" the dark forces so that the light will reign supreme. Should they actually succeed (which they cannot), it would mean the end of existence for the universe. For dark and light are inexorably connected to each other; they hold each other in existence, just as do every other polarity pair in the universe.

Beyond the dark and light forces there is only the one source. What ultimately must happen is that a person understands the true function of darkness and the true function of light in holding energy in existence. The only way this can occur is for the individual to enter into the higher point from which both emerged—the source—and then watch the energies descend.

LIFE

Once a person studies this descent, they are no longer worried about the function of the polarities of dark and light. For they understand the two go in tandem to perfect the field in which they coexist.

For instance, as my guides explained to me once, if there was no darkness of death, we could not even have a conversation. Every sound is formed of a start, a sustaining and a completion or destruction which then permits the next sound to take place.

Likewise, sometimes darkness is the best service to the source that can be offered, such as on a battlefield when a soldier is in great pain and death brings a welcome return to spirit.

Whenever it seems darkness reigns supreme, that is the precise time the interdimensional communicator engages in conversation with the energy and asks "why?" At this time, for myself, the dark force will step aside, show me the aspect of source it is working to lead the client to, then steps back in place. Now that I know its function, I can work with the client, configuring the session so that they know viscerally what they must do to find the peace that has been eluding them.

Is It Possible to Destroy One Side of a Polarity Pair?

If one pole of a merkabah attempts and succeeds at overwhelming the other side, it actually weakens the overall construct. If one side is destroyed, the merkabah itself has the chance of being destroyed, for there is now no counteraction to keep its own movement going. If the merkabah is a small one, it can dissipate into the ethers or withdraw into its own source, which can then regenerate that energy if it so wishes. If the merkabah is a highly evolved one, there are many other issues involved; there are fallback levels within itself. It can sustain its field to a certain level, but cannot experience full growth until it somehow reconstructs or replaces the missing pole. In this case, one repair method is to find another polarity within the construct to substitute for the missing pole. Finding a replacement polarity is like training the top branch of a pine tree to take the place of the point that has been cut off. The subfrequency eventually fulfills the same function as the pole that was destroyed.

Destroyed polarities is the problem facing some intergalactic worlds who have blown themselves up or who have been blown

In the world of Duality

up. This was a result of some kind of abuse of the principles of universal consciousness. According to the fables and reports of those who have had contact with these races, the inhabitants of these worlds have discovered to their great surprise that they still exist in spirit—one side of the polarity—but now have no solid form—the other side of the polarity. These beings are thus searching for a way to remanifest form so that they and their entire world soul can continue their evolutionary story. This search for a solution—for a re-manifestation of form—is the reason for the visits of some extraterrestrials to earth. Humans are good breeding stock, because of our genetic pool, and they hope to remanifest form with our assistance. The story of the mastery of energy via their evolutionary track is not over—it has simply become more difficult to achieve.

Chapter 7
Fields of Consciousness:
Collective Merkabahs

*The merkabah shape is integral
to the development of consciousness.
We can converse with every aspect of consciousness
that exists in the universe once we master the merkabah,
which is an intergalactic, or multidimensional,
method of communication and travel.*

Consciousness is composed of multiple merkabahs that are united into a specific field. Consciousness is an intelligent substance that underlies, runs through and forms all existence. It is the connector between all fields, and it is all fields. It is all shapes, at all levels of form, from solid matter to pure light. It is light and energy. It is universal mind and universal love.

Consciousness can be perceived in many ways, depending upon the capacity of the viewer and the will of that being viewed. It is tricky—and sincere. It is optical illusion. It is dreams and alternate realities.

Consciousness is God, the source, the all, the fullness and the void.

Two Aspects of a Field of Consciousness

As we said earlier, in chapter 5, every field of consciousness, or merkabah, can be perceived as a geometric form and communicated with as a living form. In that previous chapter, we focused on the merkabah as a geometric form. In this chapter, we are focusing on the merkabah as a living form, which only works because its geometry is intact and operative.

The merkabah shape is integral to the development of consciousness. We can converse with every aspect of consciousness that exists in the universe once we master the merkabah, which is an intergalactic, or multidimensional, method of communication and travel. Once we understand the merkabah, the rest is a cascade of logical results.

Once we agree on the premise that all merkabahs are variations on the original theme, all of creation can be experienced as an extension of the original source. Each level of existence has progressively segmented off to work with what it believes to be necessary subcategories, all the way down to the physical level of individual human beings. At this gross physical level, when we need to subdivide to achieve certain goals, we either birth progeny or assemble a group of other people or machines to assist in the varying tasks.

By extension, parts of our own bodies—liver, eyes, mind, etc.—are subsidiary merkabahs capable of independent thought and action. They are all directly connected to the combined life form of the human body, to the morphogenetic field of their particular type of energy (such as liver or heart) and to the ultimate source. Many healers use this awareness to correct and balance fields diagnosed by mainstream medical thinking as ill, inconscient and energetically uncorrectable.

This perception means that machines, made by humans, are also living merkabahs. They holographically contain the same universal source and so, as they evolve, can potentially perfect themselves. They can develop the ability to communicate with the other types of life forms in their environment, such as the plants, animals, humans and microlife forms of their frequency bandwidth. Many in the field of interdimensional communication are already using this awareness to communicate with and affect cooperation with the world of machines.

Every aspect of existence, from largest to smallest, whether made by nature or an "artificial" machine, has a hunger for self-perfection. This is because all contain the ultimate source, which is on a very long journey to its own perfect self-manifestation in all aspects of its own being, no matter what interim phases it passes through.

A Self-Regulating System

Mastery of the merkabah permits safe navigation of the entire frequency realm of existence. A merkabah is a self-regulating system. In merkabah work, we see a combination of what we wish to see, what we are capable of seeing, what the force we wish to perceive permits of us to see and what we are predestined to work within. These are the consciousness safeguards that are inherent to consciously working with merkabahs. The safeguards dissipate naturally as we grow in expertise until, at the highest level, as masters of consciousness, we can safely move wherever we please.

If we learn interdimensional communication to conquer and control other life forms, we will meet resistance. If we travel through true love, with the intention of assisting and sharing, we will be welcome. We are hard put to disguise our real intention when working with consciousness.

An Evolving Holographic Universe

In this holographic universe we inhabit, each part partakes inherently of the whole, or parent. However, when any part of the whole chooses to focus on a specific task, it begins to evolve its own unique expression of the master form; that is, its choices gradually alter its form. It begins to resonate at a different frequency, one which permits it to more individually utilize its potentials to achieve its chosen task. It can subdivide or replicate, and it can create holographic realities, which will also set about evolving according to each new unit's own free will.

If we are value oriented, from which perspective are we considering each evolving life form's value? If our evaluation is based on the ability to see deep into the vast reaches of unmanifest consciousness, then the originating merkabah would be considered more valuable than a subsidiary merkabah. If it is based on the capacity to accomplish a particular task that a subsidiary merkabah has been created to perform, then the spin-off version would be more capable. The question is, is it more valuable to be able to see inside the fields of infinite peace, or to know, like a United Nations diplomat, how to negotiate a peace treaty between warring nations?

If we choose to measure based on the ability to combine differing capabilities to achieve the ultimate goal—manifestation of the ultimate source—then each life form is equal and necessary to the other. Each is an aspect of the same life form, the source, like a human hand and foot, or peace in spirit and peace in a nation. Which of these aspects is superior to the other?

Moving Through Consciousness

Interdimensional communicators learn to surf the waves, fields and grids of consciousness. This enables us to travel through time and space to reach whatever locale requires our attention. This travel through multiple dimensions requires the assistance of the life forms of the fields we are moving through and seeking to work with. It requires detached travel through the frequency common to all fields—that of the core source. It requires the knowledge that all fields have one thing in common: they are *all* the manifestation of energy from some aspect of the one source seeking to express and fully experience itself and its potentials in form. Interdimensional communicators shape-shift as they move through these spaces, adapting to the energies they encounter while still retaining the memory and the integrity of their own form.

Perceptions of Energy

Multidimensional perception can be both linear and non-linear. It is not bound by any one method. Above the physical form, energy exists in round balls of information called merkabahs. When spirit is bringing down information for earth to use, it does so first within a packed globe containing all the details of that object. When we, as humans living in a linear world (right now), are able to go above the third dimension and access that merkabah, we can receive the information directly into our consciousness. Otherwise, we download it.

If we are not able to access the full field, but have sent a line of enquiry up to it, like a string on a balloon, we are in some instances able to receive strings of information in return. This information may come as flashes of inspiration or sudden thoughts on the topic as we relax on a walk, on a run, while gardening, etc. The farther that the information has to descend to reach the third dimension, the more it is strung out into a long linear thought, and the less of the whole picture we will receive.

Every object in existence has a field of energy around it and is itself a field of energy which we call a merkabah. This field of energy exists on multiple levels of consciousness. Actions on any level of consciousness can cause distortions, breaks or tears in the conglomerate merkabah. When a break or distortion occurs at one level of the field, it makes it difficult to acquire a complete picture or create an action that can move through the whole field. This is what occurs when a world blows itself up, as we discuss throughout this book such as in chapter 6 and chapter 15.

We can communicate with the fields or life forms of a merkabah in many ways. Some energy workers perceive the fields as plasma and see the energies as colors or forms, working with what we call in humans the aura.

Others perceive the grids surrounding and moving through this plasma, like the latitude and longitude lines on the globe, and search for anomalies in the grid, then correct them. Still others receive a communication from the combined light field about the situation; they have an interdimensional conversation with the field. This communication can be from an aspect of the field or from a guardian of the field. All of the above are valid ways of perceiving the same consciousness or merkabah. With experience, some energy workers, such as me, learn to perceive in all these and more ways.

In the same way, we can know ourselves as an energy form. One of the classic exercises for developing mobility of consciousness is to perceive of ourselves in all the different ways we have chosen in this lifetime—parent, child, athlete, scholar and so on. We can also know ourselves in other forms, so that we can understand how our own consciousness, which is one with all things, has chosen to experience different options. We can always assert our God-given right to understand ourselves in other forms we, or our soul family, have experienced or will experience. Some of us, called shape-shifters, are facile enough with this process that we can transform ourselves into other forms altogether. (As mentioned earlier, Merlin, King Arthur and Crow medicine women are some legendary figures said to have this capacity.)

Grid Technology

The merkabah determines the parameters of a given field: its frequency and the consciousness being investigated, accessed and/or worked with. Like stem cells, merkabahs are capable of adapting and changing as required by the field in which they are serving. Each merkabah consists of sub-merkabahs who have transformed themselves into plasma and grids. The unit as a whole will join with other merkabahs to create a collective form, taking a role of plasma or grid according to what is needed.

A merkabah is a counterrotating star tetrahedron. It is also a toroid, an oscillating flower of life, a stabilized energy field, a mandala, a piece of sacred geometry, an interdimensional travel vehicle, a conversation and translation bubble, a time-travel machine and a biological spaceship. The merkabah, being the base form of the universe, has many aspects and names. This book focuses on its use for interdimensional cooperation and community.

The merkabah permits interdimensional travel. Interdimensional travel permits us to willingly and consciously associate with our own higher self, our own self in other lifetimes, our soul-family lineage and other types of life forms who wish to assist or interact with us. It permits us to eventually travel back to the ultimate source itself.

One extension of merkabah work is called grid technology. This technology understands the universe to be formed of extensive layers of energy, or consciousness. When we examine the layers more closely, we can see they are formed of grids, and between the grid lines is plasma. If we examine the layers even more closely, we can see that the grid and the plasma are each formed of merkabahs of varying sizes, including some that are infinitesimally small. This is the same situation the hard scientist is facing when splitting an atom into ever smaller parts.

Where grid lines cross each other, they form vortexes from the force of the countering energies. In the human body, the major vortexes are called chakras. Each chakra has a different function, purpose, color and frequency. Vortexes and chakras exist at all levels of the universe.

When many grids cross, some cross points align with each other. The strong vortexes formed by these alignments of multiple cross points create a travel route through many fields. These alignments can be coaxed to coincide, or we can weave through them, like catching and riding a wave with a surfboard. Aligning these vortexes creates tunnels through the grids called, in space science, wormholes. We can surf through the wormholes to other spaces, which can be in the past, present, future or in another world. My team calls this interdimensional traveling "surfing the grids."

An interdimensional communicator surfs the grids, looking for openings or tunnels or breaks in the field, which enable them to surf to a place they are seeking. They are traveling in their own safe and secure merkabah—their own energy field, or vehicle. They are surfing frequency, moving through openings in the space-time continuum, getting off when they want, moving about and continuing on. They are always safe when they are working from the inner knowledge that they are safe—that is, when they have no fear of being trapped. They are not afraid because they know the parameters of this subtle science. They and their team move through oneness with the all. If some energy temporarily blocks their way, it is the job of the communicator and his/her inner team to study and adapt to meet the situation.

Defining the Method by Which Consciousness Manifests

Some traditions, all expressions of the one source, attempt to establish definitive terms regarding the descent of light into matter. To do so is to impose a limit on the ability of the source to develop ever-new methods of experiencing and manifesting itself. As one learns to see interdimensionally and then inspects the descriptions of various traditions, the reaction is always "Yes, but . . ." Different descriptions may be true, but they are not the only truth that can, has or will exist. This principle is true as well for the information in this book.

Some philosophies focus on descriptions of dimensions. By this they mean various demarcation lines by which consciousness can be segmented. Those philosophies specifying these separating factors may use very large or very narrow descriptors. The pioneers in this work have described what they are able to see when looking into consciousness, such as when they look inside one merkabah of a specific size (say, our universe) and then segment what is occurring at different frequencies. Some of these seers are very accurate. Some of them stopped too soon and have taken the descriptors of frequencies within one merkabah as being all that is possible for the infinite source to manifest within and from itself. There are no limits to the possibilities the source contains inside itself.

It is extremely educational to examine the demarcations of dimensions that various seers have charted. Studying their observations can make our journeys easier because doing so provides us with maps of different lands and the life forms that inhabit them. Once we have mastered a seer's method of perception, it is also educational to explore this same territory for ourselves. We may well see some things of value that the expert did not see or value.

Some traditions will take us up through fifteen or so dimensions or levels of frequency to reach the source; some traditions see seven levels, some thirty-two levels, some more. Whatever the dimension, it encompasses a particular band of frequency in which specific life forms exist, such as humans, angels, the great world saviors or the great beings of light. The particular tradition the visionary is working within determines what they will most likely see as they move up through the dimensions of that particular merkabah to reach the core levels and the ultimate source. For example, the Sufi ascent in consciousness will yield different perceptions from the Christian, the Buddhist or the Native American ascent; yet all, at their cores, provide access to the one and only ultimate source of all.

Planes of Consciousness

Consciousness, as it has evolved in its descent from spirit into matter, has been examined by many traditions. A detached scientific observation notes a descent from pure consciousness through light, to liquid light, to subtle form, to solid form. While the substance is always the same, it is called different names in different traditions. Also, the same band of consciousness contains many component parts, and different traditions value different qualities. One striking example of this is the difference in the perception of the nature of the source as understood by two traditions that have many similarities: Buddhism and Hinduism. The Buddhists perceive the source as the void from which all existence emerges, and the Hindus perceive the source as the fullness from which all existence emerges. This different perception of the same field has ramifications spinning off from it all the way down through each tradition's understanding of the function and purpose of various fields.

Some Western esoteric traditions chart the path of descent from the source as being from divine mind to divine love, to divine will, to a bridge (between spirit and the physical body), to the mental body, to the emotional (astral), to the etheric (vital) and finally to the physical.

Some yogic traditions describe the descent as moving from universal consciousness to individualized consciousness (the soul), then, in order of descent, to the heart, the mind, the vital and the physical. These yogic lineages see the heart as the seat of the soul.

Some traditions see the mind as emerging from spirit before the heart. When speaking of the mind in this way, they mean a universal mind that is a loving intelligence found in all things. Other traditions focus on love as emerging from the source before the mind, but this love is a conscious intelligence as well. A unifying statement between these two viewpoints might be that the consciousness being described is the intelligent heart—the intelligent love of the source from which we all have emerged.

In terms of the descent of consciousness from the source to the human body we now exist in, one simple yogic perception is as follows. This perception is how I primarily perceive consciousness, but it is not the only type of perception available for this work.

Universal Consciousness

This is the consciousness that always was and always will be—eternal, infinite, universal. It is the source of all else in creation. It is inside everything and beyond everything. At its ultimate source, it is one. At the point at which it becomes aware of its own existence and observes itself, duality begins: the observer and the observed.

All creation has blossomed forth from universal consciousness and ultimately returns to it. The source exerts a magnetic pull on its own existence, which seeks consciously or unconsciously to return to the source. Universal consciousness is known by many names, such as the source, God, the Supreme, Allah, the fullness and the void.

Universal consciousness exists in all other levels.

Individualized Consciousness (the Soul in a Human)

All creation is formed of particles of the source's consciousness, which are shaped into forms to meet a particular purpose.

Individualized consciousness begins when duality begins. It includes simple particles that upon the dissolution of the form return to the universal consciousness. It also includes the human soul, which is a complex form that contains the essence of its various lives on earth and/or in the universe. The choices and events happening to each soul cumulatively shape it in a very unique way, so that its experiences, as it moves towards perfection, become unlike those of any other soul. When a human's access to the power of their own soul is weak, the human can be overwhelmed by external forces. When the human has developed a strong, clear access to their own soul, the soul assumes its rightful position as the inner pilot, guiding the human into ever-greater harmony with the will of its own source.

Heart

Universal love is the next level of descent for consciousness. When love examines itself, it finds polarities within its construct: love and hate.

As each aspect of a human has direct connection to the source, people with different interests will often perceive of the human form as having emerged from different spots. For example, a philosopher sees it as having emerged from the mind; a martial artist—the don tien (just below the navel); a physical scientist—the egg and sperm. I see the heart as holding the emergence point because it is the seat of the soul in a human. The proof of this, for me, comes from the way in which an interdimensional communicator such as me successfully moves about the universe. We do so through the heart, with its soul connection to the all.

The heart is the keystone or pivotal point between the inner and outer worlds. In the body-chakra system, it is the pivotal point between the three major chakras of the mind and the three major chakras of the vital, the left/moon side and the right/sun side and the front/emotion/future side and the back/will/past side. The heart's quality is true love and oneness. It is a magnetic force that connects the soul both to its father source, the realm of spirit, and its mother source, the world or creation. Carnal love (desire) does not come from this plane, but from the vital. When the heart is weak, it either can be overwhelmed or can be indifferent to the world. When the heart is strong, it seeks oneness with the world.

Mind

The function of the mental plane is to discriminate and organize what it observes. It likes to take things apart and examine them. It searches and envisions from the inner worlds to manifest on earth. It cannot see as far as the heart, nor is it capable of as high a level of fulfillment as the heart. This is because the mind, as defined in this system of perception, separated out of universal consciousness at a lower level than the heart (universal love); that is, first there was love oneness, and then there was examination of specific aspects of this oneness. When the mind is weak, it is chaotic. When it is strong, it provides clarity and order.

Vital (Life Energy)

This is the plane of the life energy and emotions. It is the next level to evolve, below the mind, and thus cannot reach as high as the mind or the heart. When a person focuses their full attention here, seeking the answer to all their questions, they cannot achieve as full a result as those who focus on the higher levels. On the other hand, if an individual focuses only on the higher levels, they may have a difficult time fully achieving their goal in the physical world. The vital enables the soul to move about on earth. It likes to work with polarity constructs—the opposition of magnetic forces (love/hate, dynamism/lethargy)—until that life form learns to master the emotions through detachment, identification and transformation. The vital works with energy. There are many disciplines that focus on the mastery of energy, such as the martial arts and hatha yoga. When the vital is weak, it can be overwhelmed by emotions it cannot control, see-sawing between polarities. It can become rigid as a result of its effort to experience only one side of a polarity (peace not anger, or anger not peace). It can shut down in this effort, and that shutdown leads to lethargy and illness. When it is strong and disciplined, it has a calm dynamism, balance and vibrant health.

Physical

This is the plane of solid matter, where consciousness is seeking to fully manifest its intent in form. It is the playing field. The physical plane ranges from the subtle material to the gross physical. When the physical plane is weak in an individual, there is great lethargy and an inability of the individual form to help itself. When it is strong, it forms the powerful base of a form in the material world. It gives stability and determination so that vision can overcome all opposition and become material reality.

Inconscient Matter

According to some schools of yoga, matter is at its densest here. The source has packed itself so tight that at this level there is no apparent action; yet inside this level it, too, is the source. Some feel the earth game will not be completed until even this plane has been enlightened and transformed—a goal uncountable millions or billions of years in the future. The great Indian sage Sri Aurobindo defined and described in great detail the importance of this plane: when even the inconscient plane has been transformed into pure light, all earth existence will be the same frequency as the source. There being no distinction between the two, the game will have been completed, and the two will be fully merged as one.

Correcting Common Errors of Perception That Block the Process of Interdimensional Communication

Since all existence is made of light/consciousness/energy and the source is the base of all life forms, all levels of consciousness are inherently available and knowable to every form, although various levels may not be consciously present, remembered or developed.

Examining any life form is a matter of defining how the source has chosen to express itself in that particular merkabah, in its self-exploration for the ultimate purpose of its own self-realization and fulfillment.

True satisfaction comes only from oneness with the source, and so only solutions based on these premises can be permanently sustained. All other actions must change until they finally successfully align with the source.

The English language does not have an accurate vocabulary to describe these subtle processes because it is third-dimension business based. To correct this deficiency we have adopted words from other older cultures, such as *aum* and *karma*. We will sometimes hyphenate words to express the true meaning of such combined forms as *satchidananda,* which is translated as "existence-consciousness-bliss."

One result of the inability of English to express subtle distinctions is the lack of clarity in explaining various subtle concepts. Four major concepts necessary to the process of interdimensional communication and cooperation are often confused with each other in Western society. These are the nature of light and dark (misunderstood as good and evil), the process for the descent of consciousness into matter, the nature of the "other" and the "aliveness" of various objects and forms.

Light and Dark

At their source, light and dark are polar aspects of the one source. Each is an aspect of the one ultimate energy in which all forms are inherently present. Each is an essential aspect of the polarizations of consciousness that occur to create forms. Each is a very, very large merkabah.

In the Judeo-Christian West, we sometimes refer to the dark light as Luciferian or as the fallen angels or destruction, and the bright light as angelic or creation itself. We make a value judgment that dark is evil and light is good. We impart emotional and mental value judgments to the presence of darkness within a field. We also mistakenly define dark light as confused or chaotic light, which can and does appear in all fields on both sides of the spectrum.

This understanding of the nature of polarity limits how effective we can be in achieving successful results when working interdimensionally.

A more precise term for these two forces, these two polarities, these two aspects of the one ultimate light/source, is dark light and bright light. The energies and life forms of the dark light are responsible for the dissolution of form. The energies and life forms of the bright light are responsible for the birth of new form. Indian philosophy defines these two polarities as two aspects of the one godhead, Brahman. Dissolution is the task of the god Shiva, and creation is the task of the god Brahma. This culture notes a third aspect: Vishnu, the sustainer of form—that great sliding scale between the two sides.

At each level of descent into form, opposing constructs of dark and light must be present to hold the object steady. Without the one side, the other side will cease to exist, will withdraw from manifestation or will not be able to expand to its full potential. Each of these two very high polarities or merkabahs also subdivide, as do most polarities, into defining aspects within their own energy field; that is, at each point on the scale between dark and light, the energy can look at itself and define exactly what it is composed of. This composition will include, on each side, the amount of dark and light that is present in that particular space. Each point so examined creates a subsidiary merkabah within the larger form. Thus, while it may appear that an object is all dark or all light, in reality it contains both energies, as required to fulfill its task at its particular point in this complex system.

There is an often-expressed wish in our culture that darkness disappear from our lives. It would be more worthwhile for us to examine and understand the dark-light energy, enabling us to master the play of consciousness that is occurring at any particular time. This mastery would contain the dark light in its proper place and permit us to act more effectively to attain our goal.

••

EXERCISE TO UNDERSTAND DARK AND LIGHT

Sit silently and calm your emotions and mental thoughts. Focus on the heart. When you are centered, begin to examine the nature of dark and light. Study for yourself the following images:

What if there were no death, no decay, and no "dis-ease"? How would the rotation of resources exist, or the playing field be cleaned for the next group of players? How could we test what truth means, or life or love or art, if we had no means of comparison? How would we be able to harvest a crop of vegetables (and so cause the darkness of death to this life form)? How could we even voice our opinions or thoughts?

Consider the fact that every sound contains within itself the seeds of creation and destruction. Try to say your own name without the start of a specific aspect of the sound world, the sustaining of that form, and the ultimate dissolution or destruction of that form so that the next aspect of your own name can come forth. It is impossible.

Now stop looking at darkness or destruction as the enemy and instead look at it as a loving friend who, despite its ill treatment by you for so many years, still quietly and effectively serves your common need: the perfection of consciousness for the ultimate fulfillment. Thank it for its service, and if you wish, determine to work with it for your common good. Try to sustain this understanding as you examine more complex areas of your life, one after another.

∙∙∙

The Descent of Consciousness into Matter

To travel interdimensionally, it is useful to comprehend the difference in substance we encounter as we move up and down between source and matter. This can be perceived in many ways, but I like to simplify it into its main demarcations: light descends to liquid light, to subtle form, to solid form. These are the changes energy or consciousness goes through as it seeks to manifest and understand its own potentials, no matter what its composition of light and dark. This descent occurs for all physical forms in our world, whether this form is a leaf, a person or a manufactured object such as a chair. In our world every object—natural or manufactured—is the same in this regard. It is a manifestation or descent into form of the one common all-intelligent, all-aware source. We can utilize this commonality of consciousness to contact a physical form on its higher spirit level and work there to resolve differences that have manifested, begun or ended at more solid levels of substance.

Consciousness can also be understood as frequency. All frequencies have ultimately emerged from the one same source, although on an interim basis it may not seem so. Some frequencies are substrata emerging from other frequencies. Either we can enter into the frequency to directly connect with the source of all, or we can trace its linear descent through many preceding layers and on down through many more before hitting what is considered "rock bottom" (absolute inconscient matter, absolute density, absolute darkness, the solidification of light to its densest state). We can focus only at one particular small section and believe that this life form is totally linear and sequential. But once we start moving through the realms of consciousness and behind third-dimensional form, we begin perceiving in a different manner. Then what we see looks simultaneously like a spider's web and like balls of spinning energy, many inside of or part of a larger ball or balls. In other words: we can see a web of merkabahs and individual merkabahs.

The Nature of the "Other"

When one energy form looks at another, flexibility can help it adjust its perspective to that of the other form. If the energy form is not capable of broad identity, it can slip into polarity perspective: one object is good and another not good, less good or has a lesser right to exist.

It is useful to understand why all polarities and fields of existence need to exist. When we cannot understand the necessity for the existence of something, we have to correct this error of perception, or we cannot fully solve the issue involved. Sometimes correcting this error requires making an extreme adjustment to be able see into another's world, which may be operating at a specific level on principles far different from our own. Working with our guides and the understanding of the principles of the merkabah, we can accomplish this adjustment.

The "Aliveness" of Various Objects and Forms

As interdimensional communicators, we understand that to the life forms of any merkabah, there is usable light in their world. The inhabitants of any world are adapted to the frequency and spin modulations of the world in which they choose to exist or from within which they were created. When we enter any field of consciousness, we proceed from the knowledge that within itself a merkabah or life form has light aplenty; that light is simply occurring in a different dimension or world than our own.

All life forms in the universe are moving and changing, albeit at different rates and directions. All forms are struggling to become more aware and expert in their specific world. Most life forms are working in multiple fields at once. The amount of conscious awareness inside any of these fields (or merkabahs) is going to vary. To see within any one aspect of any particular field, we may need to adjust (or extend) our own frequency. We interdimensional communicators seek to fulfill this requirement of our craft.

We are also careful about making judgments as to the amount of awareness another life form has. That life form's frame of reference, rate of spin and particular frequency may simply be vastly different from ours. From their perspective, we may be seen as the unaware ones, because they do not perceive us to be as aware within their range of consciousness.

For example, we can enter into the life form of a chair and find that it has its own conscious awareness and place within the morphogenetic field of all chairs. We can then ask the chair how it is faring and find that it is upset because some ignorant, unaware human recently sat on it and tipped it forwards, weakening its front legs to a point at which the chair feels it will soon break. Who is the aware consciousness in this case?

EXERCISE FOR EXTENDING
YOUR PERCEPTUAL AWARENESS

Sit silently in your chair. Quiet your mind and your emotions and enter into your spiritual heart chakra (located in the center of your chest).

Look around you for some manufactured object that is "popping out" from the plethora of items you can see. Focus on it softly and identify fully with what its objective is: why was it made? Once you have done so, focus on what this life form's aspirations are and how well the individual object is able to attain these objectives in its current environment. What is keeping it from achieving its objectives? What is assisting it? How does it feel about you? How do you feel about it? What would happen if you simply adjusted your perception of this object and offered it gratitude for its job? What level of frustration would then be removed from your environment and what feeling of love extended? What if you did this with every object around you? How would these perceptual adjustments then send into your environs a supportive, compassionate energy of love for you to use and work with?

Why not make it a project to offer every object in your environment—including your own self and all your body parts—gratitude and love? Surround yourself with the frequency of love.

Our Limited View of
the Full Spectrum of Consciousness

Energy manifests by moving down the scale of frequency from the level of pure light to the heavier levels of physical embodiment. This descent occurs very naturally as the life form repeatedly focuses on solving specific issues involved with its own purpose for existing. Perfection develops from the base moving up through frequencies: it ascends. Once in physical form, one needs to then consciously regain, and retain, awareness of our oneness with source, while still in form.

Whatever specific plane of consciousness one is working at is relatively easy to perceive, while those planes located successively farther away—higher, lower, or sideways—are more difficult to see. This principle applies to each of us as we seek to master consciousness. We are most comfortable in the field in which we currently exist and less comfortable in fields farther away from us. This is true for the mystic trying to comprehend everyday life and for the person who has focused solely on the physical world and is now seeking to comprehend spirit. Most accomplished energy workers seek to stay mobile and facile in their ability to move among various fields of energy, seeking to constantly extend their capacity to see many ways at once.

By the time a life form reaches physical manifestation, its capacity to see and comprehend the whole of its merkabah experience diminishes, while its ability to accomplish specific physical tasks increases. The life form actually still exists at all the higher levels, but the weight of the intervening planes of consciousness acts like a fog or succession of veils and prevents it from observing this.

For example, say we are in the mountains and are looking at the progression of trees from us to the mountaintop. A thick fog roles in, and although we know the mountaintop is still there, we cannot see it. We can see the trees closest to us rather well. Then there is a sudden demarcation line, and a veil of white fog is between us and the next row of trees—and so on into the distance. The more the depth of the white fog increases, the more indistinct become the forms of the trees. Finally we can see no trees at all, only whiteness.

It is the same way with the veils, or planes, of consciousness. We can perceive the planes or frequencies closest to us. We may have the memory of there being other frequencies in front of us—like the trees and the mountaintop—but we can no longer see them, because of the density of the energies between.

When we become more adept at looking into consciousness, we learn how to extend our sight. We can identify with and teleport ourselves through the fog to whatever location we wish to examine. Even if the location is far in frequency from where we are now, we can shift to this spot and see what is occurring there. To do so, we may well need not only our own developed capacities, but also the assistance of both our own guides and inner colleagues and those of the field being sought. The capacity to establish a conscious cooperative partnership among various life forms is invaluable for this type of travel and is a trademark ingredient for interdimensional cooperation.

Chapter 8
Merkabah Sutras Collected Along the Way

The merkabah is the vehicle of vehicles, a self-contained field of light that traverses all dimensions and all activities, containing each object complete unto itself and yet simultaneously uniting all into a single all-loving whole.

It has proven impossible for me to link all of the information I have received about merkabahs and consciousness into a linear sequence. So in this chapter, we digress from the linear and offer you mini-merkabahs of information: modern *sutras*.

Are You Prepared for This Work?

When I was first learning to work with merkabah technology, it was a foreign concept to me. I did not even know how to spell or pronounce the word *merkabah*. You, too, may be coming to this work feeling unprepared. Don't worry: if this topic appeals at all, it means your personal awareness has reached a particular level of development. Even though you may not have focused yet on consciousness in this lifetime, the universe has saved your spot in your incarnational book.

When we are ready to resume any life stream of energy that our soul-family lineage has already mastered, we discover that this information has been stored and is readily available for use. Our job is to reclaim that knowledge. We learn how to enter the consciousness library (called the Akashic Records) and pick up that book of consciousness that has the information we need.

The Body Is a Complex Merkabah

Our bodies are multidimensional merkabahs. Each part—skin, bones, blood, mind and spirit—is a separate frequency field that supports a specific function. Using merkabah techniques, we can move into any of these body parts and directly communicate with that life form. We can check all aspects of our being and work to fix whatever is askew.

We contain inside ourselves every ingredient necessary to communicate and work with the different aspects of our own personal existence. We have not yet utilized these capacities. We humans are like youngsters who are just beginning to explore our own vast capacities.

••••

There are many ways to look at the merkabahs that form the human body. We are an outstandingly complex energy field, formed of multilevel merkabahs that should function together as one harmonious unit. Of course, that seldom happens for most of us. Usually we are doing battle with some part of our existence that is out of step with the rest. Merkabah technology offers us a way to come into true partnership harmony with our own existence.

••••

There are many organizations today that are working in the field of subtle energy, devising ways to cure, clear and/or optimize the complex human energy field. None of these organizations works in isolation from the other disciplines. But, should a discipline become caught or trapped inside its own methodology, it will draw up short of the ultimate goal and will not be able to solve specific issues. This has, in the past, been the situation with mainstream Western medicine, a physically based modality. In more recent times many scientists and doctors, who have seen the shortcomings of their discipline, have braved public ridicule from their professional colleagues to present alternative subtle-energy options that often provide outstanding cures.

It is not the province of this book to deal with the medical level of merkabah work. You can learn more about it from such recognized books on subtle energy as Barbara Brennan's *Hands of Light*.

Merkabah Communication

When we enter into the field of interdimensional work, we eventually have to clear ourselves of short-sighted and/or incorrect perceptions so we can accomplish whatever task has been set before us. An interdimensional communicator needs to go into every job with a totally open mindset. Every job involves beings of specific lineages, with specific capacities, wills and objectives. Some can appear very strange to our so-called objective mind, which is strongly prejudiced to Western third-dimension objectives.

••••

Most people have experienced, at some time, what happens when a merging of merkabahs spontaneously occurs. We might call it being in the "zone," where everything is lined up just right, and we simply flow into a merger with some other life form. It might have been a time when, as a child, we looked into a pet's eyes and knew we were communicating very clearly. It might have been a relaxed day in the garden when we sat with half-aware, lazy vision and were cognizant of fairies in the flowers, or of the busy work of nature all around us. It might have been a time when someone we loved dearly, a long distance away, was in trouble and called out to us inwardly for help, or was thinking especially loving thoughts about us, and we felt their presence inside our hearts.

Sexual love is the attempt to experience this merging of energy fields, or merkabahs, down from spirit into the physical existence. Indian tantric yoga includes the esoteric knowledge of utilizing this physical experience to reach up into the creative energy itself and thus come to know and comprehend the source, or God. Many life forms from non-physical worlds come to earth to experience this ecstasy. Our myths carry many legends of "gods" mating with humans.

••••

We can create merkabahs. We do so all the time with our thoughts and emotions. These can become, over time, large thoughtforms set in their ways. When we need or want to change, we must find a way to deal with these merkabahs that we ourselves have set in place. My work with land issues sometimes involves helping thoughtforms move from a piece of land they were protecting for a previous owner and either relocate or return to the source.

••••

Interdimensional communicators will often track the energy flow of a situation as it moves through one or many merkabahs. Doing so helps us to see where it is aberrant in its flow from its source and how it needs to realign to its own inherent universal core so that it can begin once again to work in a smooth and balanced manner. To accomplish this realignment, we work together with our own inner team and the life forms of the situation itself.

••••

When we explore a new field, we advance differently than we do when we explore a field in which we are already well established. But certain principles apply to both of the experiences.

All fields of consciousness exist both as a geometric configuration of light energy *and* as living life forms that are able to communicate with us, should we take the time to learn how to peacefully communicate with them. We can resolve many difficulties by simply entering into communication with the life forms of a situation and understanding the issue from various perspectives.

Taking Birth on Earth

We know how the physical human fetus develops during its gestation period. Similarly, when a soul incarnates on earth, it develops through a sequence of energy fields or planes of consciousness (merkabahs).

The soul—the direct link to the source, the spark of infinite consciousness from which the person spiritually emerged—is located inside the heart center. Between incarnations it exists inside a subtle world that corresponds to its level of development and its soul family's development and responsibilities. When it is ready to incarnate, the spark or soul proceeds through the planes of consciousness of the heart, mind, vital and finally the physical. At each point it takes on specific spectrums of consciousness according to its soul family's evolution and purpose and what it has personally earned or needs to learn or offer.

It accumulates around itself a set of merkabahs that predetermines much of what it will arrive as on earth. Remember, each of the merkabahs always includes an access point to the source of all, and these access points can be worked with at any point in the soul's descent into form. The qualities the soul accrues from each merkabah world are determined by resonances—the compatibility of frequency. These resonances can occur through the genetics of the parents, through the soul's own past-life activities (which incline it to find some frequencies more attractive than others), and from the need of high spiritual forces to send an appropriate representative for a specific task. At a high level of evolutionary development, the soul may consciously select specific frequencies as it descends. It is also possible to change core components of an individual's merkabah after birth. These changes can be made via prayers, intent, psychic alteration of the energy field, arbitration with the various energies involved and gross medical means.

Transcendence

Many traditional Hindu and yogic traditions that support self-realization focus on humans transcending the earth consciousness to return to full oneness with the source. To many, that was the ultimate goal. They were not interested in the process of returning to earth to share this knowledge with others. In general, the reason was that during the Kali Yuga this process of transcendence would occupy most of an individual's life. Only very advanced souls had the time left during a specific incarnation to turn around and bring that knowledge back to earth, serving as gurus and spiritual advisors to others.

Contemporary Western seekers following Eastern disciplines are now very often interested in a polarized, back-and-forth movement of climbing into consciousness, returning to share and then climbing some more.

Seekers who work with the merkabah are interested in being fully centered so that they can move about through consciousness to achieve specific objectives and then return home, grounding their experiences in the physical consciousness.

••••

Some Eastern and Western traditions that teach transcend work and soul journeying caution about the need to stay conn in some way to our own body during our interdimensional travels. They warn not to stay out of body more than a specified number of days. This is because they have learned that humans can forget the route back to their bodies and also lose interest in returning to the body confines. The merkabah technology is used interdimensionally precisely for these reasons. It provides us with a travel vehicle that remains intact through dimensions. It provides us with the format for connecting to different frequencies, as well as the technology to do so, and permits us to assemble the correct inner team to facilitate whatever task we are undertaking.

Soul Contracts

When a soul incarnates on earth, it comes with a soul contract. This is an agreement a soul makes in the spirit world. The soul may come as a representative of a certain party—of intergalactic beings, of a soul family, of a collective, of a thoughtform, or as a manifestation of an aspect of the ultimate source itself (such as Jesus Christ).

Soul contracts specify our particular work and how we will evolve. We all have some purpose to fulfill on earth; that purpose may be simple and small, like that of a butterfly, or very vast, such as that of a savior of a race. Contracts are made of the individual's own free will, either on earth or in spirit before incarnation occurs. Unfortunately, consciousness on earth is so heavy that people usually forget these promises they made in the spirit world. Having a purpose but not knowing what it is leads to the extraordinary sense of sadness that plagues modern society. X

For some, these soul contracts are open to renegotiation, and for others, they are not. For example, in the garden at

Gethsemane, Jesus asked for his cup—the suffering he was to bear—to be passed from his lips, metaphorically asking the Lord if such a change were possible. However, he then accepted the fact that the events of his next few days were predestined.

There are always obstacles to the fulfillment of a soul contract, and they are commensurate to the task itself. Obstacles present themselves through the law of attraction, or the law of polarities. The larger the pull to the light, the larger the opposition of the dark—until the life form learns to work with its specific task as one higher-level unit that contains both polarities harmoniously inside itself. Again we can see this dynamic in Christ's life, when on the cross he first asked, "Father, why hast thou forsaken me?" and then rose above the situation and said, "Father, forgive them for they know not what they do."

. . . .

A given lifetime may not be easy. This difficulty may not necessarily have to do with personal so-called karma. A specific person may be present in a field to change it, to learn from it, for the sake of someone else in their soul family who needs assistance or to progress through the mastery of all fields as per their personal responsibility and position in their soul family. They may have even incarnated from another world or galaxy or universe or breed of being, such as angels and fairies and nature forces, because they wanted to master or offer or experience a specific consciousness that only earth and the third dimension can provide.

. . . .

All human beings on earth, no matter what situation or status they find themselves in, are to be honored, respected and congratulated. Their simple presence means their soul lineage has mastered many preceding planes of consciousness and is now working with the gross physical consciousness. They are the chosen representative of their soul family in this dimension—a lineage that goes back through many, many previously mastered planes of consciousness to the source itself. Every soul has a contract via their own lineage to work to complete its core task of manifesting the energy of the ultimate source in some specific manner.

Breaking Free of Preconceptions

The merkabah has many uses; we apply its principles to our needs. Merkabahs of different sizes contain all the knowledge of the universe, and we can learn to enter into and explore specific issues, worlds and frequencies.

The merkabah is a mapping device for perceiving, stabilizing, clearing and balancing a field of energy. Just like a map, we can utilize the merkabah in many ways. We can look at the merkabah as a three-dimensional medicine wheel, tracking its energy from its source as it segments out into different locations within the form. Like the positions on a medicine wheel, each segment of a merkabah has its own perspective and needs to be listened to.

Another mapping method is to follow a line of energy as it moves through the merkabah, like tracking an animal through the forest. We observe how the energy behaves, for the purpose of interacting with it in some manner. Yet another mapping method is to break up the merkabah into small cubes by slicing the field horizontally and vertically, and then psychically picking up different cubes and examining the energies of that location.

••••

The longer a frequency stays inside a merkabah form, the more it grows and matures; it becomes more complex, just as we do as we grow older and gain more experience. It can also become trapped by its own complexities and subsupporting fields. This can prevent the life form from breaking loose to experience other ways of perceiving. Humans experience this type of entrapment as we grow older and become "set in our ways."

Establishing a Working Relationship with Multidimensional Life Forms

In order to consciously communicate multidimensionally and to travel to other frequency worlds, we need to accomplish a certain number of tasks. Accomplishing these tasks requires the use of inner "muscles"—of consciousness— "muscles" that are latent in all humans and which are now coming to the fore in many people.

••••

When contact with a life form in another dimension is initiated, from either side, we need the conscious capacity to stay detached so that we can observe the situation without either excessive fear or excessive enthusiasm, either of which can cloud the true energies involved. We need to stay aware of the following commonality of all evolved life forms: the experience will always be a mixed bag of consciousness. Because all life forms exist inside the realm of polarities, there are going to be many levels and layers of darkness and light intertwined. Moreover, some life forms we encounter are going to be mature, seasoned forms, and some are going to be young hotshots; some are going to present us with "problems," and some are going to offer us assistance—just like various people our own third-dimensional world.

We know we contain three basic sets of polarities: dark and light, conscious and inconscient awareness and father/vision and mother/creation consciousness. The same is true of all other life forms as well. Remember, this trio of energy polarities exists in some way inside all life as long as that life is outside the ultimate source of all.

Fields of Consciousness

Kindness and love will always win out, but we also need detached, wise observation of the field we are entering and resolute determination and mobility/agility to adapt to its specific form.

••••

When we enter a merkabah/field/world, we can encounter the life forms that guard it; the first ranks of its defense system, the "cellular membrane" of its existence. We can feel these forms as beings or see these forms psychically as light lines of energy. We can approach the field confrontationally or in friendship or in a learning mode. We can go to explore or to retrieve something we left there at some point in time or to master its aspect of our own existence.

If we approach a soldier of any country as a friend, we will encounter a person who is loyal, resolute and trained to defend a particular turf from invaders or foes of different sorts. We will appreciate those military qualities, for they keep our home safe. If we perceive the solider as the enemy or approach him with the desire to "invade" his territory to acquire some prize and then retreat, not valuing the domain but intending to conquer, then we will receive quite a different reception. We will have to wage war with the soldier, and we will be consumed with strategizing methods to win our objective.

Most classical religious aspirants during the Kali Yuga looked at advancing through the inner worlds in the second manner. Advancement to the goal of unity with the god of a religion was perceived as requiring the aspirant to do battle with the hostile forces (devils, desire, etc.) who stand in each human's way.

There is another way to advance, and we will be seeing it more and more as the Golden Age dawns. This is the path of cooperation with every life form in existence. We proceed by first honoring the life form of the field we wish to enter or pass through, both as an integral unit made up of many parts and as a living energy itself. We then approach the field with love and detached observation. Finally, we call forth our own guides and guardians, whose job it is to protect our own specific energy field, and ask them to show us what lies ahead. They will show the way

to advance and will also teach us as we go, so that we have more experience for the next such encounter with another life form. This team is ours, and it includes our own self at different levels of consciousness.

••••

Each merkabah acts like a playpen. It holds a consciousness inside, protecting it and giving it a shape. To perceive how merkabahs integrate with one another, we must move through fields of consciousness, or enclosing merkabahs, and observe their patterns.

When we step out of a specific field of energy, we perceive ourselves to be "free," but in reality we have only stepped into a different playpen.

Even the third dimension is a playpen—a very large one by now. Beyond the third dimension there are other worlds of other frequencies—other playpens with their own ascending and descending levels of awareness. Where we are determines what we perceive. What we perceive is our truth, for our field, but it may not be the ultimate truth that unites all the fields.

Often when individuals step into a new and larger merkabah, they feel that at last they know the "truth" and want to share it with everybody—to proselytize. Others may well feel these individuals know only part of the truth, not all of the truth. They don't want to participate with the first individual's truth, for their truth is far different. And they are correct, for they are living inside a different set of merkabahs.

••••

Progress through consciousness is like walking the road to a large palace. Lining the road on both sides are many buildings. Some house brothels; others house temples, police stations or food markets. Where you choose to stop is up to you. Classical religions taught the road was fraught with dangers and hostile forces. So, naturally, their seekers, marching along, keep looking for this frequency, and when they finally see a house that resonates with hostility, they say, "Aha! There you are!" and march in to do battle. The interdimensional communicator is walking along the same road, but seeking a house where there is a life form who will pleasantly and helpfully explain a situation. When they energetically locate this spot, they energetically declare "Aha! There you are!" and march in to make contact. Same road—two totally different experiences.

• • • •

When we have developed the capacity, we can enter a merkabah and with our own force of will make at least some levels of its energy conform to our wishes. This is oppression and is ultimately unsuccessful.

• • • •

A situation can exist simultaneously in many dimensions. Our intent determines what we perceive. We may choose to see a piece of land as a third-dimension form, for example, but it also exists at many other levels that can communicate with us.

Similarly, all human beings exist simultaneously at many levels and in other forms that can have knowledge different from what they are aware of in the third dimension of earth. We all have many friends and contacts in other worlds. These experiences and bodies of knowledge are accessible to us, should we choose to develop our ability to perceive them.

• • • •

Working with the merkabah permits us to see into a field of energy while remaining within our own field.

Polarities

A common occurrence for many people is that as soon as they decide they want to conquer an issue, a whole flood of obstacles and contrary qualities rear their heads and stare the aspirants in the face. "I want to be more loving," people say, and suddenly instead of having loving thoughts, they are flooded with every contrary thought on that issue. Or they say, "I want to relax and take a vacation with my family," and suddenly every conceivable problem presents itself to counter the issue. So eventually many people give up, time after time, thinking the forces are too strong against them, or they think that they are so "impure" that they can never be truly loving or so "busy" that they can never take the time for a vacation.

In reality, what has occurred is actually the opposite. They have finally found the courage to enter into a field of consciousness to master it and encountered the first entry step to that particular field of energy. That first step is locating the polarities that exist for the topic. The second is welcoming the existence of both polarities, for without well-developed polarities the topic under consideration would not itself be imbued with mature wisdom and depth. Loving and unloving thoughts balance every field. Mastery entails understanding both views in a detached manner, not being affected by either, and mastering the real issue: how to exist peacefully and at one with an energy.

The path through any such developed field of energy is highly divergent, with many roads bifurcating and turning around on each other. Such interdimensional travel is always highly individual—one of the beauties of a free-will universe in full motion.

Dark Forces

Communication begins with the frequency of our personal body system. What life forms can be communicated with depends on the perceptual range of the individual.

This perceptual range has been tailored by the needs of the third-dimension earth. Earth is an exceedingly complex merkabah of many overlapping forms and requires all of most peoples' focus to deal with its issues. Should the individual wish to perceive other planes of consciousness, it must alter the frequency range it has learned to work with thus far.

The dark forces, in their role of opposition to the light, have inculcated humans with many types of negative thoughts regarding our inherent ability to communicate with all life. They have placed many barriers to the human practice of this process. These barriers include visions of negative beings and forces standing in the way of our progress. Throughout this book we explain various ways to work with this situation, for these barriers are not the ultimate reality.

Storage Units

Because of the complexities of this world, our soul has found many ways to keep itself protected. Some ways are internal to our own personal system, and other ways come from so-called outside sources.

Each quality, capacity or event that we have personally experienced, over eons of lifetimes on earth and elsewhere, is stored somewhere in our own energy field. It is not lost to us, but we may have forgotten where it is located.

When so-called bad things happen to us, such as death on a battlefield, or rape, or psychological, physical, emotional or spiritual abuse, people may pull away from the energetically abused area. They may place the experience inside an energetic box, storing it somewhere in their energy field so that they can continue to function. In other instances, the traumatic experience may cause a tear in the person's energy field or create a wound that eventually scars over. If a hole has been made, the field leaks other energies into or out of itself. If a scar or a knot has been placed in a field, energies that used to pass through will now either logjam behind the point or flow around the spot.

Over lifetimes, peoples' energy fields become filled with holes, logjams, detoured flows and closets of boxes. For many lifetimes people can adapt and move around these energy field abnormalities. Eventually, their energy fields shift to accommodate these experiences. These adjustments show up as strange idiosyncrasies, such as the person holding their head to one side, standing in an awkward posture, viewing life only from a mental perspective and disconnected from the emotions or suffering from various allergies or personality disorders. These all indicate an abuse to the personal energy field that, when corrected, will of itself lead to a correction of the life form. The cause of this situation disappeared long ago, but the scar or scab has lingered on.

Many such situations can be fixed by an energy worker looking into a client's energy field, locating the disorder and repairing it. The disorder is rectified by simply removing the logjammed item or by repairing the tear. Some situations, however, have to be fixed by the individual on their own. They need to locate their own closets and clean them out.

Often the correction is immediate. On occasion, should the blockages have resulted in solid physical deformities or issues, the correction may not appear in this lifetime, but will in future ones.

Connectors

There are connectors everywhere in life, and the higher one goes in refinement of consciousness issues, the more these connectors are perceivable. We are all interconnected; it just depends where and at what level.

Each thought we think and each feeling we have resonate in the world around us. They can strengthen or dissipate a field of energy that surrounds and affects us. We are surrounded by webs of energy, each of which has various paths of descent and ascent through its own fields and web structures that connect to others.

Different people will perceive the same field in different ways and hence decide on different courses of action.

What If We Already Perceive Multidimensionally?

As earth moves into the next age—or world, as some traditions call it—we will initially experience a golden age of spirituality. The new world is coming whether we accept it or not. Learning the new rules for the new world is useful now, but will eventually become essential.

We are in the transition phase to this world, and it entails a lot of change. We are being propelled into the unknown. Many are already experiencing the ramifications of this energetic next stage of evolutionary development.

In the past, we could, by prayer or intent, force the images coming towards us from other dimensions to conform to a particular perception or forbid them to approach us. But as our consciousness spontaneously elevates, we are passing out of familiar territory with its familiar rules. More and more people are experiencing spontaneous crossovers between other worlds of frequency and our own third-dimensional realm. Modern society is reluctantly acknowledging the existence of other dimensions precisely because so many of us are having these crossover experiences.

On the gross physical level, this capacity to see into more rarefied dimensions is even now being measured. It is shown in the ratio between the steadily increasing Schumann frequency of earth and the steadily decreasing magnetic field of earth. The Schumann frequency, which measures the general resonance of earth, remained stable at around 7.8 megahertz for many centuries, but in the past several decades it has been steadily speeding up, resonating now, according to some calculations, above 11 megahertz. At the same time the magnetic pull of the earth has been decreasing. We are very naturally ascending in frequency modulation and thus in the capacity to perceive other life forms existing in the universe at these higher, more subtle levels. We are simultaneously retaining our ability to remain in the physical while doing so.

If you are experiencing these crossovers, you especially need to learn the science of multidimensional communication.

••••

Historically, in the Western mainstream matter-based culture, people who have spontaneous contact with other dimensions of life forms have often been regarded as insane and what they say they see as non-real imagination. This view is changing now because contact with other dimensions is becoming so common. But as recently as the 1990s, it was very common for families to advise some gentle relative experiencing this phenomenon that they were crazy, not gifted, and they had better shut down, shut up or risk being shut away. This treatment was common when there was a genetic lineage in the family of such awareness and other members had suffered when they had revealed it to the public at large.

In other cultures, especially the indigenous and pagan traditions, those people capable of spontaneously seeing and communicating with other life forms were singled out at a young age and carefully trained to properly use their extended capacities in service to the community.

 If we hear voices or see forms, they exist—somewhere in the world of consciousness. We need to find out why we are hearing or seeing them and what forms of action are being requested of us. We may have to rid ourselves of negative life forms, or learn to develop an aware communication with assisting life forms. We need to learn to control our ability to reach into other realms.

The Special Significance of the Merkabah for Old Souls

As people wake up energetically, we often spontaneously begin remembering past lives, either on earth or elsewhere in the universe. The lives we recall first are often the most traumatic or dramatic ones. We have all had them.

Usually we are granted the gift of this past (and future) life knowledge only when it is time to start making energetic corrections of some sort.

Sometimes we can look at these other lives without protection. With especially traumatic lives, we may need to find a way to maintain detached awareness. The merkabah supplies this detachment: we can place the life inside of a merkabah and, with the assistance of our guides, examine the situation from many different angles. We will need to do so in order to understand more fully what occurred, perhaps how what happened to us in that life interrelated with the social climate of that time. With this information, and the help of our guides, we are then able to make the necessary changes to our energy flow that may have started then and is impacting our present life. A simple example of this would be someone who is afraid of water discovering that they drowned at sea in a previous life. This fear may need to be harmonized with the other energy of that life: the person's profound love of the sea that made them study to be a marine biologist in this lifetime.

When we start past-life work, we need to be cautious about the difference between a true past life for ourselves and a number of other possibilities that can occur. For example, many, many people have confided to me that they are the direct incarnation of someone famous. The most frequent mentions have been St. John the Beloved, St. Peter, Mary Magdalene, Cleopatra and Joan of Arc. These people are so convinced that those past lives were theirs it does no good to point out that there might be other reasons for this identification. Some of the causes for identification with other persons' lives or famous people are as follows:

1. When we went searching for our own past life, we instead entered into a very strong universal or morphogenetic field of somewhat similar frequency.

2. In some past life, or at some point in this life, we chose to identify with a famous life as an archetypal form that helped us with our current issues. When we return to the process of examining our past lives, our energy field naturally moves into those old energy roads.

3. We are a member of the larger soul tribe that begat a significant person; this dominant field within our soul family is sometimes the first seen by a person as they attempt to access the consciousness of which they are a part.

We can enter into another's past life so completely that we know its exact details or can see events that are not even written about historically. What has occurred is a form of interdimensional travel. When we learn to work with the merkabah, we learn that we can, at will, actually enter into many different life streams and observe what has occurred, if that field has not been "locked down" by its guardians. And, morally speaking, we can enter that life stream if we have a reason to do so that all the involved inner-world guides agree is acceptable. People who have chosen to be, or have become, archetypes for human options often do not have privacy locks on their energies, for they are meant for all to identify with. In the West, one of the most dominant forms of this type of energy is the Christ consciousness and those energies associated with that mission.

Inner Affiliations

All societies and cultures state that there are other worlds besides our own in this vast universe. How and what they define these to be depend upon their intent and their consciousness, which *delineates* the worlds they perceive.

Even if a world did not exist before someone or some group began conceptualizing it, the very act of conceptualizing creates thoughtforms that soon take on a life of their own.

Sometimes more subtle worlds of consciousness have the capacity to change form at will. The worlds of fairies and elves, of gods and goddesses, of good and evil, often use this capacity when connecting to us. They will appear garbed in whatever form they know the human they are seeking to connect to will find most acceptable. They sense whether their form frightens or soothes the human and adjust accordingly. Therefore, humans, when approaching a subtle life form, must also use their extra senses, for it is possible for a nefarious force to garb itself in a beautiful exterior, to lure the human into its trap.

In these cases, the presence of one's own guides is so important. They should be a part of all your travels, no matter what dimension you're traveling in. The guides can see the reality of many situations and alert their human partner.

Some worlds are more susceptible to replication of appearance than others. The realm of angels guards its appearances very well so that others cannot assume their form and talk to humans. So, for instance, when Archangel Michael comes, you can be assured it is him or some aspect of his angelic kingdom. He will appear in different guises, according to the culture of the human and their level of awareness, but the core energy and level of capacity is always him.

Elemental forces such as gods and goddesses and fairies and elves will usually look and act differently in different cultures because of the evolving nature of their contact with that culture. These are cosmic forces that are capable of shaping themselves and limiting themselves, in accordance with the perceptual orientation of the group they are working with. For example, the thunder god has a different position and function in different cultures. In some, he is the chief god (Thor, Indu, Zeus) over all other gods, and in others (such as Native American cultures), he is simply a part of the alignment of forces.

The various wars of the gods, in which a new father figure supplants the old, come about as a culture evolves and conflicts occur between perceptual wants and needs. If a culture no longer needs a perceptual approach to the cosmic forces and stops interacting in a certain way, that aspect of that world (merkabah) goes dormant. But above time and space it still exists. Should, generations on, a group of people seek to revive the "old ways," those cosmic energies will reappear in that original guise, once again available to be worked with. This reappearance can occur with both hostile and positive forces, so be warned ahead of time, if you seek to invoke some ancient "sleeping" force.

Stewardship

We are truly the stewards of the earth, as many spiritual paths and religions have observed. Our understanding of this is changing. Stewardship does not mean lordship over and the right to control, break, destroy or pollute that which we are meant to care for. It means we have a very deep interdimensional responsibility to coordinate the needs of many worlds that all meet—or collide—on our earth, for the good of the whole.

Stewardship means working with an issue to harmonize the needs of all the life forms involved and to integrate the required change into that area's overall structure. A prime example is contemporary housing developments. Who wins when an area of woodland, home to multiple families of elementals, devas, stones, plants and trees, is suddenly decimated, ripped clean, and a housing development is dropped in? We humans don't, because such an area is now a sterile environment. Thousands of years of family structures of nature beings have just been wiped out of existence, and for what reason? Ignorance of and disregard for the needs of other worlds.

? NATURES WAY.

Change happens everywhere and all the time. Nature spirits know that well. The problem is not the change from forest to housing development but the way in which the transition currently occurs.

It is always better to avoid a problem than to have to solve it later. "Doing ceremony" is the way the indigenous cultures used to handle transforming virgin land to domestic use: they would thank the spirits and ask them to assist in the transformation process. Today, in our secular society, we could instead simply go to the property and send forth a thought thanking the nature spirits, inviting them to participate in the transformation and leaving a small gift such as some sort of sweet to "seal" our joint agreement on the matter. With respectful notification, the nature spirits can adjust and can assist in maintaining the vibrancy of the land during the transition. They also now have time to move those nature beings who are site-mobile to safe locations. Some nature beings are item specific, such as the spirit of a specific tree or plant, and notification gives these guardians time to draw in the vegetation's life force energy in preparation for its "death."

Much of my work is assisting current landowners who are faced with the problems that have occurred from inconscient land transformation. Their use of the land is often made difficult because of unresolved nature issues. This includes a common occurrence: the presence of spirits in their home. These spirits can have many origins, all of which need to be worked with. These spirits can include but are not limited to: nature spirits who used to live on the site, residents of other dimensions whose portal between their world and ours was sealed during construction leaving them stuck here as unhappy refugees and spirits from past civilizations who once occupied that site.

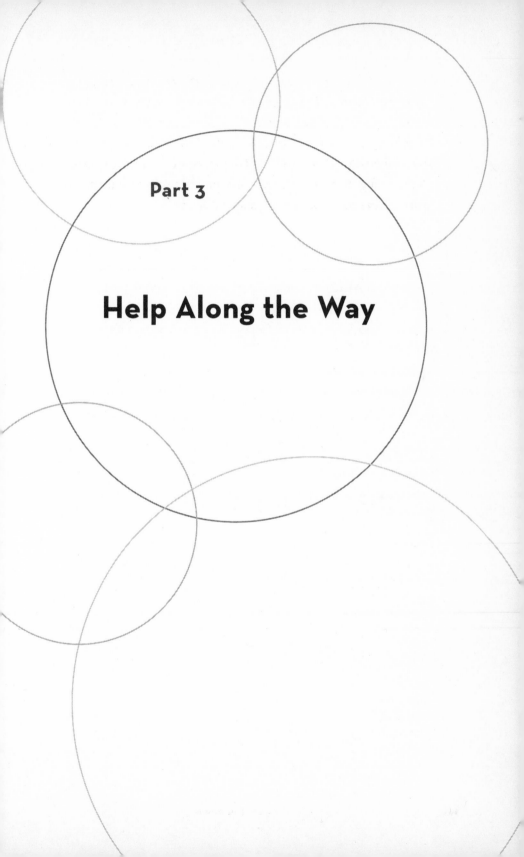

Part 3

Help Along the Way

Chapter 9
Ten Exercises to Develop Your Interdimensional Skills

Merkabahs can be used to communicate, travel and work within any space, time, field or life-form coordinate in the universe. The goal is to develop a tight, intact, healthy energy field that you can adapt as required.

You represent untold eons of life-force energy seeking to fully manifest some aspect of the infinite potentialities and possibilities of life in this universe. Your body is formed of many different communities of life forms who have agreed to join together to sustain you in their joint effort to manifest a specific energy in form. You are, energetically, a very complex merkabah.

As a soul descends for each birth, it collects along its path a mind, emotional orientation, skin type, eye color, etc. What your soul attracts to it at each point is determined by many factors, including the soul's will, its soul family's will, physical family genetics, your past development on earth and so on. It also includes the choice of the different energies of each world to join together with others, to experience themselves in community in your body on earth.

When you don't like your own body or your own life, you need to take a closer look at yourself and see what your own community is telling you. A harmonious personal community, working in peace and respect, is a happy place, just like an external community. Once you learn to be internally harmonious, you can more easily assist others and outer communities to also exist harmoniously.

The entire unit of your soul-to-body collective is a merkabah. Each aspect of this collective is also its own merkabah, and internal to each aspect there are sub-merkabahs, all the way down to and past the atoms that make up your body, each of which is a merkabah as well. All merkabahs are part of larger fields or merkabahs and contain inside themselves smaller fields or merkabahs, which they have either self-generated or brought in to work with a specific issue.

Each merkabah consists of plasma and grid. The light-field grid sustains the structure of the merkabah, and the plasma is the life-force energy that fills it. Some people perceive of the plasma as the aura. Plasma can become grid when necessary; both the plasma and the grid are adaptable components.

A mature merkabah can be formed of trillions of life forms who have agreed to cooperate. It has become, in its own world, a morphogenetic structure that goes on even while individual particles may come and go.

Once you are consciously working with merkabah technology, it is important to learn the base parameters of this discipline. Merkabahs can be used to communicate, travel and work within any space, time, field or life-form coordinate in the universe. The goal is to develop a tight, intact, healthy energy field that you can adapt as required for different situations, such as traveling to worlds you wish to visit and protecting yourself from energies you do not wish to experience.

Communicating or "talking" to life forms that have well-developed comprehension and are complex in form involves interacting with many levels and layers of darkness and light intertwined. Some of these life forms are mature and some are not; some offer "problems" and some offer assistance. A healthy dollop of caution—not fear or excessive enthusiasm, both of which cloud the true energies involved—is required when you approach any situation.

The exercises in this chapter can help you develop your capacity to distinguish and work with subtle energy fields. Wherever you are in your own personal energy-field knowledge, these exercises will give you something to grow with. They have no specific solution or goal and can be performed many times with different results. They offer a perspective for growth.

You can download a free CD guiding you through some exercises by going to our website *www.crystal-life.com.* Click on the front-page icon for this book. Inside this room you will find the CD, which you can receive for free by entering this code: YANA2012.

Down Load

Preliminary Steps

This preliminary section explains how to properly set a merkabah in place. It is the base from which you will be performing all the other exercises.

Preparing the Field

For beginners, exercises in subtle perception need to take place in optimum conditions. While you can proceed with these exercises on the train or subway, for example, it would be best for your own progress to do them in a quiet room with soft lights. This is so you can have optimum conditions as you start sorting out where your own field begins and ends.

Work in silence at first or take care with the music that is played during meditation. The use of sound is a very strong consciousness conditioner. Music is an energy field itself. It has often been utilized in the mystical and shamanic traditions as a vehicle for traveling multidimensionally. Should there be music that always brings you peace, use it, at least at the initial stages. While soft rock music or jazz may be energizing or emotionally comforting, it often utilizes dissonance as its driving force. Religious music of whatever denomination carries a very strong frequency of its route back to the source. If you are seeking to break free of a specific level of your culture's or faith's world perspective, you may wish for now to turn this music off. Later, should you choose to do so, you can go back and forth between different sorts of music and study precisely where and to what plane each takes you.

Set aside a specific length of time for this exercise; five minutes at the start is sufficient. Ask those in your community to please not disturb you. Turn off or muffle the phone and don't answer the doorbell. Say a short prayer or affirmation to yourself, requesting a positive outcome to your experiences. Saying this prayer or affirmation helps ground in the physical form the specific intent from which you will proceed.

Sit in a chair or on a couch either cross-legged (yoga pose) or with feet flat on the floor (Western style). Hands can rest on the knees or in the lap, in whatever pose comes naturally. As you progress with your consciousness work, you will learn that different hand and arm poses call forth slightly different subtle energies, but that is not important right now.

Sit with eyes unfocused, half closed, or closed—whatever is most comfortable. Again, later you will learn the differences that occur with each position, but they do not matter now.

Setting Up Your Working Space

You want to keep a clear and stable frequency inside your room or space as you proceed. That means picking up your energetic scrub brush to clean the room in which you are working and to seal that cleanliness in place. Therefore, before working with your own personal merkabah, you are going to place a merkabah inside the room, to clean and stabilize your working area.

Sitting quietly, see the energetic center of the room. See extending vertically through it a column of light, its upper source inside God the Father and its lower source inside God the Mother (which you can perceive as the core of the earth, or of the universal mother consciousness). Looking at the column of light, locate the source point within the length of the column from which the energy of the topic under consideration is actually housed—its "soul," point of origin, or "sweet spot." On the count of three, while inwardly focusing on this point, expel a soft puff of air and see a ball, or merkabah, rapidly expand from that central point to fill the room. The merkabah is pulsing with living light, and this is filling the space with high frequency energy at the level that contains the issue at hand.

It is good to hold this merkabah stable so that it does not disintegrate with the ebb and flow of energy around and through the room. Energy workers hold a circle stationary by squaring it, as we explained in chapter 5. A square, or cube, grounds the energy so that it can be worked with and examined. The numbers four (the four corners of a two-dimensional square) and eight (the eight corners of a three-dimensional cube) signify this square shape. So do the north, south, east and west positions of a medicine circle.

Place holders can also be specific energies, colors, sounds, animals, plants, minerals, gods and goddesses, saints, angels or other representations. Each tradition around the world has its own designated place holders for the squaring of the circle. If these representations are already established for you, you are welcome to use them. If not, you can always call in the four archangels, or four master energies, whose work is to protect and encourage proper growth on earth. These archangels are Michael (north), Uriel (east), Gabriel (south) and Raphael (west). If you choose to associate any of these archangels with one of the other four directions, that is fine, too.

Request the beneficial energy you have selected to hold the energies of the room merkabah in place while you proceed with your work. These positional place holders are not only life forms you can communicate with, but also very large fields of energy or merkabahs. You can see these place holders as the energies that serve each direction's responsibility. Energy workers will see the actual directional energy standing there and yet know that it is many other places as well, performing its work.

A student once told me that they were loathe to invoke Archangel Michael to assist them, when someone else might need him more. I responded that Michael is very vast with many parts at many levels and that calling on him for assistance only helps ground this energy even more for everyone else's use.

The room merkabah is now secure and held in place.

Setting Your Personal Space

Next you are going to work with the personal energy field. You are going to perceive your own merkabah. Energetic balance and full protection are the goals here, and you should make this your intent as you proceed. The process can take some time to achieve.

While seated, see coming down through the top of the head and passing out through the base of the trunk of the body a clear white column of light. This is the central channel. It is the personal version of the room merkabah you previously put in place. Even if you have to imagine it at first, see this channel as energetically existing, extending from God the Father clear across to God the Mother (either the earth core or the core of the universe). It is a clear flow of energy, and while at the beginning it may feel like a tiny pinprick, it will eventually feel as though it is four to five inches in diameter. Feel it totally cleansing and energizing you. Sit still a few moments and visualize this channel very clearly.

Next, focus on the center of this channel, at your heart center, in the center of your body. See a point of light there, even if you have to imagine it for now. This is your personal connection to the source and the seat of your soul (your soul is your central point, from which your central channel has spread out into your polarities of the universal father and mother eneriges). On the count of three, give a puff of breath and see, emerging from this point, a ball of energy—a merkabah—that totally surrounds your body; it fills the space your aura fills and then some. While in actuality it can extend to the limits of the universe, for now perceive it as a subtle ball of energy extending about twelve inches above your head and beneath your feet. You can perceive of this ball as having vertical and horizontal lines of pulsating light, much like the latitude and longitude lines on a globe, only going into the ball's center in concentric circles as well.

Next call in your personal angels, guides and guardians to be present as this process continues. These life forms are always with you, watching over you, even when you are not aware of their presence.

If you have never acknowledged the presence of these personal guides and guardians, now is a good time to start this process. First, offer them gratitude. Guides and guardians are living beings with feelings. They are serving you and your common source in a very fulfilling way: by helping their human compatriot—a life form in the greatest density of matter—master this substance and thus see and bring the infinite source and its capacities to the earth plane. These colleagues of yours protect and teach. They do not want to alarm you in any way and so serve silently until your form is ready and willing to acknowledge their existence.

If necessary, apologize as a colleague on equal footing for not listening to them in the past and even for telling them to shut up and go away (as many of us were instructed to do when, as children, we were caught speaking with "imaginary" friends). Sit silently for a little while so these energies can come into harmony with you.

When you are ready to proceed, request of all the energies involved that should your work be interrupted, the personal and room merkabahs are to remain intact but permeable. Also state now that at the close of the exercise all cords and energies are to be returned to their proper place, sealed and cauterized. This measure prevents energy from leaking through psychic cords as you return to your physical consciousness. If you forget this step, no harm; your guides will take care of you. If you are dealing with serious matters, please be sure to make this request. You do this now in case you are interrupted in your work and need to leave abruptly; the energies are pre-instructed what to do should that occur. Otherwise, you can be leaving your energy field open and may feel disoriented.

You are now sitting inside your own protected field, which is inside the protected field of the room. You are ready to undertake whatever issue you have decided to focus on.

When you have finished your session, you may, if you wish, reconfirm that the merkabah is to close. Thank your inner colleagues for their service and in some manner announce the session has ended. This need to signal to the world of energies that a session is over is why different traditions end with *amen, aum, shanti,* so be it, ho!, etc.

∙∙

EXERCISE TO REVIEW THE PROCESS OF SETTING SPACE

Set aside a period of time when you will not be disturbed. Sit in a comfortable position. Call in a merkabah to fill the room and invoke the archangels or your personal guides to seal the merkabah in place. Call in your personal merkabah and invoke your personal guides to remain present. Enter into the subject of this session. At the close, thank the energies for their assistance and announce in some way that the session is ended.

....

Exercises for Working with the Merkabah

1. Invoking Peace

In this exercise you are going to consciously create a merkabah of peace. Whenever you require a bit more peace in your life, you can go do this exercise again.

The first time you practice this centering exercise, simply sit and be. You've already placed the appropriate fields of energy around you. Enjoy the feeling of protected physical existence as well as its extension into the universe around you. Look up to God the Father and look down to God the Mother; see them fully protecting at the heights and depths of your existence. Look inside your own heart for the source of your own power. No one can take these connections from you; they are always there. They may appear to be missing right now, because of various obstructions. If so, you must believe in their existence so strongly that your intent eventually will burn through the fog, like the sun clearing the woods so that all the trees, marching into the far distance, can be seen clearly.

When thoughts and feelings come up, observe them dispassionately, ask them to be silent or ask the guides to please silence them. Sitting in silence allows you to observe what types of energy fields you are resting inside during your normal consciousness. Once you see the types of fields that are affecting you, you can decide what to do. You can see their true function and use this information in a positive way. Right now these uncontrolled thoughts and feelings are simply vibrational clutter; other frequencies existing at the same level as you are working at, and which you must learn to screen out. You do this the same way you screen out conversations around you at a social gathering to focus on the person with whom you are speaking. There may be interesting information in those other conversations, outer and inner, but right now you need to ignore them. For right now, you need to develop the capacity to discriminate between these fields. You need to tune your own inner frequency dials, much as you do the dials of a radio or TV. Then you can learn to listen dispassionately to the inner noises and decide what to do about them.

Please do not accept the Western cliché that if you hear voices and no one is there, you are insane. There are many reasons for you to hear voices, and merkabah work is an excellent method to locate what is actually occurring. Some possible healthy causes can include the inherent, natural human potential to access any point in the infinite universe and communicate with it. You may have an extra dose of this ability via your genetic lineage or via capacities inherent to your own soul's development. Unfortunately, most Westerners are not taught how to develop this very significant latent human ability.

So for now, put aside the interesting potentials of being able to listen in on all these frequencies and instead request all to be silent. Consciously tune your inner radio dials to *peace*. Keep fine-tuning your dials to that frequency which signals peace for you at this present moment. This place will change depending upon your circumstances each day. Keep that dial set on *peace* for as long as you can. Eventually, with practice, you will learn to associate your own energy field with many aspects of that frequency. The frequency will become stronger in your field so that you can tune your own being to it at will, during your workday as well as in meditation.

When finished, or at the end of the five minutes, come back into your own physical space. Thank your personal guides and release them from their task.

2. *Extending Perception of the Personal Energy Field*
Go into the room and personal merkabah formations.

Right now you are not going to analyze anything at all. You are just going to enjoy the reality of your own existence, "good" and "bad," on the playing field of Mother Earth.

In this exercise you are working to see yourself as intact fields, whole unto themselves. You are learning to perceive of yourself as a cooperative community. This may be difficult for some people because of our past cultural conditioning.

Your intent is to wash away the old stereotype of this world being based on the survival of the fittest. This perception leads to endless wars against yourself and all others. Instead, have the intent to perceive of yourself as cooperative communities of life forms. You are seeking to translate any conflicts into cooperation, any illness into well-being. Whatever flavor your work takes personally will be translated into how you will perceive not only your own personal community but also the many external communities of which you are a part—from your family to your workplace to the world. By working to change yourself, you will eventually change how you perceive and interact with your world.

Right now, work to see yourself as a cooperative life form, coexisting separately and together inside one common frame, or merkabah, or world: the personal body. For instance, look at the skin, of which you are so often unaware; it is a community of conscious beings totally dedicated to replicating itself, to stretching and shrinking, to adapting to whatever approaches it from inside or out and to operating in seeming independence from the mind or heart, which are focused on other things. Now, in your own way, according to what comes forward or to what is of interest, look at all the parts of the body and understand what they are trying to say, do and be, and in which way they are influencing you and each other. Thank them for serving you so well all these years. See what they are saying at different levels of their own existence. When you are finished, thank your guides and close the session.

3. Self and Community Oneness

Now, just for a few moments, take a good look at the human body in a totally new way. Wash away preconceptions and simply look. What a marvel you are of consciousness engineering! See what intrigues you most about this form, what irritates you the most, what is most difficult, what special talents you've chosen to focus on, what skills you have evolved, what practices and disciplines you have chosen and, better still, what you feel your center of existence to be at this present moment.

Should you feel your primary focus anywhere but in the heart, return to the heart. The heart is the part of the body that magnetically attracts all other parts into a spirit of loving cooperation. You focus here when you want deep harmony. You focus on other points when you are working on other aspects of energy; for example, focus on the mind for wisdom or the don tien, just below the navel, for powerful martial-arts energy. The heart is where all the forces of the body come together to be lovingly directed into the realm of spirit and ultimately to the individual soul and the one source.

The heart is the crossroads for energies in the human body. Its symbol is the cross, some version of which is found in virtually all high religions and energy traditions. This is because energy workers know that where two lines cross, an energy vortex occurs. When the focus of your body energies rests in the heart, when that is the convergence point, energies can balance in all directions. When you are focused in the strong heart, you are better able to act from love no matter what occurs. This great heart's love enabled Jesus the Christ to pray, "Father, forgive them, for they know not what they do."

Just for now, no matter what faith you practice, focus on these immortal words. Focus on forgiving all who need forgiving, whether you know them personally or not. Next focus on those in your own life who may have hurt you or whom you have hurt and offer forgiveness to them or ask them for forgiveness. Lastly, apply forgiveness to your own personal existence, or merkabah. Forgive yourself for not loving yourself more and for perhaps being at internal war with various parts of your own being.

Then start going through your own body, top to bottom, and thanking it for faithfully serving you for so many years—or forgive it for areas where it may have failed you. Where it has failed, ask it why and what the other parts of your existence can do to create a better situation from this time forward.

When done, thank the energies and close the session.

4. Continuing in Community

Set up your room and personal merkabahs.

From inside this field, look at yourself. See where in the personal merkabah your attention stops. Whatever place you end up, focus on it with gentle love. What need is this part of your existence expressing to you? Why is it stepping forward to get your attention?

This point is a life form of its own, and it is very real. Stay in the present moment, call on guides and angels, sit still and observe and listen to this part of your existence.

In form, this point in the personal energy field may appear in many different ways. Some ways include as a knot, a globe, a field or a merkabah complete in and unto itself, as colors or sounds or as a voice or being speaking to you from its own life source or the guides and guardians of its site of existence.

Right now, to simplify your work, you are going to look at this point as a geometric grid. You want to see what is happening to its energy field so that you can change it for the better.

Perform the merkabah exercise again, around this part of your existence. See this point with its own full field of energy, connected from God the Father to God the Mother, with a center point from which its merkabah emerged. Clearly see it connected to the source from inside itself. See this source feeding it with its absolutely pure light. When it has filled itself to its present capacity, you may, should you wish, start a communication process. But it is also enough, for now, to simply give it permission to feed itself with light, to allow it to gorge itself on the infinite light of which there is no source other than that of the ultimate source itself.

Eventually, over time, with practice, you will be able to focus on the issue represented by this point inside your own consciousness. Listen to what it has to say, to what form it has taken, what images or sub-merkabahs it has stored inside itself.

In time it will become clear to you that proceeding in such a fashion focuses you on issues inside your field that you wish to master in some way. You have chosen, or the energies of the situation have chosen, to create a marker in your own energy grid. This marker keeps an issue encapsulated until you to have the time, patience, willingness and/or capacity to inspect the matter and resolve it.

This marker, or merkabah, can be stored in many ways within your energy field. It has lodged on a line of energy going out from your heart into infinite space and time. If the field in which the issue is stored is small and on a single line of energy emerging from the source, it will be a relatively easy matter to solve.

If it is a merkabah storing energy from several lines, such as at the point where two or many cross it, then it can become a major issue for your field. It can also have grown and traveled along various levels of your grids, or built a multilevel apartment complex in some area. Should you discover the energy has done either of these things, your work can seem to be more complex. But usually you are back focusing on one merkabah form, just at another level of complexity (i.e., communities within a community, whose communications also need to be resolved for change to occur).

Any obstructions or blind or weak spots need eventually to be entered into, and the stored information dealt with in a positive way. You are learning to clean your personal house.

When you are finished, thank the energies and announce the close of the session.

5. Perceiving the Sacred Forms

Go into the room and personal merkabah formations.

Go directly to a thought or feeling that is coming forward now. This may well be a focal point, a level or aspect of consciousness that is preventing you from going into that classic "mindless" state that many Eastern traditions focus on. Every time you attempt to quiet your mind, this part of your existence may be saying to you, "Good! At last, some silence! Now listen to me—please!" This spot may also hold a cacophony of sounds—particles of thoughts in conversation that fade in and out. It is a verbal form of fog or psychic radio static.

Every second around the world, thoughts are released and float through the air until they disperse. Some last longer than others. If they are operating at your frequency, you may hear them as they pass through the personal field. You may also hear the thoughts of different sorts of life-energy fields existing inside different sorts of merkabahs. You need to start practicing tuning your inner dials. These are areas of infinite consciousness for which you have an affinity of some sort, or which have "invaded" your world in some way. Instead of attempting to block out all these extraneous sounds, which only leads to your putting up barriers, focus on each, one at a time. Learn to see and hear the different frequencies that are currently affecting you, so that you can honor the life forms they speak for and find out why you are being subjected to the frequencies at all.

When you are in your ordinary, everyday consciousness, you generally learn to tune your consciousness dials to the group level. Sometimes you set up barriers or walls to keep extraneous thoughts from entering. However, when you begin expanding your consciousness, you very often do not have such barriers in place. And you have not learned the more benign method of tuning your frequency dials. You have to learn how to proceed safely. Sometimes when people experience these internal voices, it frightens them, and they stop attempting to see into consciousness. All the ancient secret sacred traditions es- tablished ways for seekers to advance safely and taught the acolytes processes of entry to that discipline's frequency range. For instance, Christians learn to tune to Mother Mary for compassion, while Buddhists tune to Kuan Yin and Pagans might tune to Brigitt.

In today's more open culture, you need to proceed in another way. This way is still sacred, not mundane, but it is personalized to your awakening needs. This sacred way is to work closely with your own personal guides and guardians. Then, when extraneous thoughts or emotions occur that you cannot silence, you can ask your guides to protect you while you proceed, and they will assist.

So while you are seated in this meditation, you can ask your guides for assistance as to how to proceed. What are you to do next? Follow their lead, and you will have an unusual and fulfilling experience of some sort.

When you are finished, declare the session closed. — TO MUCH MENT CONTROL. Follow YOUR SPIRIT SELF.

6. Focusing on a Specific Energy

Establish your room and personal merkabah. Enter into meditation.

You are going to focus on a specific positive energy. This type of focus is an excellent way to learn to explore consciousness, for it gives you a goal to head toward. You can repeat this exercise time and again, using various positive energies and exploring each quality in greater depth.

Every quality, good and bad, is composed of one major merkabah with many sub-merkabahs. There are also many conduits, or lines of energy, that traverse the merkabah, uniting various components of the field for specific types of work. (Think of how the Native American medicine wheel assigns qualities to different directions.)

Right now, focus on the quality of *peace*. You do this by focusing on your heart center and evoking the energy of peace via chanting the word or imagining the energy.

Once you feel peace come forward, sit silently and simply feel it. When you have finished the experience of simply being, it is time to start exploring. Start looking around the merkabah and notice its details. You are in a real place, in another dimension. It has real parts that have real objects or qualities in specific locations.

Focus on what is different and in what way, in different parts of this merkabah; for example, the difference in the quality of peace when it has blossomed into a sub-merkabah, such as the peace of holding a baby or cooking a meal or praying in a temple.

Now focus on what is the same in all these merkabahs. An aspect of peace can be felt temporarily in any part of a field or more permanently if you sit or rest inside the very core of the field itself—that point where it connects to the source. You can experience the peace of holding a baby, or you can become peace by merging with the quality and letting it flow out from the source through your heart, permeating all energies.

Do this exercise several times, each time exploring another aspect of peace. For example, focus on the physical body and perceive how to find the merkabah that brings peace to the various parts of your own being, such as the mind, the emotions, the liver, the adrenals, the muscle of the right thigh. Then go back into the center of the heart chakra and observe how resting here enables you to distribute peaceful energy to all these other parts on a continuous basis.

This is an exercise for you to repeat many times, as you gradually learn to feel the peace flowing forth while in meditation, then feel it while you are in your everyday life.

When you finish, declare the session closed.

7. Nothingness

Many exercises, especially of the Far Eastern groups, are focused on bringing you into a state of total silence, a nothingness. You can fool yourself into thinking you have attained a goal above all sense perception or have reached the source. This is an inaccurate perception. What you have done, actually, is one of a variety of things. Let's focus in this exercise on just what occurs and why.

Enter the room and then the personal merkabah. Now, look around. You are actually in a "room" inside the field of consciousness, defined by its specific aspect of the total field of infinite consciousness. You know this room—its shape and size—quite well. You can ask questions of it, and it will respond.

Now suppose you were to open a door on another room— one filled with light or darkness. It would take some time to get adjusted to the frequency of that room, to what exists inside it, to its life forms and how they communicate. Until your eyes adjust, you see nothing: it seems empty, a void. That is what happens when you move through the fields of meditation. You are seeking to climb up or dive deep into infinity. But, really, it is only another field of consciousness that you are reaching, and there are many life forms there as well.

You may try to fence out all extraneous noise or visions. But what you are actually doing is creating fences at that level, and they prohibit you from seeing what is occurring. You are doing exactly what is being done in the third dimension when you fence yourself in so that you do not see and communicate with your very own guides and guardians.

Rather than fencing out, why not take another option: honest appreciation for the life essence as it exists inside the plane to which you are traveling. You may go to many different worlds that exist at different frequency levels. It all depends upon what you have a current affinity for. And any of these worlds exist at many different levels, just like your world. So you want to use care and be selective in your search. It is beneficial when doing such inner travel to invite along your own guides and guardians who have a vested interest in your success.

The classic methods of meditation stop internal chatter and help you learn to differentiate between fields of consciousness. But like so much else, it is also a double-edged sword: it can set up perimeters of defense that you must then disassemble to progress any farther. So try for yourself this method that we recommend: Go into a state of silence; stop everything from moving, if you can. Call in your own guides. And then start observing what "objects" (life forms) are inside this orderly inner space you have established for yourself.

When you are finished, declare the session closed.

8. Communicating with So-called Inanimate Life Forms

All existence is alive and capable of communicating with you. It doesn't matter whether the life form is an elf or an extraterrestrial, a tree or a rock, or a manufactured object such as a chair or a computer. Everything in existence has a form and a voice at some level of consciousness. Everything has a need to be recognized and heard.

For this exercise, select something simple in your immediate environment that is usually considered "inanimate," such as a chair or a lamp. You are going to practice communicating with it.

Go into the room and then the personal merkabah. Now focus your attention on the selected object. See it as a life form complete unto itself, with its own merkabah that has its own connections to the triune source: the father, the mother and the ultimate source. Now listen to what it has to say to you. It has a story. When the words or images start coming, don't block them as "just my imagination" or as freaky or ridiculous or frightening or exciting. Just listen, from your own heart, with a feeling of friendship for the "object," a sense of partnership in this adventure called life. There may be something the life form requests of you or some way it wishes to assist you. Listen and learn.

To get started, you can play "imagine" what the form would say if it could speak; this opens you up to the fun and play of this work. You may be correct, or you may be inaccurate; but at least you are trying, and the universe will respond.

For instance, once in a group of people all trying this experiment, one woman focused in on the chair beside her. It told her it took its work very seriously: supporting a human for some reason. It said it liked the person who had just been sitting there. But before that there had been a very, very fat man, and the chair had groaned from the effort to support the person! There are many things such a conversation can let you know, secrets these life forms share with each other.

When you are finished, declare the session closed.

9. The Difference Between Dark and Light Forces
As you work to connect with your guides, many people suffer doubts and fear they will contact a trickster or a dark force. They

have been conditioned this way by their religious organizations. This doubt and fear is a type of control that keeps people under the thumb of an organizational structure with vested interest in controlling its members for its own use.

An authentic teacher and tradition knows that individuals must use consciousness purposefully so that good will grow inside them. Purposefully working with consciousness requires an authentic investigation of the object or substance being worked with, and fear and retribution do not permit this investigation to take place. Therefore, authentic guides do not use fear tactics to connect with you. The authentic source of whatever tradition you follow, whether it is Christ, Buddha, Mohammed, Krishna or someone else, works through love and oneness. It is all too often the later-formed political- and social-order arms of a spiritual or religious organization that attempt to maintain control through fear.

We have spoken at length about the dual nature of the universe and the true and authentic necessity for both dark and light to coexist. In this exercise you will experience the need for duality for yourself. You will learn to see that dark and light work interdependently at the level of consciousness on which they are existing. For instance, darkness at its high level is offering the peace of a meditative nothingness or void, the same as light. And, for example, light at its lower levels is so mixed with inconscient consciousness that it generates its own darkness. Light cannot see clearly at this low level and so wanders about lost, seeking someone or something to show it where to go. It is that blind state, where we humans have resided during the Kali Yuga, that gave traditional religion its stronghold; these organizations each said it knew the way home, and we grasped at that extended hand for help.

Well, there comes a time when each soul must seek the specific way home for itself. Every true tradition teaches students that this search occurs and seeks to prepare them for this step, this way to approach their own internal true growth. The lower levels of every religion have their place as a method of controlling and encouraging proper growth. But because no one practicing at this level can truly see, there is much darkness mixed in with the light. It is a mishmash or soup. To start sorting out what is authentic, one must go above the level at which this mixture is occurring, look at the reasons why, sort the forces into dark and light, understand their true necessity for being and then transcend the issue once and for all. Bitterness or hatred or revenge or negation is not a way to succeed in this process. Detached observation and love for all are the only process that will work.

Go into the room and personal merkabahs.

Ask to look at some part of your life that is currently an issue for you. When it comes forward, sit in silence and observe it in a state of detachment. This observation, in and of itself, can take a long time to master. You must sit silently and calmly, surrounded by the protection of your own guides, and look at the issue at hand. When you learn to sit silently and observe the energy, you learn to see it as a field complete unto itself. It is a merkabah of some sort, with its own connection to the father and the mother sources and its own center point connecting it to the ultimate source. When you relax, it will relax. It will slow down, lower its own defenses and permit you to look inside it. It can, if it so wishes, explain its own function to you much better than any other life forces can because it knows what it is responsible for, what it can do and why it exists.

Fear of the unknown and of "hostile," "evil" or "dark" forces are what keep you from using this process more often. If you start perceiving *anything* in creation as evil and without performing a beneficial function for the ultimate source of all, there is no end to the power of separation. It can make one part of one faith feel that another part, following the same leader, such as Christ, is wrong and evil, or make you fear your own vitality or mind or ego as evil. You can even consider one follicle of hair that will not stay in place as evil!

Different aspects of consciousness represent different ways to approach the same topic. What you want to start doing in this exercise is perceiving these different ways.

When you are finished with this exercise, declare the session closed.

10. *Working with Clients*

All seasoned grid workers have some method they use to keep their personal energy clear, balanced and protected. We will review some common methods in this section, primarily as they pertain to working with merkabahs.

In general, the more advanced you are working with merkabahs, the less you need to worry about utilizing intermediary protective steps and the more quickly you can get to work. This is because, through practice, you have gradually set proper procedures in place. They now automatically occur. Experts can quickly, simply and safely link their consciousness to that of the field with which they wish to communicate.

The ability to quickly link comes from working through the heart chakra. Any other location in the body can only keep you linked to life forces within its frequency range, such as the mind or the emotions. These locations are not sited as near to the source as the heart is. The heart has the widest range of motion and travel available to it. It is thus the most practical spot from which to work. The heart is called the seat of the soul, and the soul is that part of the human always in direct contact with the source. Therefore, the heart has access to the soul when it needs to call in additional information about a situation that has occurred.

Some philosophies consider other locations in the human body, such as the third eye or the naval chakra, to be the seat of the soul. These are actually the source points for that specific aspect of the human life form—the mind or the vitality; each aspect can take you into its source, but not to the ultimate unified source for the body "unit" as a whole.

In the human life form, the heart center is the seat of the soul—the individual's connection point to the infinite source, but this may not necessarily hold true for other life forms. Each life form's original source point is its point of connection, via the common source to all other life forms and spaces in the universe. While poised inside their own source in their own merkabah, accomplished interdimensional communicators can simultaneously enter into the energy field of whatever frequency they choose to explore.

Merkabah work requires a comfortable partnership with subtle energies who can help you to successfully navigate many different interdimensional worlds, when it is beyond your current capacity to do so safely on your own. Currently, these energies are known as guides and guardians. Technically, as we have explained before and throughout this book, our guides and guardians are really our inner colleagues.

Grid workers, energy workers and interdimensional communicators learn to work with their inner colleagues in all matters, both in their private personal work and when working with clients. These colleagues will alert the practitioner if there is an issue of concern and caution is required. Sometimes when the situation is very dangerous, the practitioner's guides will work with the guides of the client, and together all team members determine a solution.

When one is working with a client who has issues that might possibly cause problems, such as a serious illness or an emotional issue, an energy worker can proceed in another way. Ideally, a healer should be clear on all levels of his or her existence. What the client's issues are should not matter. But right now, at our present human level of awareness, this is not always the case. We all have issues that we must deal with, and, in actuality, working with clients helps the practitioner see and clear personal issues we may not have realized we harbored. When you enter into your client's issue and you are not clear yourself, the energy of the issue cannot pass through you like a breeze; it sticks somewhere and can begin to gradually cause you problems, such as headaches, anger, disease and so forth.

One day in the far future many of us will be working in manifestation in a perfect state of consciousness, but not yet. This is why the fallacy of perfect awareness via identification only with God the Father—that is, not joined also with God the Mother— has caused so many problems for some gurus, roshis and priests. They thought they were totally clear and protected and sallied forth, only to be trapped by the gradual accruing in their fields of their devotees' or parishioners' issues, which they had not fully cleared from inside themselves and which they could not admit to, because of their discipline's demand that a leader be perfect and infallible.

When, as a practitioner, you feel cause for concern, you can proceed as follows. This is also an excellent way to work with a group to establish a common resonance for clear communication.

Establish a room merkabah, with God the Father and God the Mother positioned as the heaven and earth polarities. Then stabilize the globe inside a square or cube, putting a cosmic energy in charge of the north, south, east and west sides.

You should also call in all beneficent forces who feel they have a say in the topic under investigation. If you are working on a very serious issue, you can next create a merkabah that is the common issue under investigation; create it as a field resting inside the room merkabah, complete with its own directional guides.

Next work with the client or audience to visualize themselves as individual merkabahs and have them call in their own guides.

Then request that each individual, from their heart center, throw a line of light into the heart center of the common merkabah (the issue or the room). State that each person is invited to freely offer their soul group's knowledge to the group effort, to feed the common topic with love and oneness. Ask that all offerings be accepted and directed toward the one common source of all, which is at the heart or core seed of the issue. Ask that each person receive back what is required for their own progress. Ask that anyone entering the room be immediately included in the circle, that anyone needing to leave may do so, and that at the end of the process each person's own guides and guardians do whatever is needed to maximize the positive experience for each individual. All cords are to return to each individual, with whatever treasures of light each needs, and all cords are to be sealed. Request the guards of each direction to disperse the merkabah as appropriate to the matter at hand. Seal this request, such as with an "amen," "aum" or "So be it."

Now start the work.

Chapter 10
Personal, Social and Spiritual Support

To truly succeed in this work, we need to maintain both the consciousness of the exploring child and the wisdom of the ancient sage.

Personal

Different worlds have evolved specific methods for working with their energies. These methods, or "rules," are integral to their world, but do not necessarily apply to other realms. This holds true for earth as well, where many perceptions and ways of operating within a specific culture have evolved. Therefore, when we start to travel and work interdimensionally, we need to stay open to the possibility that the same concrete situation may have very different underlying purposes and ways in which it evolved. We need to remain detached from the concrete reality so that we can explore the lines of energy feeding into the situation. To truly succeed in this work, we need to maintain both the consciousness of the exploring child and the wisdom of the ancient sage.

We cannot simply follow directions about how to make something work, like a manual on how to fix a fan. Instead we need to consult about the situation with our own inner and outer colleagues, guides and teachers and with the guides of the situation, and then decide with them the best way to proceed.

When exploring the writings and teachings coming forth from the many groups now starting to communicate with other realms, we often get different reports about what takes place in various realms. Each report comes from the focus of the individual doing the reporting. Even different individuals communicating the same information directly from a major energetic source, such as Archangel Michael, will report it slightly differently, because of their own evolved lines of communication and interest. Archangel Michael, like many spirit guides, has many different aspects and levels.

Tuning Your Inner Radio

When I was growing up and I would sit silently to meditate as I had been taught in Quaker meeting, I would often hear a cacophony of voices fading in and out of my mind. People would tell me to silence the mind, but every time I tried, I heard only more random voices saying a wide variety of random thoughts, seemingly unconnected to anything in my world. Or I might get moral judgments about myself and my behavior, often negative, as that was the nature of the Christian society, or morphogenetic field, in which I lived at that time.

Whenever I broached the subject of hearing voices in a very general way, the cultural message of that time was that only crazy people hear voices, and they are sent to asylums. So I kept silent about it, as most people do even today in our society. I learned how to silence the voices, putting energetic barricades at every point I heard a voice or saw a life form. This method of dealing with the situation served its purpose at the time. But I have learned since that it is not the highest or best solution.

When I grew up, I joined a yoga group that practiced *bhakti* yoga (devotional yoga, or yoga through love of God). Our instruction was to reject the mind and focus on the heart, which exists at a higher frequency or plane of consciousness. We were told to go above thoughts to the silence of infinite consciousness. I did this as well, blocking any sounds or images that appeared, struggling to fence in my ascent through consciousness to comply with the consciousness road the teacher was providing us. Yes, I could experience the universe as the classic *Neti-Neti*—God is "not this, not this." The result, for me personally, was a barrenness. Some twenty years into my yoga practice, I began exploring other modalities. This exploration freed me of a reliance on "rules" and allowed me to observe what was actually occurring. I observed that above "thoughts" are fields of consciousness which can make their presence known through geometric form, light, sound or beings who can communicate non-verbally with humans. This state is partially described by the yogic term "contemplation," which is a state beyond meditation where seekers begin to study the various fields or states of consciousness into which they have journeyed.

I learned, through years of personal introspective practice, that we can selectively tune the so-called random thoughts and images that flow through our consciousness. We are like radios, receiving many frequencies at once. We need to be taught how to tune into only one frequency at a time. We can then learn to turn the dial to receive the frequency we are interested in knowing about and communicating with.

Some of those locked away in Western insane asylums are people with an affinity for multidimensional communication who have had no one explain to them how to control what they are experiencing. No one has shown them the simple process of tuning their own inner radio to separate the different frequencies that they are naturally capable of receiving.

When learning to tune our own internal radios, we become aware that people can pull in both positive and negative information within any particular frequency. Knowing how polarities work is of great assistance here.

Depending upon one's own propensity and training, people go naturally towards a particular frequency level inside a field, and we make our judgments assessed on that. For example, if we come from a rigid moral, judgmental background, we tend to see that aspect of a field. If we go seeking power and the dark side, we are drawn to that. If we go seeking oneness and full partnership with all life forms, we will find that.

When we go into any dimension, we are first aware of a shift in energy. This energy can appear as light or darkness, depending upon our point of focus, our point of entry, why we are traveling there and what we want accomplish. Our intent attracts to us specific frequencies that reside inside that field.

The experienced inner traveler eventually learns that we have to work with any energy in its full spectrum of options: dark and light, good and bad and the varying degrees of intensity between. Otherwise, we can only go so far before we are brought up short by the presence of other energies we do not have the option to explain or understand, because we refuse to acknowledge their existence: "I only see the good in people; I refuse to see their faults," etc.

The Right to Shift Focus

We are aspects of the source, each seeking to master the third dimension and to accomplish very specific, complex tasks. I often hear religious people say that they do not understand something and that they "do not have the right" to seek for the truth themselves; they imply that seeking the truth is for more exalted humans than they. However, as manifestations of the one source exploring its own existence, who has more right than ourselves to both search for the truth and to ask for help while doing so? Who is this "other" more worthy than we ourselves are?

There are very few places in the universe in which physical form has evolved to as sophisticated a level as it has on earth. Earth is not a punishment, as many of the lower levels of all religions try to tell us. It is an opportunity for consciousness to manifest its individual capacity down into the gross physical level of existence. Earth is a reward.

This reward comes with copious assistance from other life forms in other realms. Some of this assistance comes from the internal lineage through which our souls have evolved. These lineages extend up to the source itself. They have invested eons of time in evolving this part of themselves to be able to manifest in solid form. We are their evolutionary progress. Does it make sense that these life forms would abandon their eons-long investment? That they would tell the parts of themselves who have achieved this level—physical manifestation of spirit—that these physical forms are now on their own? That these inner colleagues would say, "Sorry, don't ask for help?" It is not logical, efficient or pragmatic for these inner colleagues to do so.

Religion

This is a conscious universe. It can appear not to be so if we succumb to the unaware attitude that only those things existing in our frequency of perception are real—the attitude of "If we cannot see it, it does not exist." This is the downside of accepting the reality of any frequency world. As we adapt to master its needs, we lose the breadth of sight to simultaneously see other frequencies. We gradually get locked into its small segment of consciousness. We need to focus and stay free of the focus.

When we were in the age of darkness called the Kali Yuga, now just ending, and consciousness was very dense, humanity in general did not have the capacity to see through the heaviness of physical form to the higher levels of consciousness. A few very rare individuals, such as Jesus the Christ, Buddha and Krishna, came to various societies to teach about these more subtle planes. How were these rare people able to see so clearly when the rest of us could not? Why have billions of people based their entire lives and careers on the teachings of these evolved beings? Many explanations have been offered, such as the exalted leaders were favored children of God, they were born with an extra portion of light, they came from a very pure lineage that had kept the original high-level human genetic codes intact, they were sent directly by the source or they came from intergalactic societies that have a connection to and responsibility for earth's safe development.

Whatever reason you personally believe, the end situation is the same: these rare teachers could see beyond the physical world, and they told the rest of us that other worlds do exist and are meant for us to know and work with.

Because the majority of humans of their era were not capable of comprehending their knowledge, society translated it into terms it could understand, losing the original, multifaceted meaning of the original statements.

Organizations grew up surrounding the base teachings of these people. These organizations sought to codify their founders' universal insights, to assist others who were aware of the physical realm alone. This codification has, time after time, limited the full breadth of the original insight, just as we do when we identify with a merkabah at its source versus at different points in its descent to earth.

Obeying the rules that organizations codify around a founder's inspirations can help individuals make progress through the self-discipline required. But as our consciousness expands and we begin to access the energy of many religions and philosophies for ourselves, the evolved rules often become straitjackets binding us and preventing our further growth. Then we need to inwardly identify with the founder's consciousness and learn directly from that source, putting aside all the accrued rules.

The consciousness fields of Jesus the Christ, Buddha, Krishna, Archangel Michael, Melchizedek, Metatron, the Ascended Masters and the Great White Brotherhood are some of the cosmic consciousnesses that are currently working with people on an individual basis, teaching them directly how to proceed according to their own situation and circumstances. These fields are very real. They exist and will communicate in a very tactile manner with those focusing on them. Some, such as Christianity, are very complex and have evolved and manifest now at many different levels.

We can enter these fields at one point, but we can give ourselves the option of exploring other frequencies as well. Why? Well, true devotees of Jesus the Christ, for example, should want to understand all aspects of their Lord's existence, not simply the ones they initially focused on.

Religious and Philosophical Definitions

In the world that is now passing, various religions and philosophies looked into spirit, and their great visionaries charted roads they saw or felt would take them and others to the source. They often charted the way back to matter that occurs within their merkabah or world. If we want to get to heaven via the Christian or Islamic or Hindu faith, there is a certain road with specific markers that will get us there. However, what is often not understood is that the road will take us to a specific merkabah, *but* that is not the only merkabah existing at that frequency level that offers the option of being safe in "heaven." A Christian heaven looks different from an Islamic one, but both are correct descriptions—for their merkabah. Merkabahs can exist complete unto themselves without interfering with or negating any other road inside any other merkabah.

Exploring any merkabah of any size, if done properly, takes us back to the ultimate source itself. The source is the origin of all life, and all merkabahs are the manifestation of some aspect of the one source. To prove to its devotees that the source is inside all, some traditions will have seekers meditate on a rock and will consider seeing God there as representing remarkable progress. The interdimensional communicator knows this truth—that all is the source—and travels to whatever field and frequency is required to work with whatever issue is being studied.

Our Changing Perception of Organized Religion

As we become a global culture, any religion's claim that it is the only way to the source is seen for the incomplete statement that it truly is. All religions are *a* way; none are the *only* way. Earth's open global culture, and the coming into the open of many secret esoteric societies, has helped develop a broad base of information about the nature of consciousness and spirit. This is permitting a new discipline, spiritual science, to develop.

The process of comparison, direct experience and growing expertise is permitting us to more fully understand the nature of the source. How does all this integrate with the belief of various religions that theirs is the only one destined to arrive in heaven? Let's look at this topic from the perspective of merkabah technology.

Most religions believe in some central figure or form or consciousness or energy from which all has emanated forth. This source is a merkabah. Energy within it descends from spirit to matter via a series of circles emanating from the holiest of the holies. These emanations emerge in both circular and linear form; that is, from the source there are various realms, located at various distances from the center, populated with those existences who work in service to that particular source. There is a ranking system of dominions. Within each dominion, there are forces assigned to different positions: top and bottom, right and left and so on. Closest to the source are the broader life forms: those who have charge over more dominions. Farther from the source are life forms who have charge of more specific realms or worlds.

All religious merkabahs begin with a frequency of perception that grows into a self-contained ball of energy. It contains the answer to numerous riddles of life within itself, at precise locations. Heaven is at point x, hell is at point y, angels are at point b, good boys and girls are at point m and bad boys and girls at point p. Those not of this religion do not get to participate in this field of energy; they are lost souls, the abandoned, the damned. Within any specific religion there are subsidiary merkabahs: different sects, communities, leaders, study groups and so on. To belong to this religion, one must be initiated, baptized, swear allegiance to the leader and so on. In some way, the applicant must accept the consciousness of the merkabah and request entry into it and protection from it. This is also the experience one goes through when joining any group that has formed or is forming a community, or merkabah, such as an inner city gang or a country club clique.

Each religion is a morphogenetic field that supports the efforts of its occupants to understand the nature of spirit as it exists in that realm. A different religion, existing inside a different merkabah, may have different rules, and thus what its occupants learn may be different.

Those with some vision point to their visit to their religion's heaven. In this location, they saw only members of their own faith. They give this image as proof that only members of their religion will ascend to heaven, and the rest will be found in some less desirable spot. Heaven, as many religions currently perceive it, is also a specific location inside their religious merkabah. It is, therefore, populated by beings who have thoroughly identified with that energy. This does not mean those of other religions are damned—just that they are occupying a different merkabah. Each way is "true" for that energy field. It is, however, incorrect for a person to believe that their way is the only way and that the rules of their world (merkabah) apply to all worlds.

Religions tend to isolate individuals within that group's perceptions, believing theirs is the best workable model for behavior that will have the beneficial results of oneness with the source, or of earning credits by pleasing the source and of bringing peace to themselves and the world. But has this isolation worked? Many of the great wars of our planet have been fought because of religion. Centuries ago the Crusades enveloped all of Europe and parts of the Middle East. Today's wars are devoted to contests of religious or philosophical perceptions—Islam versus the West, Islam versus the Jews, Islam versus the Hindus in India and Pakistan, Islam versus Islam, Christian versus Christian, etc. There are many subset versions of this process, such as those in which very conservative Christian sects will not meet officially with other denominations of their own parent religion or gather in unity with those of other religions. Even inside such sects, isolationism continues. Sect members are taught that only special ones among them have the right to speak directly to the leader or to God; all others must go through these "chosen" few.

Once we focus on separateness, there is no end to the segmentation that will eventually occur.

God and Partnership

The recent patriarchal religions have often seen God as a supreme male of vengeance, guilt and power who demands obedience and repentance. The common people have no access to Him; He can only be approached through those selected to speak His will. This concept of God has permeated much of our world's social structures and has caused many of the problems we have today, including the abuse of natural resources and of "others," however a group may define them.

The currently emerging understanding of the original source views all religions as different aspects of one common energy. This source offers us free will. We are free to build or destroy—to do as we wish. But the great secret is that when of our own free will we align ourselves with the core energy of the situation—which means the core energy of the universe—we are happiest and most content. We will soon be seeking to align ourselves with the source of everything that approaches us in our lives, to replicate that same feeling of honest satisfaction. And that is the trump card the source has placed throughout its own creation. Alignment with the source of all existence, all being, all power, all knowing, is the only truly and eternally satisfying option for all, dark or light.

It is the energetic maturity required to approach this awareness that stymies us. We need to exist inside a field of high enough frequency to perceive this reality. Astrologically, earth is approaching such a period, called by different traditions the Second Coming, the Ascension, the Golden Age, the New World, the Fifth World and so on. It is a time when the whole world will be infused with greater light offering more clarity to our understanding. We can flow into this shift very naturally, overcoming, dismantling, destroying and/or enlightening the current murky fields of energy that the earth is experiencing now—if we choose to do so. But many are so thoroughly "trapped" in the old frequency that a considerable shaking up is required to dislodge them from their old perceptions.

Partnership and Hierarchy

To successfully work with merkabah technology, most of contemporary humanity needs to shift from being focused primarily on hierarchical polarities, such as those found in formal religion, to cooperation and partnership, as demonstrated by many groups working from a spiritual/scientific perspective.

The hierarchical approach is excellent for its purpose, which is defining the patterns within a field. The partnership approach is excellent when we are seeking to establish cooperation among the fields with which we wish to work and communicate.

A hierarchical perspective creates power struggles that never end. If we lodge inside the hierarchical consciousness, we are inclined to say that the father consciousness is better than the mother consciousness, or vice versa. Pursuing this energetic viewpoint, we eventually reach a point at which we are saying, when looking at our hand, that the thumb is more useful and thus better than the little finger, that the heart is better than the mind, that a Hutu is better than a Tutsi and thus has more right to live or that a human has more rights to alter a piece of land than the elemental who has overseen and protected it for thousands of years.

The partnership perspective works differently. It understands that all fields of consciousness, or energy, have an important part to play in the ultimate perfection of the one common source. It perceives that each of us contains the entire universe inside ourselves and is thus complete within ourselves. Nothing can be excluded in this viewpoint, for all is a part of the one source and is also our self. *Any* aspect of creation we have not accepted is a life form whose purpose we have not yet fully comprehended. The partnership frequency also has its problems, of course, for when everyone works as equals, it becomes trickier to reach a joint decision.

This awareness of the ultimate oneness of all does not mean we have to accept any specific life form into our world. In fact, recognizing its true reality, we have the free-will right to ask for protection from life forms via our guides and guardians while we work on comprehending their consciousness, rules and operational methods.

For example, a spiritual aspirant can comprehend the world of pimps and prostitutes or drug users and dealers without necessarily participating within these fields of behavior—*unless* the field contains a reality that individual or their soul group has collectively or individually decided they need to fully experience to master for their work. Then one or many from that soul group may be sent into the fray, in some role or another, to sort out the situation on an experiential level. This participation does not necessarily mean playing one of the "leading" roles; it can also mean taking a supporting position. Thus, we could choose to work in a service reclaiming these lives, such as in a shelter for the homeless, in a home for unwed mothers, or doing work like Mother Teresa's work with the homeless. Once we have known and lived the energy, we will have mastered its frequency modulations, fully respect it for its contributions—dark or light—to the one unified source and no longer be affected by it. We will accept and respect its contribution to the whole picture of energy. When it arrives in our life, for some function, we will recognize it and be able to deal with it while remaining detached.

Speaking for myself, I can say that any time an energy affects me adversely, I understand it is a frequency I have not yet mastered. I will usually work to do so, as the opportunity permits.

The Role of Prayer and Intent

We are aspects of the source seeking to accomplish a very specific, complex task: the mastery of third-dimensional reality. As such, we have specific rights, including being able to call for assistance and to have that call answered. From time immemorial, humans have invoked assistance to comprehend and deal with what occurs on this planet called earth. Right now, most of us have to work through our own past patterns to receive this help, and doing so may not be easy.

When we know that we need help but are not able to see or feel the location of the source of that help, or of the answer, we often use the process known traditionally as prayer. Every wish we make or dream we have is a form of prayer. It is an intent projected forth into universal energy, and it will always, like a fishing line with a hook on the end, lodge itself inside some field of energy.

What we perceive in our lives comes from our prayers and intents, even if we are asking as a child asks for a bike. What we ask for will receive a response. The answer will sometimes be yes and sometimes no, just the same as when we ask for something in this world of another human being. If we ask for something that is not possible, we may not get it.

The church presents us with morality plays, the commercial theater with dramas or comedies, all focused on what happens when we get or do not get or appear to get/not get our prayers answered, and what happens when we pray to different types of sources (the devil, God, gluttony, fame, etc.).

Traditional religions tell us that God answers all prayers. Folk knowledge tells us not *all* prayers are answered: it depends on how we phrase the prayer or accompany it by action. There are, for instance, the thousands of children who ask for a bike for their birthday and don't receive one. Or the person who keeps praying, unsuccessfully, to win the lottery until, one day, the joke goes, God booms forth from the sky, "I could use a little help. Buy a ticket!" There are also cases in which the answer to the prayer is given, but fear rejects the answer.

For example: about fifteen years ago, when I was in Bali, I visited an ancient temple and sat to meditate for a long period of time. The guardian spirits of the temple spoke to me, said that they were very pleased with such devotion from a Westerner, and offered me a boon—it had to be practical. So I thought about it and, since I was having difficulty understanding finance at that time, requested assistance in understanding the true spiritual nature of finance. That night, during sleep, I felt a rush of energy come towards me. Its intensity startled me, and as I fought to keep it away, not knowing what it was, it gradually morphed into a red dragon and dozens of temple statues came alive, all roiling around inside a merkabah that kept dancing towards me and then back. I woke up frightened. This merkabah of energy appeared to me off and on over the next few years, and I suffered heart palpitations every time it approached. Finally, one night, after I began doing interdimensional work, I followed my own advice and stood very still when the energy approached. It became still in return, and we began communicating. To my wide-eyed surprise, I discovered it was a merkabah with the gift of financial understanding; it had been sent in answer to my prayer and could not leave until I accepted the gift. My prayer had been answered, but I had been too afraid of the energy to see the answer in front of my eyes!

What really happens, from an energetic point of view, when we send forth a prayer or intent of any kind? It depends upon what part of our energy fields we choose to project the thought-form from, how developed that part of our field is and how intense our wish has become.

A classic instance would be wishing for success in some given field, such as being a musician or an artist or a businessperson or an athlete. What is the point of the wish? At what level do we wish to succeed? If the source answers our prayer, will it do us any good—or will it form problems more severe than those we are currently involved in?

Many people are praying for our earth to stay permanently the way it has always been (to their perception). That is not possible; when perceptual capacities increase, as they are doing now, the old perceptions that are resonating at a much lower frequency are no longer relevant to our needs.

Connections and Prayer

The results we receive from our prayers and intentions also depend on how strongly connected we are with our own inner colleagues: our guides, guardians, higher self and collective energetic family consciousness. Our results also depend on what forms of energy we have set up or have had set up for ourselves, in other lifetimes perhaps, and must now move through to reach our goals.

For example, many women are in the process of recovering from the witch-hunts of the Middle Ages in Europe and from many other kinds of trauma at the hands of men, who for centuries have treated women as dirty, filthy, unclean and/or unworthy. Many of these men were the spokespeople for the so-called light side, such as traditional religions. What form this trauma took for each woman must be worked through, as does the collective consciousness of this experience for all women. As women represent the creation consciousness, their experience is also related to the general abuse we humans, as a whole, have been exerting on Mother Earth. So the women will have to work through that field as well.

For men the issue is different. For example, they have always been taught to fight—to fight off predators, to protect the family or the country. And this issue, too, is a morphogenetic field of consciousness that we, as a collective whole, have to move through and master before we can put it to rest.

Dark and Light Knowledge

There is no such thing as a free trip anywhere in the universe. There is always a price to pay. With the dark forces, it is control by them. With the light forces, it is the responsibility for our own independence and free will. Should one wish to shirk their own self-knowledge or responsibility, the dark forces are more than willing to step in and take over. They tell us that if we just do as they wish, they will do the work for us.

Even so-called religious orders can develop a darkness of their own. All the subtle orders and mystical knowledges require self-discipline. We often have to learn this self-discipline by following a regimen set up by a teacher. But sometimes a group slips over into controlling the individual, dictating what the person can say and think and using mind control or emotional control to confine the person inside a very specific frequency. This entrapment is a very high, subtle form of darkness.

Darkness is a teacher as well, leading us to experience negative situations until we are so tired of them that we are willing to call forth our own personal strength and rectify the situation.

It is comforting to feel that one can mindlessly follow a perfect teacher and in that way reach the light. But all teachers, inner and outer, are fallible in some way; if that way is detrimental to your progress, you must retain the detachment to see that. Mindlessly following any teacher can lead you into darkness. Never give up the independent free will to make the final decision. Decisions, even in a religious group, are still ultimately the responsibility of each individual.

Free Will and Cocreating Reality

We, as life forms connected to the source, have free-will rights. What we all too often fail to realize is that since all forms in the universe are also connected to the source, they have free-will rights, too. All life has evolved from the same parent source as we have. All life forms have much the same issues as we do: the need to survive, to succeed and to experience joy and fulfillment.

The need to cooperate for the common goal becomes important when this situation is factored in. In making our own decisions, it is important to first establish that we have aligned ourselves with the ultimate goal of the source: its own perfect perfection.

Once we feel aligned with this viewpoint, then we can focus on understanding the alignment of the other party in whatever analysis we are undertaking. There are many possible alignments and motivations. These can include clear free-will opposition to the goals of the source, serving the source through love, serving the source through darkness, serving the source through oneness, serving the source with needs that supersede or are secondary to our own.

The only way to get a clear understanding of how to proceed is to examine a situation in a detached manner. All too often we humans have been encouraged to ignore or block our awareness of the opposing force in our situation, especially if we perceive it to be a dark or negative force. This makes our ability to discern and deal with the core issue almost impossible.

During the Kali Yuga, when consciousness was dense and actions were often locked into the physical realm, what we consciously thought and perceived were limited. Now, however, as we develop our conscious ability to see and act on other planes as well, we need to take greater responsibility for what we think, feel, intend, pray and focus our will upon. We are now consciously affecting other planes of existence.

The source of all will ultimately win for that is its objective. Our contribution can make this process more or less pleasant; with our thoughts and actions we can set up, avoid or correct the alignment of energy. The more closely we are aligned with the source, the more powerful we become and the more personal responsibility becomes a necessity. If someone is fully aligned with the source, they will ultimately "win" in any situation, for they can now only act from oneness with the will of the all-powerful source.

A classic situation that illustrates this is the battle that will sometimes occur between a black magician and a spiritual master.

The black magician will have identified with the dark forces and may have climbed up very far in that hierarchy. If he goes up against a spiritual devotee who has focused only on the light, it would be an interesting battle, and the black magician could win. Battling against a spiritual master is another matter. The spiritual master will have worked to comprehend both the dark and the light forces, to see beyond that duality to the higher source of both. The spiritual master has the better chance to prevail because their way encompasses and understands the energy being projected by the black arts.

The black magician, on the other hand, is not capable of fully comprehending the spiritual adept's knowledge of light. Should the black magician begin studying the light in order to conquer it, they would be transformed by the experience, for they would pull into themselves the consciousness of the ultimate source, which is all love. The black magician loses either way: either the spiritual master defeats them through their knowledge of the light, or the black magician defeats him/herself. Many famous spiritual masters in history have come to their expertise in this roundabout way, setting out to acquire the ultimate power first through darkness and then becoming transformed as they discover that to be truly all-powerful they must incorporate the light as well. Eventually they rise above the polarity of dark and light to the infinite source of both, the ultimate Light itself.

Your Legacy

The only heritage any of us can acquire or leave behind is frequency—the resonance with which we live our lives. Family will come and go, friends will come and go, we will come and go, but what we leave behind, as our legacy to this earth, is the frequency with which we perform our tasks and live our lives. This frequency pours into the collective field and creates a strong energy that becomes a permanent aspect of our earth and our universe.

How you handle any energy—fear, love, friendship, community, commerce, war or land use—feeds into the overall field for that energy and becomes a permanent part of our world. What do you want to leave?

Chapter 11
Support from Guides, Guardians and Inner Colleagues

We all have guides and guardians of our very own, whether or not we choose to acknowledge them. . . . Establishing a working relationship with guides requires time, effort and trust.

Very often, when I am lecturing on the topic of guides, individuals in the audience will ask if I can see their guides and what do they look like. When I look at some of these unaware audience members, I see soft angel wings folded over their shoulders, surrounding and protecting their hearts. These are the gentle folk, somewhat bruisable, whose angels are encouraging them to live in the heart by surrounding them with loving care. When told of this, many people are vaguely aware of the situation but have been refusing to acknowledge it, because cultural conditioning tells them that such events are only "imagination."

Another image I often see is standing behind people are guides with their hands over their mouths. The guides are showing me that their person has told them to shut up, and, this being a free-will world, they have complied. The guides are still there, still protecting, but not speaking to the human.

Most people in contemporary Western mainstream society were taught in childhood that voices and apparitions are things to be wary of. They have been told that such voices and images are dark forces, or are imaginary. And for goodness sake, please don't ever tell anyone you can see them, or you will be locked up like Uncle Joe or deemed crazy like Aunt Meg. The fear inculcated in children is often greatest in those families for whom extended vision is an actual occurrence. These families have often, in their lineage and thus in their cellular memory, had problems with their community or religious affiliation in the past and wish to spare their children the same experience.

This is a free-will world. Guides and guardians of the light comply with an individual's free-will mandates. If an individual repeatedly requests, "Don't talk to me," their guides eventually will not. It is usually only in an emergency or in a situation we have not been able to resolve at a material level that we seek help from other realms, very often unconsciously or as a great cosmic call to the universe for help. It is then that these forces will very often instantly come in and assist, because we have sincerely, from the heart, asked. As the Bible says, "Ask and ye shall receive." When we are lucky, we are aware of this assistance and continue to work with these guides on a conscious level. This is how I and many other innovators of today's alternative technologies re-established contact with our own internal lineages. We had a crisis and called on the universe for help. The universe responded, and this time we listened.

Establishing a Relationship with Our Helpers

We all have guides and guardians of our very own, whether or not we choose to acknowledge them. Upon initial conscious contact, they often act like big brothers or protective parents: they take care of and watch over us. Eventually, when we are energetically grown up and are comfortable existing in interdimensional society, they become our friends and colleagues.

Initially, when we go seeking our own guide or guardian, with true sincerity, the strongest force present in our field will respond. When we do so in a group setting, such as at a workshop focused on working with your guides, the power of the group all seeking the same goal will strengthen the ability of each member to value conscious connection with their own guides.

Often, when I am working with a large group of people, I will consciously ask my own guides to please contact the guides of the audience members and give them some sign of their presence. When the exercise is complete, many in the audience report a variety of occurrences. These vary according to the individual's orientation, receptivity and capacity. The guide may make a person's finger tap; it may take on the appearance of a beloved relative who has passed over to deliver a message. A person may experience an angel speaking to them or a spiritual teacher or totem figure contacting them. Guide contact can include a feeling of light or love or peace descending into a person, a shimmering enveloping them like sparkles of light, colors appearing around them or before them or sounds or voices giving them a very specific message, such as "live in the heart" or "all is well." In the effort to make their presence known, our guides will work through whatever sense is most highly developed in their human colleague. Then, as we get used to each other, our interactions expand so that we are able to understand the guides via more of our senses.

Establishing a working relationship with guides requires time, effort and trust.

The forces of light are often taken for granted. Although these forces are always with us, they are usually benign, and so we need to be diligent in recognizing their presence in our lives. After guides have helped humans to clear up the old horrors in our lives, after we have clung to them for survival, after we have become comfortable with ourselves and our improved lives, there comes a time when we are in danger of forgetting about our guides' presence. The crisis is over, and we revert to our old ways. We need to be diligent about maintaining contact at this time.

Life forms working from the dark side do not need to comply with the non-interference mandate of free will. This is part of their allure. They seem able to do whatever they please and get away with it. They are spokespeople for desire and hence are often aggressively selling their wares to a human. When we tell the dark forces to be quiet, they do not have to comply. Thus, they are frequently the voices people hear first, since they have shut up the "good" voices. The best way we can defend against the agents of the dark light is to consciously choose to work with the guides and guardians of the light who have either been assigned to us or who reside inside various fields of endeavor.

There is a saying that God protects children, madmen and fools. There is much truth in this. When we are content to stay within a field of energy, we are protected to a certain extent by the forces, some good and some bad, that control that field. Inhabitants of our world have to date behaved like good children, content to play inside our third-dimension playpen.

But as our world elevates in frequency, we are being forcefully moved out of our old playpen and are being presented with many options of where to go next. Energetically, we are becoming teenagers, and, as we start exploring and moving about in other fields, it is important that we know energetic protocols and that we have a good guide. We should also invoke or pray for protection. There are many, many forces at work in the universe, and there are always accidents, tricksters and malevolent forces to be on watch for. Virtually all traditions include prayer and invocation to call in the presence of protective energies. Some prayers are elaborate, others simple. Some evoke each guide by name, and others evoke the guides as a group.

Many American dowsers use the following invocation before starting work, and listen carefully to how their guides respond, making necessary energetic changes before proceeding: "Dear spirit guides and guardian angels: May I, Can I, Should I proceed with this work?"

A very simple prayer to guides you regularly work with is "Dear spirit guides and guardian angels, please be with me."

If you wish to call on specific guides and beings to be with you, I recommend concluding with the following general invitation:

". . . and any spirits or beings of the light who feel they have a right to speak or participate, welcome! I apologize for not invoking you by name, and I ask for your blessings and benevolent participation as we proceed."

I do this because, from experience, I have discovered that the old fairy tales are correct: it is always the fairy godmother you forget to invite to the party who feels insulted and causes problems!

Honoring Our Free Will

Our guides, guardians and inner colleagues are here to help us navigate through the fields, as per our needs. When they cannot solve the issue themselves, as is sometimes the case with practitioners assisting a client, the guides know whom to call in for assistance. They have a very large realm of energies to work with.

Guides and guardians of the light do not want to control us or take away our freedom. If a subtle life form ever approaches and in any way starts to take away free will, stop right there. This is a trickster, an agent of the dark light or a life form with an agenda of its own. Our own authentic guides and guardians know that for progress and sustained cooperation, free will is the only option. They also know that just as we need help to comprehend the universe, they need our help to act on earth. We are the life form that has been given the mandate to comprehend and master the potentialities of the third dimension. For our inner colleagues to continue the lineage of light from the source to the ultimate goal of full consciousness manifestation, they need us to develop full mastery of consciousness, right here on earth. Our inner colleagues can assist us, but because they do not have density or form as we have, they cannot interact with matter the way we humans can.

Communicating Versus Channeling

There is a technical difference between communicating with our guides and channeling a life-form energy. We need to be aware of this difference as we move forward. Channeling technically means providing a channel through which a substance can flow. Communicating means we are establishing a dialogue with another life form.

Channeling can occur when higher life forms need to present some technical information to humans and cannot find a way to otherwise communicate it. In this case they must find a willing human counterpart to process the information through. If they locate someone from their own family lineage and the energies are compatible, the individual can channel without too much effect on their health. If the life forms cannot locate such a channel and the information is deemed critical, they must find a human vessel who, of their own free will, accepts the task, even though it often means a gradual degradation of their own personal health. Oracles, in the past, provided channeled information from other worlds via the cultural parameters of their civilization. Up to the present time, many people seeking information about other worlds willingly accepted roles as channelers, either consciously (they are aware of what was coming through) or unconsciously (the entering life force takes control of the body to present the message, the human stepping aside or being energetically overpowered, returning to command of the body only when the channeling life force leaves). Today the human race has energetically matured to the point where we are able to enter into direct communication with these other worlds, and for many, channeling is no longer required. Direct communication is always preferable because it requires that the human extend their own personal capacities in a conscious manner.

Sometimes people say they are channeling when they really mean they are communicating; it is a matter of semantics. Then there are the people who think it is fun to call in some life form from another dimension and who do so through a Ouija board or through channeling whatever wanders through the universe and happens to hear them. This is an open invitation to tricksters and dark forces. When we approach the topic as a game, we can't expect a high-level consciousness to respond. Our intent draws to us a matching consciousness from other realms.

If an unknown energy tells us that they are trustworthy and we should listen to them, and it is an insult for us to test them, ignore them! True guides work with us, providing us with ways to test them to verify who they are and what their capacities and abilities are. They will work with us to develop our abilities to perceive them, communicate with them and work confidently with them. For example, they may tell us what will occur next week, which may be so far from anything we feel would occur that we disbelieve them; then, when circumstances all come together and the event occurs, they will remind us that they can provide us with that service. They may show us what is occurring around us, which others may be disguising; they do so by opening up our third eye or heart center and permitting us to see or feel the truths.

True guides often have a very good sense of humor. They want to be our friends and confidants and will frequently joke with us or casually communicate about issues we are working on together. They are very much like us, only on a different level of consciousness. Therefore, if a life form approaches you very seriously, pontificating great truths and being very rigid, be extremely vigilant; this situation can very soon turn into a power issue, to your detriment.

It is not the pattern for true guides to dictate to us what we must do in this third-dimensional realm. Guides and guardians usually do not know all the nuances of how to adapt to the third dimension unless they have themselves spent time in the human form. We are the part of the collective that is handling this function; it is our human job to master the fine points of the third dimension for our collective spiritual family. Guides know how to look into each situation and see the energies involved— where the energies have come from and how they have arrived at just this spot. Guides can see what is occurring around us, and, as many are either above the time-space continuum or know how to become so, they can let us know the probable future of a situation. Once our energy has descended into the gross physical plane, resulting in something such as cancer or a broken bone, it is more difficult for them to assist us. The physical situation represents the descent of a specific frequency or thoughtform that has worked its way through many levels of consciousness and is grounded in physical matter. At this point help must be more extreme from the inner worlds, but it is available, circumstances on all planes permitting. There are many cases where, when once prayed for intensely enough, cancer has disappeared and broken bones have instantly healed.

Different Types of Guides

Guides, guardians and inner colleagues are a collective nomenclature that encompasses several different categories of life forms. Many are connected to our own soul's evolutionary development.

In various cultures and religious sects, some types of guides are more acceptable than others. Our guides are willing to adapt to our cultural expectations if it will get their human's attention and cooperation. So the higher self might say it is an angel, for example, or a saint, if their person does not believe in such a concept as a higher self. As the human gets used to communicating with their guides and if the human finds it culturally acceptable, the guides gradually help the human to understand their true nature. Staying open to all possibilities ensures our ability to get on accurate, familiar grounds with our own guides.

Some guides are integrally connected to our personal energy field, and we cannot get rid of them even if we try. Some guides are voluntary, and we or they can withdraw from the arrangement. Some guides we keep for a lifetime, and others we stay with for a short or longer journey.

All guides have specific functions, and while we can ask anything of any guide, they cannot always give it to us. This can be because the request is not their area of expertise, because it is not for our higher good or because some other situation that intersects with ours has precedence.

Personal Soul Groups

We can work with representatives of all the following personal soul groups:

The higher self. We exist as a full spectrum of consciousness right from our own descent from the ultimate source until our return to the ultimate source. This true self exists throughout all time-space planes of existence that we have ever or will ever experience. We may disconnect from an awareness of this lineage when we fully absorb into any plane of consciousness to concentrate and work with the principles therein. We forget what is occurring elsewhere because we are focused on the specific event that is occurring where we are. But we also have the innate ability to disconnect from a specific task and reconnect with that which we are in totality. That totality partakes of all the wisdom and knowledge of the universe. It wishes and needs to feed this knowledge into whatever specific task it is participating in, so that it can perfect its job efficiently. It has a stake in our observing correctly and proceeding in the correct way. We can trust this higher-self lineage, for it is of us and for us.

Our own soul-lineage collective. Each of us has descended from the source in a particular linear path. When we are looking up from our earthly perspective, we can trace this lineage back through ever-widening forms of life. It is somewhat harder when we wish to track the descent and subdivision of vast consciousness down into our tiny physical form. It is harder because the higher levels of consciousness are vast and as each level segments itself to focus on specific issues, so we need to keep refocusing on which segment eventually led to us.

Each lineage on earth has, ultimately, one prime directive from the source. What each of us as an individual aspect of our collective has inwardly agreed to master is very specific. We may have unconsciously forgotten this, but it is latently there. When we "awaken" and once more know and understand the forces and priorities that are pushing on us to master what urgently needs to be mastered, it becomes easier for us to focus on the necessary tasks.

Our current birth family. Our specific birth family unit has certain tasks they have been entrusted with by their genetic and soul lineages. We participate in all these lineages when we incarnate into a family line. A specific incarnation is not by chance or by mistake; our birth family has been chosen for us, or we have chosen it ourselves. We have certain lessons that need to be learned, and the best situation for learning these has been presented to us. This is true even of abusive or difficult family situations. The reason may not be a "bad" one—that is, it is not necessarily a karmic payment for "bad" actions in the past—but it may be a difficult one precisely because we need to master a difficult situation in order to grow in our personal overall goal of universal service, whatever that may be.

Over time, this continual reincarnation process permits us, in our larger existence, to comprehend on a working, operational level the full scope of our potentials; it gives us the opportunity to master them. The goal, remember, is to ultimately be a fully aware conscious life form, an embodied aspect of the one ultimate source. We are collecting life experiences on a genetic resonance basis that will stand us in good stead forever, into the future and the past and in all dimensions.

Our own past and future incarnations. Most of us have lived before and will live again. We chose to specialize in specific functions in each of these lifetimes. Sometimes we may need the qualities we developed in a past or future incarnation, and we can call upon that consciousness to assist us in our present lifetime. Whether our role was to be a warm-hearted mechanic in one life and a cool mental mathematics genius in another, it was our choice, or our lineage's choice, based on what we needed to do next to master the intricacies of our own personal growth.

Sometimes the lessons we must learn in this lifetime are ones that appear to be very difficult. We will learn more efficiently when we can see this life in relation to all other lives. For example, we might be a beggar in this lifetime to offset the misuse of power over others in a previous lifetime, or we might be rich in this lifetime to see if we know how to properly steward our abundance of resources. Learning about ourselves helps us face the decisions we must make now, so that this lifetime is even more worthwhile.

Our soul family. We, in our unawakened human consciousness, may have a strong desire to pursue knowledge in a specific way. When we start consciously working with our guides and lineages, this intention may totally change. When we re-establish conscious awareness of our soul family, we are often told about their overall goals and the function we agreed, before we incarnated, to come to earth to perform for the collective. At this time our work may shift, and however humble or grand it is outwardly, it inwardly feels totally "right." This is because our work is our own soul's goal.

When we are in ignorance and disconnected from our sources, we may feel a vague dissatisfaction with whatever we choose to do, as if no matter how outwardly appropriate the course of action, it is somehow not quite right. Once we start working with our own soul family, we may have to make some adjustments to the ways we work and to our perceptions. But from then on, these adjustments will, guaranteed, lead us only along the path home, through the morass of illusions, to find our real purpose for being on earth.

Whenever someone says they see no reason for life or for their life, and that life is meaningless, or worse, too painful or too worthless, this is the clue that they have not yet made contact with their own true inner reality. Making contact with our own lineage and colleagues is the most fulfilling and rewarding experience we can achieve. All our true reasons for being now come into the open.

Guides and Guardians from Various Worlds

We can also connect with the following life forms and energies:

The guiding life-force energy of various topics. Every field of endeavor and every individual have a core-level desire to perfect themselves in a spirit of harmony and love. It is very useful to go to the core of any form with which we are seeking to interact. Doing so cuts through a lot of lesser aspects of consciousness with their attendant obstructions and takes us to a place of harmony. Whether we are seeking to be the best pianist or the best mother, the field itself has its own guides and guardians that can help us achieve our goals. When we cannot see the ultimate goal inside the field, our intent to attain that level can attract to us appropriate life-force energies who will gladly assist us. It benefits them to have their field used to its maximum potential, and they will assist us to grow in understanding to the best of our potential. We can draw upon the collective universal knowledge and life-force energy of any field: we simply need to locate where this information is in the universe.

Various worlds who are meant to assist humans with their tasks. One major world in this regard is the angelic realm. This world is very close to the human realm, and every human has at least one angel assigned to them when they incarnate.

Nature spirits. There are life forms responsible for all aspects of earth's existence, including the spirit of earth herself. Humans can connect with these life forms to accomplish specific tasks. These life forms include the devas and the various worlds inside the faerie kingdom.

Guiding spirits of various realms and planes of consciousness. If we are seeking peace, dynamism, health, etc., we can enter into that world and work with these beings.

Guiding spirits of the animal, mineral and plant kingdoms. Traditionally, many folks have connected to these spirits in order to obtain their help with the development of specific qualities or to access specific types of energy.

Many other inner worlds. Everyone is different, and the guides that come to assist you will always be appropriate to your life story, whether that story includes origins on Arcturus or a connection to the world of quartz crystals or an affinity for Athena from having been her high priestess in some past incarnation. When you start working with your guides, stay open. Expect to be surprised, so don't be surprised when some strange occurrence takes you someplace you never even heard about before. Just listen and be open.

Other Types of Guides

In addition, other types of guides help us along the way:

Outer teachers, guides and traditions. Many people have preceded us in our search for knowledge, and if we call sincerely to the universe, the universe will locate the correct teacher for us. This teacher may appear to show us how to perform a specific task or we may study with them for a very long time. When we have completed our learning, we move on to the next teacher, who could be a pet, a child or a bad work situation—whatever we require to master our next level of self-perfection.

Always carefully examine any inner or outer teaching and teacher. Most paths, to have converts or students, have mastery of a particular spectrum of consciousness. But there are many aspects to mastery. How has this teacher taught this group to work? By exclusion or inclusion?

We are evolving right now out of a culture that could not see into the fields of consciousness. Like a band of blind people, we had to trust others to show us the way forward. All too often, if someone spoke forcefully and had a bit of wisdom, and we felt ourselves make some progress right at the start, we would "buy in" to their world. Too often, that easy access would turn sour, for as the road took us deeper into that group's energy we would discover what the leader had the group purposely hide from our sight.

Having learned from sad experience, our culture has developed ways to test these teachers and their groups. Here are some directional markers:

Do the teachers ask their students to study only their teachings because all others are false? Do they state that their group is the only one with the truth and all others are false? Do they state that other paths, teachings and teachers are "fallen" or wrong and that only they are right? Do they work to separate us from family, society and loved ones by telling us these other people are inferior or dark or fallen and will try to take us from light? Do we want to be guided by the principles of this teacher's group, as these are manifested in all levels of its work?

There is a difference between focusing on our own discipline to master its techniques and isolating ourselves from all others. For example, a piano player might focus on classical studies, but that does not make jazz or country less authentic. The same holds true with the study of consciousness: there are many different approaches, each equally valid but different.

Mentors, assistants and oppositional forces. Besides guides and guardians, there are also mentors, assistants and oppositional forces. All of these exist ultimately inside our own larger life form; they have simply separated themselves out to perform different tasks for the one overall consciousness.

The Nature of the Life Forms You Will Be Encountering

There is a common perception in groups existing in denser ranges of consciousness that the forces of other worlds live in nontime structured realms, are manipulative, dangerous, dark and need to be controlled by us. This is an incorrect viewpoint that emerged during the Kali Yuga.

When we go into another world to establish communication, it is to our advantage to do so with a sense of partnership, fun and true respect. If we go in to trap a life form from that world to do our bidding, we are for sure going to incur the wrath of the beings in that realm. Just as we on earth go on a hunt if someone takes one of our people captive, the life forms in other worlds will often go on the hunt for anyone harming one of their colleagues.

Just as some people attempt to manipulate the life forms of other worlds, there are beings in some other worlds who will seek to do this in our world. But in most instances these are the exceptions, not the rules. We on earth may be familiar with some worlds because of the abuse some of their life forms have exacted on earth. But not all individuals in those worlds are like those abusive life forms, any more than having a pirate attack you on your first visit to earth means all earthlings are pirates.

Now, as to time. Time exists all-where inside creation, no matter how rarified the consciousness or how different it is from our perceptions. Once we have a structure, no matter how subtle or vast, this indicates change from the ultimate unmanifest source has occurred. Change indicates a sequence, and a sequence can only occur through time. So when we say we are going above time and space, where all is one, we mean we are going above linear time.

It requires an adjustment of perception for a human to see into other dimensions, and some dimensions are so very different that it appears nothing is there—no time, no space, no form. However, this is not true. There are no voids in an ultimate sense—just different types of time, space and form. Scientists are discovering that even the so-called black holes in space have life forms of a different sort.

Once we start working with subtle energy, we begin to comprehend the fluid nature of time and space. For us on third-dimension earth, the subtle energy structures have grown and replicate in one way, while in other dimensions, also having free will, they may have evolved in other ways. Their time configurations and sequence may be different from ours, but they do exist. Otherwise there is no growth or change possible for that world, and that cannot be. The simple act of moving or communicating requires a change to occur. As my guides explained to me, they and I could not even be having a conversation if there was no time. A concept or word has a start, middle and end. That has to be so, or one concept would never stop to allow for the next to begin.

While a life form can seem eternal from our world's point of view, it is that life form's way of proceeding. It may simply have evolved different structures from our own human way of proceeding. Cosmic forces, angels, gods and goddesses and faeries are not eternal. They simply live in a different time-frame from our own. These life forms change and evolve, in their own way. They, like us, are an expression of the same one uncontainable source seeking to experience and perfect its own self in all its aspects.

The Intent of Our Connection

When we wish to communicate with any other life form, whether with our own inner colleagues or with those we are to assist or be assisted by, it is important to be aware of our intention. We can be very effective when we start from our own heart within our own merkabah. Study the intent that is found there. If this intent is for a good purpose, then proceed. But if there is an overlay or blockage that feels like detrimental power or lust or unjust monetary gain, then rethink the matter, for this overlay of energy that is trapping us will draw these forces from inside any field we explore. A comparable force will approach us from that merkabah, attracted by the frequency with which we have entered its domain.

Once we have accessed the pure love that resides inside all hearts, we need to check with our inner colleagues to be certain they agree it is proper to proceed. If necessary, because we cannot yet see the frequency of the world into which we must enter, ask these inner colleagues to communicate with the guides and guardians of that world. Proceed by a community-level connection of the merkabahs—a joint effort. When we do so in this way, all the parties involved can cooperate for the joint benefit of all the worlds involved. Whatever issues come forth can be dealt with using a communal approach for mutual benefit.

Becoming Friends and Colleagues with Our Guides

Once we start working with a guide or two, we will begin to notice the differences between them. Each guide has their own personality and area of responsibility. Guides can also be perceived as merkabah forms. Thus, Archangel Michael exists as one very large force or merkabah and equally as many smaller forms that have segmented out to fulfill different responsibilities—different parts of the one whole. When we call on Michael for protection, the form that responds will be Michael, but it may very well be one aspect, or merkabah, within his overall life form. Today we are fond of calling this concept *holographic reality;* that is, an aspect of a field, when broken off, will contain the whole field, and yet the field itself is still whole. Thus, when we invoke Michael and he is present with us, he is not diminished in any way as a total life form. We can ask for Michael to stay with us, and if we have his agreement, he will stay. We don't have to worry that we are taking him away from any of his other work. An aspect of his life form stays with us, yet in the larger sense he is still serving in many other places simultaneously.

When we begin working with our inner colleagues, we eventually learn that we are participating in a partnership. In a partnership all members need to be listened to, respected and have their basic needs met. Both we and our inner colleagues have free will; we both are serving together for the supreme force or light of the universe. It is our free-will choice to assist the other, and we are not absolutely bound to do so. We have either agreed to work together before the human part of the team came to earth or, if we are working with a new guide, we will show the guide that we are worthy material to be protected, taught and worked with. Often, when humans first learn they have had guides all along, they need to have it proven to them. In such a situation, the guides will propose appropriate tests. For me, this involved the guides telling me certain facts that would occur in the near-term future, many quite odd, which, much to my surprise, proved true. It also involved their showing me the underlying energies of certain situations, and then assisting me to change my own energy to adapt successfully to the situation. Kezamm! All of a sudden the energy of the still-occurring situation would pass through me like air; there were no energetic hooks left for me to snare the energy as it flowed on.

However, once the guide has met the test, you need to keep your part of the bargain, and begin to trust in the guide. Over time, through the situations you meet and solve together, this bonding grows strong. When you are first establishing trust in your guides, it is important to understand that we have nothing to fear if our intent is pure and we are pure of heart. Our guides often become our friends and colleagues. They will joke with us and keep us company when we are bored or alone or afraid or tired or unsure. They will show us precisely what we are able to offer the partnership. This contribution by us will usually be a service to the source that only a third-dimension life form can assist with. Our guides know not to push us too hard, although we sometimes have to remind them that the third dimension has certain restrictions other planes do not, such as eating, sleeping, relaxing and bringing in sufficient money to pay our bills. Likewise, our guides honor our need to check their credentials and to sometimes go above them to confirm the validity of certain procedures they have advocated. After awhile, both we and our guides know each others' personalities and capacities. Working with guides doesn't involve drama; it is just doing good, solid work with a friend.

Should the guide who approaches us be a trickster or a hostile force, they will eventually reveal themselves. We may find that our "guide" begins to usurp our free will. It may demand we obey it in some form instead of leaving the option of doing so up to us. It may start to threaten us or demand we perform degrading or destructive acts to others or to ourselves. It can be difficult to get them to leave at this point. So at the start we want to guard well our own intent and the nature of the force with whom we are establishing contact.

From Our Guides' Perspective

Guides have free will, just as we do. Thus, if we have misbehaved very badly, our guides have the right to withdraw from us. If they have been assigned to us for this lifetime, or if they and we have agreed prior to birth that we would all work together as a team, they will have to remain in our energy field. However, they have the free-will capacity to distance themselves from our gross physical misbehavior. For example, a person who sadistically murders others would be unlikely to have open communication with their true guides. When such a person sincerely seeks to change themselves, their guides may be coaxed to come forward and directly assist the individual in this process.

Until we learn to perceive consciousness multidimensionally, the forces that want to assist us will very often adjust their appearance according to our current level of perception. These forces may take on the guise of a guide if our particular cosmological perception does not allow other aspects of ourselves to exist and communicate with us from other dimensions. The significance of the form is less important than the fact that they get our attention and trust so that we are willing to communicate with them.

When we are still perceiving solidly within third-dimensional reality, there is no doubt whatsoever that we need outer help to move through all the many segmented fields that exist. When we move into the realms of subtle energy, our options can expand. They can also narrow, should we choose to proceed in a narrow, linear manner.

For example, we could choose to proceed to the source through the lineage of a particular doctrine, whether it is political or religious. In this case we *will* ourselves to see only one particular line of ascent to the source and to avoid all other lines on the way. As we progress, we are increasingly fenced in to that perception, if we are proceeding by an exclusionary method of study and believe that only our way is correct. We choose to proceed through levels of forces that have been defined by those who have explored and mapped that path before us. How do they know the path? Because they have examined and grounded the forces of this particular line back to the source and have stabilized a particular way back for others to follow.

Therefore, we will of necessity have to fight the vital forces Buddha encountered before his final enlightenment. Or we will feel the necessity to die in battle to attain heaven, as some militant sects believe. However, we do not have to proceed in this way; we can choose to proceed otherwise. We can get to the source by other routes. And sometimes, even though we will ourselves to follow a particular route, we will be unable to follow it for long if it is not inherently our way. As we move up in frequency towards spirit, it will feel wrong, and we will lose interest.

When we are ready to define for ourselves the unique personal manner in which, of sheer core necessity, we must go forward—when the ways we have been taught no longer satisfy us—then it is time to strike out on our own, and we will need to make contact with our own inner colleagues.

Our intent is the first clarion call to these individuals. Determine this intent from the very highest level of perception that you can right now. That intent will become the defining way you will proceed, at least for a time, and it will leave its mark on you and your family lineage. Should you choose a dark way, as some do, at least for a time, that way will eventually require you to master these forces until you learn for yourself the shortcomings of this chosen route. The way of light also has its own shortcomings for those wishing to fully reach the goal, and many of us have explored the deficiencies of this approach as well before learning the course corrections necessary to go on. Eventually, however we started, we must go above both dark and light, to where they might merge in the absolute source. (LIFE)

. . . .

EXERCISE TO CONTACT YOUR GUIDES/GUARDIANS

Allow one full month for this exercise.

You are going to work to re-establish contact with your own authentic guides and guardians. Establish this intent and mark it on a calendar. One month—you will not give up in attempting to establish communication for this length of time. You will be doing many other things during this period and other exercises, but this particular intent will also be there and will be ongoing.

Sit silently and center yourself. Now speak inwardly to the guides, as if they were there. Even if you do not know that they are there, pretend, imagine and give them shape or form. Engage them in conversation. Ask them what they do, where they are from. Listen to their responses. You are seeking to engage their attention, to bring them forth from the inner worlds. After all, they may have been "goofing off" just like you. You are attempting to initiate a higher work-order schedule for them, and they need to toe the mark, the same as you need to do.

It helps when you solidify this process. So here is a checklist to complete. You might want to write this out on a separate piece of paper and leave space between each line for your response.

1. The life form I wish to contact is:

2. The reason why I wish to contact this life form is:

3. The goal when we achieve contact is:

4. My commitment toward achieving this goal is: (circle one) 1 2 3 4 5 6 7 8 9 10

    (Clue: if you say 7 or less, it is highly unlikely you will contact your guides. Your commitment has to be very intense.)

5. Beliefs I need to hold to accomplish my goal:

6. Beliefs I need to eliminate to achieve my goal:

7. Date goals will be reached:

Strategies (Example: "I will believe in the presence of my guides and will read about subtle energy every day to familiarize myself with this topic.")

Specific actions (Example: "Every day I will sit for five minutes and center myself. I will request my guides to come forward to communicate with me, and I will be open to their responses.")

Chapter 12
Tools of Use for Interdimensional Purposes

Energy tools usually interact with the consciousness of the user. They are only as effective as the individual using them. We can use a hammer to build a house or to hit someone on the head.

In this chapter we are going to discuss energy tools, which we define as any thing or being who assists us in the operational use of consciousness to achieve a particular objective.

Certain tools work better in specific dimensions and less well in others. When we are shifting dimensions, we need to ascertain which tools we will work with.

Modern Sutras on the Nature of Energy Tools

In the third-dimensional world, we have had to create tools that can succeed with gross physical matter. This ability to shape and control physical reality is one of the "bonuses" of the Kali Yuga. Since most of us could not see much beyond the third dimension, we had no choice but to develop tools and processes that worked with gross physical reality. This has resulted in the development of such disciplines as the arts, sciences, politics, athletics and the military.

Just as our dimension has parameters that require a specific type of solution, so do other dimensions. In all instances, working with the energies of a specific dimension or world will bring us into contact with a wide range of consciousness conditions and solutions. Many dimensions require solutions far different from what we have developed for earth in the third dimension. For the most part, the worlds each of us will be entering in the course of our work, and the kind of reception we will receive once we step into that field or frequency, depend to a large extent on what our intent is, what our inner lineage is and with whom we choose to align ourselves in our work.

••••

Beyond solid matter, energy becomes supple. It is capable of shape-shifting, to different degrees, as it wills. If it should so will, it can descend into the subtle energy appearance of many different beings. To comprehend the true energy behind the subtle form, then, we must be able to go to the level of its key structure, to the heart of the matter—or rather *its* matter.

••••

Until we can see clearly and properly, it is possible for dissonant forces to distort our awareness. We will have thoughtforms passing through our consciousness and shaping our perceptions, uncontrolled by us. Thus, it is important to have bona fide guides, guardians, energies and forms assisting us and for us to learn how to proceed safely in new territories.

••••

In this new age we are entering, in which we will be more aware of higher frequency life forms, it is important for us to be able to perceive energetic structures and to effectively and safely interact with them for our overall success. How we do this will depend upon our own character development to this point. Whatever way we choose, we are bound to make so-called mistakes, which, as most of our mothers have told us, are the only way to wisdom. Mistakes are only mile pointers showing us which way to go or not go.

•••

Just as we are sometimes making mistakes, so too are all the other persons and disciplines now seeking to comprehend the new capacities and opportunities earth is experiencing as it cycles into this new age of heightened awareness. While well intentioned, even the great seers do occasionally make perceptual mistakes. So, as the Buddha himself has told us, never believe something an expert has told us just because that person is an expert: always test the advice for yourself.

•••

Just like us, every generation has pushed the envelope for personal exploration. They have been sometimes wrong and sometimes right and sometimes right only for their time and culture and not right when their insights are applied to a later or different culture. For these reasons it is also inappropriate, in our radically new culture, to blindly accept our past earth religions and philosophies as being 100 percent universally true, without questioning the context in which their statements were made.

•••

Energy tools can help us to see the actual structures involved in a situation. They can help us retain awareness as we work. They can increase the efficiency with which we act and learn.

Tools are also alive, just like all other life forms, manufactured and "natural." They are used by us, under our command, to achieve a certain objective. They are not meant to usurp our free will or our choice as to what to do with them. Energy tools usually interact with the consciousness of the user. They are only as effective as the individual using them. We can use a hammer to build a house or to hit someone on the head.

Different Types of Consciousness Tools

We are in the initial evolutionary stages of the new science of subtle energy. As with any science, we are starting by mapping the field and determining ways to proceed. We are developing ways to scientifically prove the validity, purposes and potentials of these fields. The following information is presented in this light: a summary of some of the subtle energy tools currently being explored.

Mathematics and Sacred Geometry

Mathematics and sacred geometry are among the core-level universal disciplines, or life-forming processes, that are being used today in innovative ways.

All cultures have metaphysical groups who focus on the occult power of numbers to affect energy and matter. A proper use of numbers, in specific sequences and in geometrical relationship to each other, can shift the energy of a person or location. The Indian science of numerology is one such discipline.

When we go back through form, past the aura, we reach the shape of the underlying structure. We are working with this concept as the merkabah, but as we've said already, it has been called many other names, including the mandala, the medicine wheel, the hologram and the flower of life.

The highest geometric form in virtually all cultures worldwide is the star tetrahedron, also called the Star of David and the Seal of Solomon. It consists of two intersecting triangles—the start of polarity in the universe. From there the forms start splitting to perform various actions. The world of sacred geometry has mapped the diverse manners of splitting, replicating, duplicating, negating, competing, destroying and cooperating. An exploration of any book or study of sacred geometry, or of yantras and mandalas, will help us learn much about the nature of energy movements, but is beyond the scope of this work.

One can look at the initial geometric form, the merkabah, as a shape holding any type of energy. An internal study of this shape, should one wish to proceed through geometry, will reveal many patterns of possible interaction both within the field and among fields both internal and external to any particular form.

At the start of interdimensional communication, using the merkabah is helpful. It, too, is a tool. When we are comfortable in moving among fields, we may very well decide not to use the merkabah at all, but to directly perceive of the field in a different way. That works, too.

Some of the newer disciplines working with the principles of sacred geometry to transform matter include BioGeometry®, founded by Dr. Ibrahim Karim of Cairo, Egypt. BioGeometry® has created a vocabulary of geometric forms which, when focused on, can correct the distorted energy field of some part of the human body. Dr. Karim comes out of the Islamic community, which is one of the most advanced in the use of mathematics and geometrics to convey energy. One reason for this is that Islamic culture forbids the depiction of God as a human being, and so, instead, Muslims use geometry, mathematics and pattern to describe that energy.

Another discipline that uses these bodily geometric forms is Reiki, which originated in Japan. Reiki teaches its practitioners to draw "in the air" symbols of beneficent universal energy forms, using these forms to clear human energy fields.

Light and Sound

Light   Many fine companies are working with light devices to tune in to and alter energy. Light comes at all levels of consciousness. By working with different frequencies, we can feed and nourish the body, mind and spirit. A merkabah, when looked at from the perspective of light, is light in motion.

Light is used extensively in most subtle-oriented cultures. Laser beams are the start of such work in our contemporary Western cultures. Light can be beamed through crystals and tailored by metals, ceramics and other devices to store and channel information and energy. Interdimensional practitioners such as myself "space travel" via light to other worlds and places.

Sound   Every merkabah has not only its own shape but also its own sound field. It generates a resonance or frequency, which can be perceived as a sound or as light.

The original start to a merkabah is two intersecting Stars of David. Each of these triangles, when seen three dimensionally, is a spinning cone of energy. When viewed from the end point of either cone, looking towards the other side, the direction of the spin is the same.

The elegant simple beauty of this form is that when the two cones meet, their energies are spinning opposite to each other. If each side is clear and operating in a balanced manner, the friction between the two keeps each side clear and spinning. The counterrotating spin whirls out the debris from the other's field. As long as the two sides are equally balanced in this symbiotic partnership, there is perpetual motion. But if either side seeks to dominate or falls "ill," the balance is thrown off and the issue of imbalanced polarities starts.

Each pole has its own sound and also a harmonic made up of the two fields moving against each other. This sound changes at different points within the slopes of the intersecting cones. Those sensitive to sound can enter into various worlds by tuning to that frequency or sound. We may need assistance in locating this frequency, especially if we are journeying or in new territory. We also need assistance in grounding and sustaining the frequency long enough for us to identify with it. There are many methods for proceeding via sound. Sound workers use tools such as pendulums, music, tuning forks and singing bowls. They work with inner guides, too. Sound workers report that the most beautiful sounds they have heard are the choirs of angels, orchestras of the gandharvas and the sounds of the planets.

Technology

Zero-point Technologies   These are technologies that are seeking to address the pollutions of our world by placing objects in some form of a hyperbaric chamber. The energies are adjusted, over time, to rebalance the object to what is termed its original zero-point condition. This means the original state of perfect balance for that object, the one that existed before it was thrown out of balance via interactions with other life forms. When these zero-point-balanced objects are then placed in a human energy field, they resonantly assist in rebalancing the human energy to its original wholeness. The current problem with this technology is that the object, when placed near an imbalanced field, will gradually degenerate out of its own balance. When using these objects, be aware that they need to occasionally be recalibrated. This situation will eventually be corrected, as we learn more about this science.

Other tools, such as geometrics, ceramics and stones, can also bring energy fields back to zero-point balance. But balanced fields created in this manner can also go out of balance, if an imbalanced energy of another frequency is introduced.

Dr. Masaru Emoto's work with water is a variation on this concept. He uses prayer and intent to purify water. He has found, however, that unless the prayer is continued, the water will gradually degrade in quality upon prolonged contact with the still-present polluting factors of its environment. He can correct the field but it can become imbalanced again if the correction is not repeated on a regular basis. The ability to establish, maintain and act from a place of balance is an ideal goal for all life forms as well as for humans.

Bioceramics   One of the best examples of the use of ceramics to adjust frequency is ancient Egyptian faience. From a particular combination of ingredients, the way the mix was grown and how it was fired, a substance was fashioned that could resonantly clear energy fields, never wear out and never clog up. It was self-sustaining and self-clearing. When placed near other objects, the ancient faience formula could clear and balance the fields of those objects. The ancient Egyptians often combined faience beads with gemstones and gold in jewelry and objects, creating energy fields that could enhance health in various manners. Today, companies such as Biomagnetic Research, out of Globe, Arizona, produce a modern faience-like ceramic that is combined with stones, metals and grids to clear energy fields and is especially effective for mitigating the effects of computers and emf. My own company, Crystal Life Technology, Inc., uses many of these ceramics in combination with specific stones to clear and enhance various energies.

Other companies are also working with ceramics as energy clearing devices and may "grow" the ceramic base with specific bacteria. These ceramics are often paramagnetic. This is useful because the new communication technologies (computers, cellphones, wireless routers, etc.) are usurping frequencies once used by the human body. This means the human no longer has access to these frequencies, which causes physical harm to some people. The paramagnetic resonant ceramics permit life forms to harmlessly share a frequency with others.

Dowsing Instruments   Dowsing instruments are among the oldest recorded energy tools. Pendulums and dowsing rods are depicted in the artwork found in ancient Egyptian pyramids and tombs.

Working with a pendulum is an excellent way to find a frequency or a world. Many subtle-energy practitioners favor pendulums for locating something that we know exists, only we do not know where it is or how to get there.

The secret to using a pendulum, as in all subtle-energy tools, is to work with it in a cooperative manner, without seeking to overpower its information with your own willpower. Once you lose your detachment, it is more difficult to acquire accurate information. Dowsing is an ancient discipline, a huge morphogenetic field of information with its own guardian energies. Many experienced dowsers invoke the dowsing system before starting their work while others invoke the presence of their personal guides. If you wish to learn more about dowsing, log onto the American Society of Dowsers website: *www.dowsers.org*. The society has chapters in many states, and these chapters offer classes on using pendulums. You can also log onto my website, *www.crystal-life.com,* and download a free booklet on dowsing, "Letter to Robin," by master dowser Walt Woods.

The Natural World

Objects in the natural world around us can make excellent tools. Each evolved from the source—just like us—and one of their functions is to hold a specific range of energy in place. They can work in partnership with us to help balance and clear specific aspects of energy. Natural objects commonly utilized by humans include crystal and stones, natural fibers and metals, herbs and essential oils. Those of us who have a favored way in which to heal ourselves, whether stones or nature or animals or food, would do well, in part, to examine our relationship with that world. It can be of service to us in some way.

Be aware that these natural forms can also be unbalanced through use or conditions surrounding them. They need assistance occasionally to clean and recalibrate themselves.

Guides, Guardians and Inner Colleagues

True guides, guardians and inner colleagues can also serve as "tools." They can serve as leverage to exact change in different worlds that you need to go into. They can show you how to use the tools of each dimension when you need to go there. Like physical tools and our own body, this group will not usurp your free will. Should any life form say it is your "guide" and then demand that you serve or obey it, watch out. These are not authentic guides, but energies disguising themselves for the purpose of energy domination.

The Body as a Tool

Physical Exercises, Postures and Breathing (Pranayama)
These are excellent for realigning our human energy field to accept and receive subtle energies in a balanced way. Hatha yoga, the martial arts and meditation techniques teach direct ways to perceive and work with subtle energy.

Initiations, Ordinations and Attunements   Each group has its own way of perceiving and moving through energy. If we share this information with others, a group ascension is possible for us all. Therefore, today most groups in the subtle-energy field practice an open process of attuning others to their particular aspect or knowledge. Once we have received the attunement, we have the knowledge, internally, of where that body of information exists within the universe. Should we so wish, we may now locate and work with the field. The more we work with an initiation process and the more frequently we go into the field we have been granted access to, the stronger will be our identification with the energy of that field.

DNA/RNA Restructuring   This is a field that many interdimensional workers are focusing upon. Essentially, the issue here, from one of the major viewpoints, is as follows. Originally, we had a larger number of DNA strands; twelve or its multiple of twinned strands, twenty-four, is usually the number cited. The human being of today was formed from the joint genetic banks of twelve different races, heritages or lines of descent from the source. Each strand represents the capacities of that line.

Because this lineage was so potentially powerful, it became uncontrollable, and in the course of its evolution, it was wreaking havoc not only on its own world but in many other realms as well. Therefore, one of the high intergalactic councils made the decision to remove some of the strands and disassemble others until humans were mature enough to receive back the remaining components.

This theme of the removal of something from humanity is found in the ancient texts of virtually all cultures. It is referred to as the lost chord, the lost sound, the missing cord, the Tower of Babel and so on. Our junk DNA is the disassembled DNA that remains in our system, waiting to be reassembled and activated.

In addition, different genetic lineages were given different aspects of the strands to hold for humanity. Others lie inactive in our human energy fields, waiting for us to wake up to the levels of consciousness at which they exist.

This is still a highly experimental science, and while many groups have part of the answer, we are still working at effective, measurable ways to go about this restructuring. It should not take us long to do so. Different groups with an affinity for different aspects of the vast human-energy potential have had much success in some ways. They can see the codes and remove blockages in some ways but not in others, yet. Even the removal of some blockages can be a significant way forward for us in terms of consciousness advancement.

The Human Consciousness   This is the highest level tool we can work with. Our own internal development enables us to work with energy better than any other tools available, but it takes lifetimes of work to master.

Various Protocols for the Same Issue

When energy workers participate in a group session for healing or exploring, they generally start with the premise or agreement that they will focus on a specific issue or frequency for the purpose of understanding it. If some of those chosen to participate are not able to see into that frequency, then they will not see the same experiences as those who are able to tailor their view. They may see other objects because they are focused on a different spectrum of frequencies.

There are many ways to see and feel the issue: some practitioners will see the effect in the aura; others, such as me, will see the effect in the person's "light grid." When different practitioners look into the chakras, for instance, they can experience vastly different ways of seeing because they have different types of inner sight. Most ways are accurate in their approach and level of perception.

Some practitioners will look into the field and see the actual incident that caused the situation; or, if it is a highly protected area because of the trauma and the destructive energy enclosed in the energy cyst (like a physical tumor), they will converse with all the guides involved, including the guardian of that particular energy field, and discuss what should be done.

Very often when the karma has been paid, the knot is still existing because it is an energetic scab or scar; it can simply be removed. Like a logjam in a river, removing the key log will allow the other logs to be released as well and the energy (water) begins moving freely once more. If there are still lessons to be learned, all the guides involved will discuss the best manner to approach this issue. Action will be decided on and discussed with the client.

There are a variety of courses of action and energy tools that can be used in the same situation, depending upon the family lineage from which the energy worker has emerged and to which the client belongs.

. . . .

Helping Earth Visitors

Most of today's energy workers have helped beings from other worlds adjust to the human form. When beings from other worlds attempt to incarnate on earth, they may either step into an already manifested being (called a walk in) or they enter the fetus of a female and are born into the human condition and often, as with the rest of us, forget where they originally came from along with the task they incarnated to perform. The density of the earth consciousness, to sustain form, is so heavy that it is very hard to be naturally aware of spirit; this is a craft that must be learned.

The process of incarnating in a fetus has its own challenges. If the life form is very different from the human one, the genetic memory of the original form may prevent a full identification with the human form. Sometimes this is extreme, and the fetus is aborted, stillborn or severely malformed.

Other times there is a small deviation such as a slight misalignment of the nervous system.

Oftentimes, while not remembering exactly who they are, these people feel they just don't belong on earth and that they don't fit into their bodies.

One individual I assisted was from a world where they had two hearts and were round beings that rolled when they walked. She was a bit round in this lifetime as well and could never quite balance herself when walking. Another individual came from a world where the life forms existed in a gaseous state and she had difficulty staying in her physical body; her consciousness kept flying up and out. In both instances, the situation was resolved by taking the individual back up in consciousness to their own world, then slowly bringing them back down again, this time making the necessary adjustments.

. . . .

As we proceed through the process of full integration with the energies of existence, we come to know that all tools are a part our own extended consciousness. Tools can take us into different parts of our own extended merkabah field, which is universal in size. They can teach us to perceive and work with what is inside any field. Any tool we pick up has something to teach us about the options life offers. All we have to do is listen and ask the tool what it can do for us. To do this, a capacity for multidimensional communication is essential.

No matter what the tradition, no matter what country or culture, once we move away from seeing only physical form, we begin working with the energies underlying matter.

Chapter 13
The Importance of Resonance

*Frequency and resonance are the
interconnecting links between all worlds.*

In all the disciplines, ways are coming forward to affect, change, enhance and embed energy in fields. All these new (and ancient) technologies make use of the same principle—resonance— within a specifically defined field of consciousness. Sending a frequency through a field will alter it in some way, good or bad.

The Toroid

Frequency and resonance are the interconnecting links between all worlds. The simple concept of toroids shows us how they work.

A toroid functions as an energy coil that stabilizes an accretion of cycling frequencies. It starts as a simple pattern of rotating energy into which other frequencies are introduced and incorporated, gradually making a full, complex and integral cycle. We are living toroids—frequencies that circle intact as we move through our daily lives. Our basic toroid shape emerges from the soul, and we overlay it with multiple frequencies that bring us through the energy patterns of the heart, mind and vitality into the body. As we go through our day, we pull in frequencies from many different activities and integrate them into our body's particular frequency range. A merkabah is also a toroid.

Our modern technology transmits information through frequency. As a society, we are not considering how our bodies and our earth are being affected by the increasing number of artificial frequencies we are creating and sending through the air. We are bombarding ourselves with multiple artificial frequencies without considering what frequency band they come from and how they interrelate within our personal environment. Cellular phones, for instance, vibrate on the mental frequency and are interfering with our brain's functions. What must we do to adapt this useful tool to protect ourselves on these frequency bands?

Children are walking energy antennas attracting specific frequencies from the regularized appearance of specific tonal vibrations in their lives. When spirits are young and supple, they are more susceptible to frequency changes than when they get older and more set in their energy patterning. Expose our children to specific frequencies, and they will adapt their energy systems to these. They will rapidly incorporate frequencies into their complex energy toroid, where it becomes integrated into their personality. We are exposing our children to negative, destructive energies, presented to them through programs carried by our entertainment and technology industries, and then we complain when they act in the same energetic manner as the shows they are watching. This is not freedom we are allowing into our children's lives; it is unwitting slavery to the negative forces of nature. The negative side of the spectrum of consciousness is using our willingness to tolerate these "entertainment" frequencies to do irreparable damage to our society and our culture.

We need to be more responsible about the frequencies with which we surround our children. Since both parents are working in most of today's families, we need to be especially careful in choosing our children's caretakers. Today caretakers are not only human; they also include machines. It is extremely important for us to pay more attention to the frequencies of television shows and video and computer games along with the frequencies of the machines themselves. Are our children watching shows whose frequency devalues the sacredness of human life? That condition our children to seek the energetic thrill of violence for violence's sake? Do the machines themselves work at a resonance that usurps bands of energy used by other significant functions, such as the heart or the solar plexus?

Machines

The wide use of electromagnetic devices, at home and work, are part of the proliferation of artificial frequencies that are hindering our naturally evolved energy fields from receiving their full supply of energy from the source, earth, and earth's atmosphere. Our current electrical systems and our microwave satellites circling the earth to facilitate communication via cellphones and other electromagnetic devices are sending out artificial frequencies that are blocking, for some sensitives, access to the natural frequencies that reside at these levels.

If a life form utilizes the frequencies currently being usurped for our growing globalization of artificial electromagnetic fields, it is going to be affected by a lack of access to those wavebands. This is true of those life forms who draw sustenance from the wavebands currently being usurped by artificially constructed products, such as nylon made from petrochemicals, chemically based household products, and perfumed items containing artificial scents made of chemicals. These products are creating frequency fences that prevent some life forms from having access to their old homelands and others from passing through, much like the fences put up by homesteaders in the old Wild West prevented wild animals, native people, and ranchers from moving freely from one place to another, as they had in the past.

Today's commercial communication technology is unconsciously constructing frequency fences. However, other sectors of society are seeking to consciously use the principles of sound and frequency for different purposes.

Some groups, labeled as the "conspiracy theorists," believe a secret world government is working with intergalactic civilizations to control the population via frequency principles. This nefarious alliance is united by the same goal: power, finance and world dominance. Confronting these efforts, they say, are those mounted by the Galactic Federation, which seeks to protect earth's natural evolution from the interference of various intergalactic predators.

Whether you believe the above scenario is real or fiction, there is no doubt that some of our own world governments, including the United States and Russia, are already using the principles of frequency emissions to create military weapons. These weapons have been reported on by various mainstream media. The weapons are based on scientific data about which frequencies control precisely which aspects of the earth's and human's energy fields. Altering these frequencies in some way will cause very precise changes in behavior or field integrity. The arsenal of some countries include, for example, weapons that can be directed at a crowd and, while not appearing to do anything at all, cause the blood of the advancing individuals to start boiling. Other frequency weapons can cause diarrhea or massive headaches in an advancing army.

Whatever the cause, the proliferation of man-made frequency devices is already taking its toll. Many people are experiencing immune system collapse; high levels of stress; the growth of tumors, skin lesions and rashes; and other bodily aberrations as the human energy field attempts to adapt to the frequency invasions. With the proliferation of satellites beaming frequencies down and up, no place in the world is safe. If we can make a cellphone call from the top of a mountain, it means even that isolated location is being affected by artificial energy fields.

Our animal friends are also affected by these frequencies. Many people have commented on the recent unusual migratory patterns of birds and other animals. Some breeds are wandering about aimlessly, seeming to be lost. Others are wintering over in areas they usually leave. This is because there are tiny microcrystalline structures in the animals' brains that act as compasses and homing devices, causing them to head to the specific frequency location inbred into their systems. These frequency modulators are, unfortunately, operating at the same resonant tone as many microwave satellite emissions. The artificial technology, stronger than the animal's own naturally evolved systems, never varies in frequency as does a natural biofield, and so the animal loses out. Humans in tall office buildings filled with floor upon floor of electronic and microwave devices, all emitting the same relatively low-level, short-span range of frequencies, also lose out.

Today, energy solutions for people sensitive to these frequencies include a great number of resonance tools. The benefit of our current situation is that those who are suffering most have had to go outside the current box of medical perception, which does not work, to find alternatives that do work and that can give both relief and restoration of health. These people are the canaries that miners used to take with them into the mines; when the bird stopped singing or died, the miners knew there was a gas emission, and they then had time to leave before they were affected as well. I am one of those early canaries, and restoring my own health was my entry point into the knowledge of resonance technology.

Solving Modern Problems
via Resonance Technology

Which of the following remedies are already being practiced in today's alternative medical community, and which are concepts whose time will soon be here?

1. A person is born with a very low immune system. They are placed in a protected environment and played special music, day in and day out. The music contains the notes and sounds of a healthy immune system. Gradually, over time, their own body learns to listen to these healthy notes and reconfigures their field. *Done. See the work of Canadian Nicole LaVoie.*

2. A whole field of children are fed discordant music, filled with messages of anger and resentment; the messages are contained not only in the resonant notes and the rhythm, but also in words fed into the music backwards, then played forward, to disguise them. The children become argumentative; is it any wonder? *Done. Listen to the music of such groups as the Grateful Dead, which for a while, at least, was purposely delivering negative subconscious messages, reversed, in their music.*

3. The water in a local lake is polluted. Fish species are dying, and the bacterial count is so high that swimming is discouraged. A local group does a ceremony and takes a vial of blessed water, specially handled with power and intent, and pours it into the lake. In a few months the lake is clear. *Done. See the work of Dr. Masaru Emoto.*

4. A woman fears having anything close to her neck, and her panic is getting more intense as she grows older. In the course of some remedial energy work with an energy practitioner, it is discovered that there is, lodged high

above the left side of her head, a "knot" of fear in her energy field. The energy worker, who is capable of working above the time-space continuum, sees that it is related to a medieval lifetime in which the woman was an herbalist. In the mass hysteria of the time, the herbalist was condemned as a witch and hung in front of her community; the current woman is now approaching the same age her herbalist self was when she was hung. *Done, over and over, by energy practitioners working with private clients throughout the world.*

5. The national communications company installs a large regional cellphone tower at the edge of a small mountain village. Villagers begin reporting unexplainable massive headaches, nausea and illness in themselves and their animals. An expert in sacred geometry is hired to study the situation. He installs specific geometric devices in specific locations, and the health of the village is restored. *Done. See the work of Ibrahim Karim and Biogeometry®.*

6. A person has just been convicted of having sexually molested a child. Their punishment: to be tattooed on the left wrist with a very specific biogeometric symbol, which resonantly, from its form alone, will correct the person's aberrant behavior. Held for a few weeks while the form is tattooed and the energy settles in, the person is then released, no longer affected by that aberrant energy field. *Not yet done, but won't it be wonderful when it occurs?*

· ·

EXTINCTION OF SPECIES

In just the last two hundred years, since the onset of the machine age, life began to change for us all. Instead of a world dominated by nature, we started to control exertions of energy to improve our lives. Machines now do our work and transmit our messages through "empty air." The critical gap in our knowledge is that this air is not empty. It is full of living organisms, living particles made of the same energy source as ourselves.

When we humans tap into frequency bands and use them, we should consider, first, the function of that frequency and, second, what happens to us and the creatures of that frequency when we move into their domain.

We need to learn what forms of life and what functions exist on separate bands of sound frequencies. For example, every bodily organ is the manifestation of sound in form and playing its specific resonant note can actually help a sick or injured organ to return to health. Usurping its frequency can also interfere with its healthy functioning. This is what we are doing to extensive living organisms and our own organs with all the communication devices we are pulsing into our atmosphere, from computers to HAARP. It is time for us to responsibly exercise our human fate in its stewardship function of caring for our earth.

We are not alone on this earth of ours, and we are interfering with and killing off life at various frequencies, invisible to the physical eyes, just as surely as we are killing off the thousands of physically visible endangered species that are disappearing from our earth every year.

Looking into the Future

Imagine it is two hundred years in the future. The knowledge of resonance tools and theory has thoroughly evolved. You are heading to work in your vehicle, and as you enter the "parking lot," you must pass through a simple-looking frame of very specific dimensions through which a blast of frequencies is being emitted. As you do, you are cleared of any little particles of energetic debris you have accumulated on your trip to work. Feeling quite good, healthy and energized, you continue to your parking space.

Now imagine you are on a transport ship between worlds and, like the characters on *Star Trek,* are being beamed back up from your scientific work on another world. Inside the device, as it beams you back up, is a special filter that uses frequencies to clear your energy field of any exotic life forms—bacteria or more complex—that were looking to reappear with you.

All of these devices are resonance or frequency tools that are going to become part of our culture in the future. There are, already, many visionaries, including me, making and selling variations of these tools. They help humanity deal with the wide group of frequency issues of which we are becoming aware. These issues include basic energy-field balancing; the elimination of negative or polluting frequencies that come from brushing up against other life forms; the conscious efforts of other people or life forms to interfere with our right to a healthy, happy and prosperous life; and the increasing pollution of the natural frequency bands of earth through artificial substances, such as electromagnetic and chemical products.

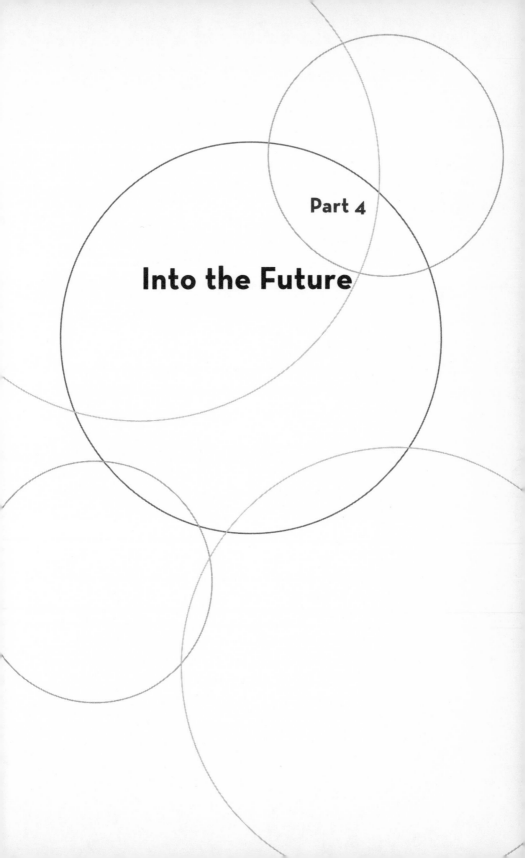

Part 4

Into the Future

Chapter 14
Earth Changes

Light will always, ultimately, win out. . . . We can choose, right now, at this critical juncture in time, to travel the path of peace and light.

While it is possible to go backwards in time and see what has occurred, it is far more difficult to go forward in time and accurately predict the future. The future always contains multiple probabilities, which are at some times more varied than at other times. These future probabilities are still in subtle thought or emotional form and have not yet materialized into third-dimensional reality. It is usually our own choice which reality we decide to "ground." The rest of the options remain as unfulfilled possibilities, like dreams or a fetus, and are absorbed back into the ethers as that spot in space and time is passed by. They will always exist as parallel realities and worlds, but the same life-force energy will not be available to them from the point of decision forward. This is how my lineage works with time. It is not the only option available.

Throughout the ages there have been times and situations when humans have been able to change the probable future. There have been other times when the flow of energy is so intense and powerful that we cannot. Our present era is a combination of both. Earth is at a particularly complex, powerful and critical juncture point. This coming age of spiritual awareness is predestined. We cannot control this outcome. It is an astrological event of such magnitude that not one prophetic culture of our past has been able to see past this restructuring. It will be an age so new in concepts, strategies and behavior that no one inside the older earth energies can even imagine it.

What we personally and culturally choose to do will affect how we experience this period. We can fight the change or move with it.

There was a time, several decades ago, when the direction of the change could still be manipulated. We have passed that juncture point; we made our decisions and our world is experiencing the effect. Those who are aware that the change is occurring are more easily able to adapt than those who are struggling to keep the world the way it had been.

It is wise to understand that earth herself is changing in her basic alignment. The direction of true north keeps shifting so rapidly that air flight charts, which help pilots orient via compass position, keep being redrawn every couple of months instead of every couple of years. This earth shift is changing the location of ley lines along which energy and information are transmitted; and the intersecting vortices on which power spots have been built. Earth is being affected by the magnetic field of the sun which is itself shifting; by the reappearance of celestial bodies in our proximity that we have not seen for tens of thousands of years; and by the approaching centerpoint alignment of our galaxy. All these developments, and more, are shifting the interrelationships of all the energies on earth. We who live on earth will change with her.

Most of the great mystery schools have taught that this particular period would occur at this precise moment in time. This is the time referred to in some traditions as the ascension, in others as the end of the world, and in yet others as the start of a new world. We are in the end times—and the beginning times. It is a time of great change: wherever we are, at whatever level, whatever we are trying to accomplish, it is all changing.

Those societies prophesizing this time include the Christian, with its second coming and talk of ascension. The Tibetan Buddhist, Hindu, Mayan and Hopi traditions tell of the end of time for this particular world; the calendars of all these traditions conjoin on this period, cited by various experts as beginning as early as 2007 and lasting to 2012, 2022 or even 2040. Many prophets, including Nostradamus, have foreseen this particular age. They have had two visions regarding it: One is a time of great wars, earth destruction and economic upheaval. The second is a time of great peace, love and harmony. Some see these visions as sequential. But others have suggested these are two alternate possibilities and even two parallel realities coexisting at the same time.

Light will always, ultimately, win out.

We have the free will to choose to not pass through the destructive phase before reaching the ultimate triumph of light. We can choose, right now, at this critical juncture in time, to travel the path of peace and light. It "simply" requires enough people choosing this option. This would bring that morphogenetic state into place that is called by some the second coming of the Christ consciousness: a time of peace. Philosopher Gregg Braden is one of the most knowledgeable advocates of this viewpoint.

Those astrologically and astronomically astute point to the fact that the magnetic pointer located in the center of our galaxy is approaching the exact middle point: a time of great balance and clarity. Others point to the presence of a twelfth planet now approaching us: Planet X or Niburu. The most ancient of teachings, from Hindu and Tibetan Buddhist archives, have explained that when this planet appears, some say only every 26,000 years, a golden age comes with it. One of the most physical explanations for this planet's effect is that its own frequency is so high and so powerful that it pulls on earth, extending earth's perceptual parameters to greater bandwidths. Other cultural interpretations posit negative events occurring with the appearance of this planet. My inner colleagues have explained that much of this diverse interpretation comes from intergalactic politics as to the nature of the change; the change itself is not questioned by any of these groups.

The Change Is Now

Many prophetic secret societies and traditions began as groups whose job was to covertly preserve sacred earth knowledge that at various times other groups wished to destroy, or that the unaware society of their time considered to be "evil" instead of enlightening. These societies saved their knowledge via verbatim memorization of ancient teachings, or in the very secret storing of documents and artifacts. To preserve this knowledge, which other groups were determined to eradicate, some secret societies had oaths vowing they would kill any member who divulged their secrets to others. Sometimes, like everything else during the Kali Yuga, these original high purpose oaths became methods of control.

Well-known groups who have attempted to preserve secret knowledges include the ancient Egyptian and Greek temple societies, the Judaic Kabalistic community, the Catholic Jesuits, the Christian Masons, and some indigenous South American tribes.

Very often the leaders of secret societies are in close conscious contact with the inner world guardians of the information. Starting several decades ago, most of the societies with secret information were asked by these guardians to start making portions of their knowledge available to the public. This is because the information is now required to assist us during the change of the worlds we are experiencing. Most intriguing is the South American knowledge of the signs of the coming earth changes, and what we can do to work with various possibilities to escape the direst scenarios.

••••

Now, in this time of change, earth culture is ready to explore new solutions to long-standing issues. These once-secret knowledge bases are very useful tools for us to integrate in finding equitable and workable solutions.

Added to the release of secret knowledge is the natural increase in human awareness that is now occurring. Many people are retaining their connection to the lower frequencies, yet expanding into the higher ones as well. This broader frequency band permits us to see the life forms previously hidden to us. This expanded vision enables us to see the truth behind many high walls built during the Kali Yuga. So far we are seeing the revelation of hidden lies, in all fields, from religion to government to business. We are being forced to restructure and to tell the truth, at least on the third dimension, for consciousness is becoming so transparent there is no other option. The old solid, stonelike structures are no longer so solid; we are seeing the air between their molecules and what lies behind.

Our scientists tell us that the magnetic field of earth is lessening and shifting. With this lessening, the forces holding us inside our established fields are also lessening, and this is permitting shifts in frequency perception to occur more readily. The barriers are lessening between dimensions, and we are more easily able to see other life forms than we were just a century ago.

This critical change-of-consciousness period has other aspects to it. We are just on the brink of beginning conscious communication with beings from other worlds—not only through interdimensional communication, but also through the advanced technology of extraterrestrials who are preparing to make themselves known. As we mentioned in an earlier chapter, earth has been in quarantine for countless eons, as the Galactic Federation sought to permit our evolution to proceed unimpeded by outside forces. This quarantine time is almost up. We are of interest to many intergalactic groups, some good and some bad. The bad want to exploit us. The good fear that we are destroying ourselves with our weapons of mass destruction and thus wreaking considerable havoc on intergalactic society. Remember, we are all connected, and what affects one affects all.

At the same time, we are experiencing an environmental crisis on earth. We are dirtying and are now in the process of destroying our own home, earth. Our actions are bringing into the mix the inner earth energies—the nature spirits and elementals—who are coming forward to work with all who can perceive and understand them. They also know there is only one earth; if we destroy her, we destroy them as well.

Each human being is part of a long lineage of life forms stretching down from the source itself. We are part of a cascading series of choices and specializations enacted by our greater selves to master a particular aspect of universal consciousness. We are cogs in giant galactic wheels, and if something happens to us, our entire lineage suffers. So there are many beings from other realms—aspects of our own self and our own lineage—working secretly on earth to help ensure everything turns out for the best.

Personal Choice

We as a culture and as individuals have the opportunity now to choose which probable future we will move into. For a short distance down each road we still have the option to change. But after a certain point, our choice will have defined itself, and the other options will disappear from view. While we will be able move about then, it will be more difficult; our course will be set until the next juncture point occurs, and its options will be predicated on what our last choices were.

While change is assured in our near future, the actual look of that change is still to be decided. There are many different options. We could destroy our world entirely. We could create a

Mad Max/RoboCop future with a total breakdown in society's structure, in which darkness prevails and the human spirit struggles to control the chaos rampant everywhere.

But I believe, like many other visionaries and especially those in direct contact with higher life forms from other realms, that humanity will survive—with a little help from our friends—and that we will actually move into a future of peace and extended consciousness, of a world organized on the principles of light and love. In this probable world, we are aware of the energetic structures behind form and work with them for the benefit of all.

In a way, it is our choice which future we will invite. In another way, we have no choice at all. We have no choice because, at this juncture in our form's evolution, we are at the control of fate, of destiny. It is the free-will choice of those of us inhabiting earth right now to be a part of this change of the ages. But, still, we forget who we are and why we came. So in this state of amnesia, of forgetfulness, each person must decide whether to change or stay behind. The choice we personally make determines whether we experience the hope of the new world's arrival or the despair of witnessing our current world's failure.

We may believe that our individual choice will not affect the whole, but it does. If we choose to retain our ties to the old consciousness, then, yes, we will help hold onto a world in chaos as the old forms deteriorate. But if we choose to take the leap into the new world perception, we will be entering another consciousness, with an entire lineage behind it that is helping to create a new world of enlightenment and peace.

Our Current World's Legacy

Each of us—each structure, body part, plant, tree, person, culture, discipline and religion—has participated in exploring some aspect of infinite consciousness on earth. None of the disciplines has been capable of comprehending and encompassing all of this reality, which is infinite in nature. We have thus far attempted to fathom its essence by breaking down forms into smaller and smaller parts, looking for the source.

Now we are entering the age of partnership and community, in which all the disciplines we have worked so hard to develop will be integrated. For this integration to occur, we must work at a level of awareness that sees all as one, each aspect fulfilling a particular part in the play. To successfully fulfill our role in this new age, we need to follow a process of integration and acceptance.

All these forces combined are bringing with them the capacity to see into other dimensions and realities and to communicate with the life forms there. Just now we are learning many ways to correct frequencies that hurt or injure by balancing them out with other frequencies. Future earth society may well see violence and crime met not with punishment, but with such simple means as analyzing a person's genetic structure, then tattooing on them a set of geometric symbols that will correct and balance them back into harmony with their own soul frequency. When life forms listen to their own internal source, they flourish.

We have now taken our first steps into the new age of conscious awareness, and as many predicted, the perceptual barriers between dimensions are thinning out. This intergalactic, interdimensional universe we are now seeing has a broader set of rules than we needed to work with before, as well as some eternally old ones. To be successful now means we must be aware both of the immediate moment and the broader fields of consciousness that are affecting us. Since these energies affect us, whether we wish them to or not, it would help to have a basic understanding of their workings. Imparting such understanding is a function of this book.

The Human Story

Looked at short term, the human story often seems too painful to endure, and escaping via meditation into the so-called higher realms appears a valid option. But it is not. Eventually we all must return to the work at hand, which is the transformation and perfection of this realm. That can come only by full identification with both the mother and the father polarities of existence.

This particular age we are in now is a critical one. Much depends on how we work through the very serious issues that are facing us. However, we are not alone in our battle. The significance of this phase is so powerful that we have here, on earth, right now, many, many very high life forms who have come to assist us. More are parked in the subtle energy realms, assisting at these levels by adjusting frequencies, feeding us information and keeping those of hostile intent as far away as possible. We may be still immersed in the amnesia that comes with human birth, but other life forms are ready and waiting for our memories to reawaken and recognize them once again.

The End of Earth?

Because of the need for concrete living examples to show the way forward within the third-dimension environment, and because of the way the universe has thus far worked to preserve life on earth, it seems unlikely, to my group of guides, that the experiment will be called off and earth destroyed, as many have projected. It is also unlikely that there will be a split of the worlds into those remaining in the third dimension and those who have "ascended."

Many of those who master these lessons will be returning. Why, when the lessons are finally beginning to be mastered, should the experiment then be called off? The point of the lessons, not only for individuals but also for the whole of earth, must be understood. The knowledge we have gained passing through the Kali Yuga was a necessary component for a full mastery of physical earth and its unique opportunities.

Ascension Technology

Many ascension philosophies are preaching of a time of only light, of ascension to an ideal heaven where only good exists. Although heaven is real and exists in all religions for its proponents, it does not exist as a sugary place of only good things. This truth has many implications for the new world now emerging, with its emphasis on the workings of consciousness, and especially for the field of ascension technology.

Ascension technology is a new science evolving from the efforts of many different traditions seeking to comprehend the nature of the world we are entering. In this world, there is no question that we are ascending in consciousness—whether we go willingly or kicking and screaming. In the old world, to comprehend this period, different traditions couched the information in fable or imagery appropriate to the level of comprehension of those receiving. We do not have to rest in these incomplete descriptions now, but can expand on the concepts, giving a fuller view.

According to the prevalent information in some segments of the Western Christian community, those who have faith or have been saved will ascend, and those who have not will descend. Other religions have segments of their faith with similar stories. While this idea is true, in a way, it is incomplete in another way. If we identify fully and truly with our faith, it will help us to ascend into its core, and we will adapt well to the changes taking place. If we rest in the false aspects of the religion or do not seek comprehension, we will be "left behind" as far as our current comprehension of what is occurring.

One aspect not understood in a simple description of this process is the presence and purpose of the dark forces. In a simple way, of understanding, the dark forces are cast down into hell, while the good forces are ascending. In terms of merkabah construction, there is truth to this; the two polarities are extending their range in opposition to each other. But what is not comprehended is that these two polarities are both serving the one source; they are, therefore, both of the same source. Anger or fear or rejection of the dark forces only slows our personal ascent.

All life forms have the same need to grow, evolve and return to the source. It does not matter whether they are of the dark or of the light. All are ultimately of the one source, the void or fullness from which dark and light emerge and return.

Ascension is not based on destruction, but on understanding and correctly incorporating all of life, for the common goal of full awareness and full manifestation of the one common source.

At the highest levels of consciousness, the lords of darkness and the lords of light are both perfect polar expressions of the one common, infinite, eternal, immutable, omniscient and omnipotent source. Each side has responsibility for the continued existence and growth of its domain. Each is compelled to eternally oppose and balance out the other side, or neither side can continue to exist, let alone grow and expand in capacity towards the one ultimate goal of all life forms: perfect conscious union with the source while in manifestation.

From their own great, core-level love of source, the Lords of Darkness have worked well to counter, or polarize, the work of the Lords of Light. Both wish to see God the Father's highest vision united with God the Mother's deepest level of matter. If darkness and light do not perfectly counterbalance each other at any specific level, the awareness of the nature of consciousness cannot fully occur at that level. Instead it remains, for a time, as a partially evolved potential and does not yet become a fully manifested aspect of the one source.

Rising above Polarities

To master any aspect of consciousness in our third dimension, we need to harmonize the polar opposites of whatever issue we are focused on. This is accomplished by going above the issue to either that plane of consciousness preceding the issue, or to that point of time just before the issue began. We must then be able to hold the full spectrum of options within our consciousness, without being swayed by any aspect of the spectrum. Because we now hold the solution inside ourselves, in the physical body, this consciousness is more easily attainable by everyone else around us and in our world.

This is How we can go the world!

This means we are establishing a whole new level of human life on earth—beings who have accepted the reality of all polarities inside their energy field, including the most extreme levels of dark and light, evil and good. From this point of all-acceptance, they can ensure that no one is stifled in their wish to learn these lessons for themselves and provide a positive environment for everyone to do so, instead of one that rapidly degenerates into illness, death or destruction.

The ultimate goal of full manifestation of the source, in all its majesty and beauty, will then become a grounded, visible, physical reality; other less evolved beings can see that manifestation of the source is both fulfilling and capable of being achieved.

Chapter 15
Intergalactic Contact

The ability to communicate and cooperate with other life forms is a perfectly normal extension of our current human capacities.

There are blue airfield lights in the pine woods to my left as I drive, a bit too fast, down the deserted Maine highway. I have traveled this road many times; it takes me between my family's summer place in New Hampshire and the Portland airport.

Today, however, I have misjudged my travel time. The Portland airport is still thirty minutes away, and I am worried about getting there in time.

The blue lights confuse me. How can the airport be here, in the middle of the thick, June-green forest? Where am I?

I feel panic as a second blue light suddenly appears and streaks through the woods directly at me.

••••

I look to my left, out the car window, filled with a profound sense of peace and a strange confusion.

I see no lights in the deep pine forest. Why did I think I had seen some? Why was I afraid? I look at the car clock. I'm not going to be late for the plane. Why did I think that? I'm actually fifteen minutes ahead of schedule.

I am aware that I am confused, but also feel very strongly that this does not matter: all is fine now.

The beauty of the trees, birds, insects and plants that border the quiet country road are profoundly pulsing their energy towards me. I put aside my confusion, enjoy the peaceful energy and continue my trip, content to stay well within the speed limit.

••••

And so began my journey into the world of multidimensional awareness.

Ask me if I believe in the presence of extraterrestrials, and since that lush summer day, the answer would be yes. So do millions of people who, like me, have experienced contact.

Soul Contracts, DNA and Politics

It took me a few years to remember the events of that day, and I still don't recall them all. What I do know now is that the blue lights were frequency beams, set up by an extraterrestrial civilization called the Arcturians. At that point in time—the mid-1990s—they and other Galactic Federation member nations were seeking humans with their civilization's particular genetic strands in their DNA. It was a period when many humans were being "upgraded" to more easily adjust to the world changes soon to come. The type of beam I encountered is tripped when the specific frequency being sought passes through it. The human is then "rescued" and often recalibrated. This means the energetic distortions and ripped-out or scrambled DNA are fixed and made active so that the human has far greater access to their own genetic potentials. They are no longer limited to the narrow human band of third-dimension frequencies, but have the option, should they so choose, to comprehend and understand the far wider bands of frequency in which other life forms exist.

Once assisted in this way, the human is returned to continue their evolutionary path on earth. The galactic scientists continue on, separately, doing their pickups and recalibrations elsewhere.

How extensively a human assimilates this "systems upgrade" and what course they choose for their own life determines how much and what kind of progress they will make from there on out.

Sometimes the individual retains conscious awareness of the recalibration experience, and other times the information is blocked, at least for a while. This block occurs for several reasons, including the difference in the human's and assisting civilization's structures of consciousness. As humans, we are not yet sufficiently developed to comprehend beings in far different frequency signatures than our own. Awareness can also be blocked for the sake of the individual, whose own cultural training on earth may include the perception that such contact is hostile and whose entry back into their own society would be jeopardized by a sudden expanded awareness. In these cases, as the individual grows in awareness following their internal genetic restructuring, the memory gradually returns. This was my situation.

There are many intergalactic civilizations similar to the Arcturians doing pickups and genetic realignment for those of their lineages who are evolving here on earth. Our media chooses to publicize or fantasize about great conspiracies and manipulation by hostile extraterrestrials. Going unpublicized, mainly for self-protection, are the hundreds of thousands of people who are being helped to successfully transition into this new world rapidly approaching us.

This is a free-will universe, and if up to that day in Maine I had chosen a different path of development, my evolution after that time might have been different. But I was given an opportunity to comprehend more about the spiritual nature of the universe, and I took it. That acceptance has taken me, since then, far out of the relatively normal life I had been living and into a totally new understanding of our lives on earth and our parts in the cosmic plan.

Everything—*everything*—in this book concerns human capacities that are a normal growth of human evolutionary development. We have all experienced some part of the experiences described throughout this book, whether we choose to bury them as imagination or block them for fear of being considered insane or, more benignly, different. In my case, I was gifted with an unexpected awareness upgrade, so that I finally understood that my subtle experiences were not imagination but reality vibrating at a different frequency than that of ordinary human beings.

One of the results of my upgrade was a greater capacity to comprehend the nature of consciousness, a topic that had always interested me. I took a giant leap forward in my ability to comprehend consciousness, for I could now not only palpably see and feel subtle consciousness, I discovered I could also communicate with consciousness in an internal conversational manner.

When this leap occurred, I discovered that many ideas I had thought were mine were actually being offered by various members of a group of life forms, each of whom had their own distinct personality and purpose in my life. They are not the extraterrestrial scientists who picked me up; these life forms call themselves my colleagues and emphasize the fact that we are equal partners, and they are working through me to serve earth. We all have similar internal teams of colleagues who are always present and are seeking to assist their human partner.

My inner colleagues are of the Metatron-Melchizedek lineage, like I am. I had sensed and ignored them many times before in my life because, like most of us, I had been trained by parents and peers to consider these experiences imagination, perhaps tinged with madness.

These colleagues are real life forms: forget the superstitious tales we have all heard in our youths. They simply live in other dimensions. Because of the free-will mandate of the universe, they are not permitted to consciously converse with us if we have told them to shut up! If we have asked them to be quiet, they stay around in our energy field—that is the contract we have made with them before we came to earth—but in normal circumstances they remain silent.

When I first became aware of these beings, we went through a testing stage, where I ascertained their validity and purpose. Once I verified their positive intentions, we began our serious work together. They told me then that everything I needed to know, they would teach me. They appeared to be keeping their promise.

But then, one night about a year later, I attended a workshop by an interdimensional communicator from another branch of the Melchizedek lineage.

The topic was intergalactic politics, and the woman speaker explained many details about the different interdimensional worlds and how politics and power are not anomalies of earth. As in all else, earth embodies in the solid, third dimension the energies that have formed in less solid realms. A great many very ancient and powerful energy forms and interdimensional worlds have staked out a presence on earth, for all the reasons such a political move connotes. Support, destruction, rampage, profit, assistance—there are life forms here for all these reasons, juggling for position, during this period of intense earth change.

I heard about the Pleiadians, the Arcturians, the Lyrans, the Sirians and more intergalactic societies. I learned about the current battle involving the Reptilian races, the differences between the dark and the light grays, about deceit and counterdeceit. My head was swirling with all this information!

But when I walked into my home after this lecture, I experienced a sudden outburst of anger. She knew so much and was from my own lineage!

Now, the Melchizedeks have a wonderful sense of humor, as many who work with them have observed. They use this to help humans relax during the learning of what is an immense subject. So in response to my anger and confusion about all the knowledge I had just acquired, but not from them, and the "everything" that I wanted so much to know about, I felt them smile and gently enter my energy field.

In an instant, they pulled my consciousness in through my heart chakra and out into the dark, star-filled universe. Great galaxies were swirling in all directions and life forms of all sizes and frequency were richly pulsating. I was a part of it all and understood that everything is the expression of the one ultimate life form we call the source, or God.

"In just what part of 'everything' did you wish us to begin?" they gently chided, pausing to let me contemplate the peaceful, loving vastness of the scene. They then brought me back into my body.

Enlightened and awed, I understood that what I need to know will always be provided, at the right time and place but not necessarily in the way I expect. Expectation predetermines outcome, and I have been taught to avoid it.

I then received some more instruction. Sometimes, they explained, the right way to learn means learning from others on the outer plane in what they are experts on, through their own internal family lineages. Humility and a willingness to learn from *all* others is necessary in a job such as the one I have contracted for.

They then went on to explain that the intergalactic races I learned about that evening all have vested interests on earth. As in earth politics, beings on one side will often project evil intent on the other, no matter what the ultimate objective is of each. I was to be careful about assigning the qualities of "enemy" and "friend" to any group. Taken long term—and universal time can be *very* long—the situation is much like that between Russia and the United States: sometimes they are allies, sometimes they are opposed, and each has its own perspective that needs to be understood. All are expressions of the one source. The necessity to see above duality will exist even when earth consciously enters galactic society.

My contract, my objectives, and most of my inner colleagues are different from those of the workshop leader's, and I needed to stay on course with my own work

My colleagues reminded me of the soul contract I had made with them some time before. This contract, which was open to renegotiation by me at any time, was determining what part of the universe our team had chosen to focus on.

I had contracted with them, as a member of one of the galactic civilizations that helped create earth's original genetic make-up, to welcome all who wish to contribute to the richness of the earth field. It was not to matter what world they themselves are affiliated with. I had contracted to help all life forms adjust in partnership with each other for the highest good of a specific situation. What I needed to accomplish this, my colleagues would provide, one way or another. This is the "everything" that I can expect from them. They have never failed in their promise.

The World That Lies Ahead

One of the topics that has interested me is the much-talked-about change of ages, said to be occurring sometime around AD 2012—with a time-frame spanning from 2007 to 2022 and even 2042. On occasion, my colleagues and I have discussed this change of ages. They have explained to me that when an energy form is in the chaos of change, it is easier to affect its field than when it is stable and set on a particular course and direction. Earth, as it moves into the twenty-first century, is in major change. It is at the end of a very long cycle.

Some yogis say it is a 26,000-year cycle and that we are leaving the lowest phase of it, called the Kali Yuga, or the age of darkness. This phase signals the end of the one cycle of time and the beginning of a new one, which always starts with a Golden Age of Spirituality. This new energy is introduced at its purest, and from there on out, it grows into form. Finally, by the other end of the cycle, matter is the densest, and the good and bad aspects of the force have solidified and are the base of consciousness for the next cycle when it begins.

The Native Americans speak of this time as well, saying we are at the end of the fourth world and about to move into a fifth world, where everything will work differently. The Mayans and Toltecs speak of a new world that will start around AD 2012 and will be so different they cannot describe it. The Christians talk about the second coming of Christ, a time of ascension when true brotherly and sisterly love will prevail after a period of profound chaos and destruction. Those with an astrological/astronomical bent speak of how the yardarm of our galaxy is about to cross the center point, where it will pause for a moment. Then, they posit, there will be a reverse in the rotation of all fields as it pendulums out the other side.

Since my experience in Maine, I have learned that the future will not be a Mad Max world of turmoil and also will not be a religious utopia. It will be a time when humans are a conscious part of a very evolved cosmic society. We will become responsible stewards for the world we are entrusted to work with and through—earth. This will be a world where the needs of all life forms—whether manufactured, of nature, or of humanity—are responsibly listened to and worked with in partnership.

All these simultaneously occurring fields of life are waiting for us to mature into our responsibility as true earth stewards. We will not be stewards in the current understanding of the word, which is filled with patriarchal bias about a human's right to manipulate nature. We will be real stewards who, before we act, listen to and consider the needs of all involved.

Coming Forward with This Information

I kept silent about the Maine incident for many years, for all the fear-based societal reasons that keep most contactees silent. I am speaking out now for several reasons.

First, those who have known me since childhood may say, "But she was always the most ordinary of people. How can she know how to talk with all these life forms? Why, I remember her when . . ." So this speaking out answers their question: How can this very ordinary kid I grew up with know these far-reaching concepts?

Second, I want it to be very clear that the ability to communicate and cooperate with other life forms is a perfectly normal extension of our current human capacities. It is a part of our evolution. It is not a nonhuman ability. I am still a perfectly normal, ordinary human being. I have simply been fortunate enough to have had my personal evolution helped along its way.

Third, this is a critical time for earth. We humans are beginning to wake up to an awareness of intelligent life forms beyond our own. This is part of the ascension of consciousness foretold by so many traditions. We need to understand what is occurring.

In my life, I have learned that this is a free-will universe we live in, and if we ask for something in a gentle and open manner, backed by knowledge and strength, the universe will cooperate.

Interdimensional consciousness . . . communication . . . cooperation.

Listen. Can you hear the many life forms waiting and hoping we will work with them in the great partnership era of earth that is now emerging?

ABOUT THE AUTHOR

Atala Dorothy Toy, A.M., P.P., has served as Secretary of the Board of Trustees of the American Society of Dowsers and ASD Marketing Director. She is a co-founder and board member of the Institute for the Study of Interdimensional Cooperation (ISIC) and the founding president of Crystal Life Technology, Inc., begun in 1996 to provide the public with subtle-energy information and tools. Crystal Life Technology now operates as a store in Geneva, Illinois, and has an award-winning website, *www.crystal-life.com*. Atala Toy speaks frequently on subtle energy and future earth scenarios and is a professional subtle energy land consultant and personal consultant. She is the author of one previous book, *Explorations in Consciousness*.

Atala was brought up as a Quaker, graduated from the Quaker-founded Swarthmore College, is a practicing yogini of over thirty years and a member of the Labyrinth Society, the A.R.E., and the Theosophical Society. She is a Melchizedek priest.

At her website, *www.crystal-life.com*, you will find a link to a free instructional CD to guide your work with other dimensions. Here you can also learn about upcoming workshops, see photos of interdimensional life forms and post your own interdimensional photos on the crystal life blog.

TO OUR READERS

Weiser Books, an imprint of Red Wheel/Weiser, publishes books across the entire spectrum of occult and esoteric subjects. Our mission is to publish quality books that will make a difference in people's lives without advocating any one particular path or field of study. We value the integrity, originality, and depth of knowledge of our authors.

Our readers are our most important resource, and we appreciate your input, suggestions, and ideas about what you would like to see published. Please feel free to contact us, to request our latest book catalog, or to be added to our mailing list.

Red Wheel/Weiser, LLC
500 Third Street, Suite 230
San Francisco, CA 94107
www.redwheelweiser.com